John Bunyan, George Burder

The Holy War made by King Shaddai upon Diabolus

to regain the metropolis of the world - Vol. 1

John Bunyan, George Burder

The Holy War made by King Shaddai upon Diabolus
to regain the metropolis of the world - Vol. 1

ISBN/EAN: 9783337286248

Printed in Europe, USA, Canada, Australia, Japan

Cover: Foto ©Lupo / pixelio.de

More available books at **www.hansebooks.com**

THE HOLY WAR

MADE BY

KING SHADDAI UPON DIABOLUS,

TO REGAIN

THE METROPOLIS OF THE WORLD:

OR, THE

LOSING AND TAKING AGAIN OF THE TOWN OF MANSOUL.

BY

JOHN BUNYAN,

AUTHOR OF "THE PILGRIM'S PROGRESS," ETC. ETC.

WITH EXPLANATORY, EXPERIMENTAL, AND PRACTICAL NOTES,
BY THE REV. G. BURDER.

Embellished with Seven Superb Engravings.

PHILADELPHIA:
J. B. LIPPINCOTT & CO.
1868.

JOHN BUNYAN'S

ADVERTISEMENT TO THE READER.

Some say the PILGRIM'S PROGRESS is not mine,
Insinuating as if I would shine
In name and fame by the worth of another,
Like some made rich by robbing of their brother·
Or that, so fond I am of being sire,
I'll father bastards; or, if need require,
I'll tell a lie in print to get applause:
I scorn it; John such dirt-heap never was
Since God converted him. Let this suffice
To show why I my Pilgrim patronize.

It came from mine own heart; so to my head,
And thence into my fingers tickled;
Then to my pen, from whence immediately
On paper I did dribble it daintily.

Manner and matter too were all mine own,
Nor was it unto any mortal known
Till I had done it. Nor did any then
My books, by wits, by tongues, or hand or pen
Add five words to it, or write half a line;
Therefore, the whole, and every whit is mine.

Also for this, thine eye is now upon,
The matter in this manner came from none
But the same heart, and head, fingers, and pen,
As did the others. Witness all good men.
For none in all the world without a lie,
Can say that this is mine excepting I.

I write not this of any ostentation,
Nor 'cause I seek of men their commendation;
I do it to keep them from such surmise,
As tempt them will my name to scandalize;
Witness my name, if anagram'd to thee,
The letters make Nu hony in a B.

JOHN BUNYAN.

PREFACE BY THE EDITOR.

Mr Bunyan was a wonderful man. Called by divine grace out of a state of ignorance, vice, and obscurity, he became, without the aid of human culture, a most useful minister of the gospel, and a very eminent writer:—a writer so eminent, that though he has been dead more than a century, his works still live, and are deservedly popular; particularly his allegorical works—the Pilgrim's Progress and the Holy War. Few books have ever been so often printed, or so much admired as the former. In that charming work, the christian life is represented under the figure of a journey, and the pilgrim is conducted through a thousand remarkable incidents, from his native city of Destruction, to Heaven, the city of God. In the Holy War, the same subject is treated in a military manner. The fall and recovery of man are represented by two remarkable revolutions in the town of Mansoul. The human soul is figuratively considered as a beautiful and prosperous town, seduced from its obedience to Shaddai, its builder and governor, by the stratagems of Diabolus, his inveterate enemy; but the town, after a tedious war, is again recovered by the victorious arms of Immanuel, the king's son. This military view of the subject is strictly consonant with the sacred scriptures, which represent the christian life as a warfare, Christ as a captain, the believer as a soldier of Jesus Christ, the preaching of the gospel as the weapons of the holy war, and the graces of the Spirit as so many parts of the heavenly armour. Mr Bunyan was better qualified than most ministers to treat this subject with propriety, having himself been a soldier; and knowing, by experience, the arts and the hardships of war. Indeed, he has conducted the whole work with singular ingenuity and skill. He displays throughout, his accurate knowledge of the Bible and its distinguishing doctrines; his deep acquaintance with the heart; and its desperate wickedness; his knowledge of the devices of Satan, and of the prejudices of the carnal mind against the gospel. He proves himself to have had an extensive knowledge of christian experience, of the power of conscience, of the excellency of faith, of the misery arising from doubts and fears, of the danger of carnal-security, and of the necessity of crucifying the flesh, with its affections and lusts. The grace and love of our Lord Jesus Christ are sweetly delineated in the character of his Immanuel; and the powerful influences of the Holy Spirit are finely described in the character of the Secretary. A vast fund of experimental religion is treasured up in this book; while the instruction is conveyed in the form of entertainment and amusement; and occasionally, a smile excited by the singular propriety of the unusual names assigned to the numerous characters introduced.

To render this edition of the Holy War more agreeable than any former one, the same method is pursued as in the Editor's edition of the Pilgrim's Progress. The work is divided into chapters of a moderate length, an improvement which this work certainly wanted. Proper pauses are necessary to relieve the attention of the reader, as well as to allow time for reflection, and to assist the memory. A considerable number of explanatory and practical notes are subjoined, intended to render the author's designs more conspicuous; to impress a useful hint, which might otherwise be passed over too hastily, and to point out some of those latent beauties, which might else escape a cursory reader. In attempting this, the Editor has availed himself of the author's *marginal key*, with which he has endeavoured to unlock every division of the curious cabinet, and to expose the valuable contents. From the very favourable reception which his edition of the Pilgrim has obtained from the public, he entertains a hope that the present volume may prove equally acceptable and useful.

GEORGE BURDER.

Coventry, Jan. 30, 1803.

JOHN BUNYAN'S

ADDRESS TO THE READER.

'TIS strange to me, that they that love to tell
Things done of old; yea, and that do excel
Their equals in historiology,
Speak not of Mansoul's wars but let them lie
Dead, like old fables, or such worthless things,
That to the reader no advantage brings:
When men like them make what they will their own,
Till they know this, are to themselves unknown.

Of stories I well know there's divers sorts,
Some foreign, some domestic; and reports
Are thereof made, as fancy leads the writers;
(By books a man may guess at the inditers.)

Some will again of that which never was,
Nor will be, feign (and that without a cause)
Such matter, raise such mountains, tell such things
Of men, of laws, of countries, and of kings;
And in their story seem to be so sage,
And with such gravity clothe every page,
That though their frontispiece says all is vain,
Yet to their way disciples they obtain.

But, readers, I have somewhat else to do,
Than with vain stories thus to trouble you;
What here I say, some men* do know so well,
They can with tears of joy the story tell.

The town of Mansoul is well known to many,
Nor are her troubles doubted of by any
That are acquainted with those histories†
That Mansoul and her wars anatomize.
Then lend thine ear to what I do relate
Touching the town of Mansoul, and her state;
How she was lost, took captive, made a slave;
And how against him set, that should her save;
Yea, how by hostile ways she did oppose
Her lord, and with his enemy did close:
For they are true, he that will them deny
Must needs the best of records vilify.

* True Christians.   † The Scriptures.

For my part, I myself was in the town,
Both when 'twas set up, and when pulling down;
I saw Diabolus in its possession,
And Mansoul also under his oppression.
Yea, I was there when she own'd him for lord,
And to him did submit with one accord.
When Mansoul trampled upon things divine,
And wallowed in filth as doth a swine:
When she betook herself unto her arms,
Fought her Immanuel, and despis'd his charms:*
Then I was there, and sorely griev'd to see
Diabolus and Mansoul so agree.

Let no man, then, count me a fable-maker,
Nor make my name or credit a partaker
Of their derision; what is here in view,
Of mine own knowledge I dare say is true.

I saw the prince's armed men come down
By troops, by thousands, to besiege the town;
I saw the captains, heard the trumpets sound,
And how his forces cover'd all the ground:
Yea, how they set themselves in battle 'ray,
I shall remember to my dying day.

I saw the colours waving in the wind,
And they within to mischief now combin'd
To ruin Mansoul, and to take away
Her primum mobile† without delay.

I saw the mounts cast up against the town,
And how the slings were plac'd to beat it down.
I heard the stones fly whizzing by my ears;
(What's longer kept in mind, than got in fears?
I heard them fall, and saw what work they made,
And how old Mors‡ did cover with his shade
The face of Mansoul, and I heard her cry,
Woe worth the day, "in dying I shall die!

I saw the battering-rams, and how they play'd
To beat up Ear gate; and I was afraid,
Not only Ear-gate, but the very town
Would by those battering-rams be beaten down.
I saw the fights, and heard the captains§ shout,
And in each battle saw who fac'd about:
I saw who wounded were, and who were slain,
And who, when dead, would come to life again.
I heard the cries of those that wounded were
(While others fought like men bereft of fear.)

‡ Death.   § Lusts.

ADDRESS TO THE READER.

And while the cry, Kill, kill was in mine ears,
The gutters ran not so with blood as tears.
  Indeed the captains did not always fight;
But when they would molest us day and night,
They cry, Up, fall on, let us take the town;
Keep us from sleeping, or from lying down.
I was there when the gates were broken ope,
And saw how Mansoul then was stripp'd of hope.
I saw the captains march into the town,
How there they fought, and did their foes cut down
  I heard the prince bid Boanerges go
Up to the castle and there sieze his foe;
And saw him and his fellows bring him down
In chains of great contempt quite through the town
  I saw Immanuel when he possess'd
His town of Mansoul: and how greatly bless'd
The town, his gallant town of Mansoul was
When she receiv'd his pardon, lov'd his laws.
  When the Diabolonians were caught,
When try'd, and when to execution brought,
Then I was there; yea, I was standing by
When Mansoul did the rebels crucify.
  I also saw Mansoul clad all in white,
And heard her prince call her his heart's delight;
I saw him put upon her chains of gold,
And rings and bracelets, goodly to behold.
  What shall I say? I heard the people's cries,
And saw the prince wipe tears from Mansoul's eyes;
I heard the groans and saw the joy of many:
Tell you of all, I neither will nor can I;
But by what here I say, you well may see
That Mansoul's matchless wars no fables be.
  Mansoul! the desire of both princes was,
One keep his gain would, t'other gain his loss;
Diabolus would cry, The town is mine;
Immanuel would plead a right divine
Unto his Mansoul: then to blows they go,
And Mansoul cries, "These wars will me undo!"
Mansoul, her wars seem'd endless in her eyes,
She's lost by one, becomes another's prize;
And he again that lost her last would swear,
Have her I will, or her in pieces tear.
  Mansoul thus was the very seat of war;
Wherefore her troubles greater were by far
Than only where the noise of war was heard,

Or where the shaking of a sword is fear'd!
Or only where small skirmishes are fought,
Or where the fancy fighteth with a thought.
    She saw the swords of fighting men made red,
And heard the cries of those with them wounded,
Must not her frights, then, be much more by far
Than they that to such doings strangers are?
Or their's that hear the beating of a drum,
But need not fly for fear from house and home?
Mansoul not only heard the trumpet sound,
But saw her gallants gasping on the ground;
Wherefore we must not think that she could rest
With them whose greatest earnest is but jest:
Or where the blust'ring threat'nings of great war
Do end in parlies, or in wording jars.
    Mansoul her mighty wars they do portend
Her weal, her woes and that world without end;
Wherefore she must be more concern'd than they
Whose fears begin and end the self-same day;
Or where none other harm doth come to him
That is engag'd but loss of life or limb:
As all must needs confess that now do dwell
In Universe, and can this story tell.
    Count me not, then, with them who, to amaze
The people, set them on the stars to gaze;
Insinuating with much confidence
They are the only men that have science
Of some brave creatures; yea, a world they will
Have in each star, though it be past their skill
To make it manifest unto a man
That reason hath, or tell his fingers can.
    But I have too long held thee in the porch,
And kept thee from the sunshine with a torch.
Well, now go forward, step within the door,
And there behold five hundred times much more
Of all sorts of such inward rarities,
As please the mind will, and will feed the eyes,
With those which of a Christian, thou wilt see;
Nor do thou go to work without my key.*
(In mysteries men do often lose their way)
And also turn it right; if thou would'st know
My riddle, and would'st with my heifer plough;
It lies there in the window. Fare thee well,
My next may be to ring thy passing bell.

              * The margin.

CONTENTS.

Chap. I.—The original beauty and splendour of the town of Mansoul, while under the dominion of Shaddai. Its noble castle described. Its five gates. The perfection of its inhabitants. The origin of Diobolus. His pride and fall. Revenge meditated. A council of war held to deliberate on the best means of seducing the town of Mansoul. Diobolus marches to the town, and sits down before Eye-gate. His oration. Captain Resistance slain. My Lord Innocence killed. The town taken   11

Chap. II.—Diabolus takes possession of the castle. The Lord Mayor, Mr Understanding, is deposed; and a wall built before his house to darken it. Mr Conscience, the recorder, is put out of office, and becomes very obnoxious both to Diabolus and to the inhabitants. My Lord Will-be-will heartily espousing the cause of Diabolus, is made the principal governor of the town. The image of Shaddai defaced, and that of Diabolus set up in its stead. Mr Lustings is made lord mayor, and Mr For-get-good, recorder. New aldermen appointed. Three forts built to defend the town against Shaddai   21

Chap. III.—Information of the revolution carried to the court of King Shaddai. His great resentment of the rebellion. His gracious intention of restoring Mansoul. Some intimations of this published. Care of Diabolus to suppress them. His artifices to secure the town, and prevent its return to Shaddai   36

Chap. IV.—Shaddai sends an army of 40,000 to reduce Mansoul, under the direction of four captains, Boanerges, Conviction, Judgment and Execution, who address the inhabitants with great energy, but to little purpose; Diabolus, Incredulity, Ill-pause, and others interposing to prevent submission. Prejudice defends Ear-gate with a guard of sixty deaf men   48

Chap. V.—The captains resolve to give them battle. The town resolutely resists, and the captains retire to Winter-quarters. Tradition, Human-wisdom, and Man's-invention enlist under Boanerges, but are taken prisoners, and carried to Diabolus; they are admitted soldiers for him under Captain Any-thing. Hostilities are renewed, and the town much molested. A famine and mutiny in Mansoul. They sound a parley. Propositions made and rejected. Understanding and Conscience quarrel with Incredulity. A skirmish ensues, and mischief done on both sides   60

CHAP. VI.—Lord Understanding and Mr Conscience imprisoned as authors of the disturbance. A conference of the besieging officers, who agree to petition Shaddai for further assistance. The petition approved at court. Immanuel, the King's Son, is appointed to conquer the town. Marches with a great army, and surrounds Mansoul, which is strongly fortified against him   72

CHAP. VII.—Immanuel prepares to make war upon Mansoul. Diabolus sends Mr Loth-to-stoop with proposals for peace. These proposals being dishonourable to Immanuel, are all rejected. Again Diabolus proposes to patch up a peace by reformation, offering to become Immanuel's deputy in that business. This proposal also rejected. New preparations made for battle. Diabolus expecting to be obliged to abandon the town, does much mischief. Ear-gate, violently assaulted by the battering-rams, at length gives way, and is broken to pieces. Immanuel's forces enter the town, and take possession of the Recorder's house. Several mischievous Diabolonians are killed   87

CHAP. VIII.—The principal inhabitants hold a conference, and agree to petition the prince for their lives. The castle-gate broken open. Immanuel marches into Mansoul. Diabolus is made prisoner and bound in chains. The inhabitants, greatly distressed, petition again and again. At length a free pardon is obtained, and universal joy succeeds   101

CHAP. IX.—The liberated prisoners return to Mansoul, where they are received with great joy. The inhabitants request Immanuel to take up his residence among them. He consents. Makes a triumphal entry amidst the shouts of the people. The town is new-modelled, and the image of Shaddai erected   118

CHAP. X.—The strong holds of Diabolus destroyed. Incredulity, Forget-good, Lustings, and other Diabolonians

apprehended, tried, and executed, to the great joy of
Mansoul   129

Chap. XI.—Mr Experience is made an officer. The charter of the town renewed, and enlarged with special privileges. The ministry of the Gospel regularly established under the direction of the secretary. Mr Conscience ordained a preacher, and his duty particularly specified. Directions how to behave to the ministers. The inhabitants clad in white, and receive many other distinguishing favours from the Prince. God's peace is appointed to rule. The unexampled felicity of the town   145

Chap. XII.—Carnal-security prevailing in the town, a coolness takes place between the inhabitants and Immanuel, who being greatly offended, privately withdraws. Godly-fear, who detects the cause of his removal, excites the people to destroy Carnal-security. Measures are then taken to induce Immanuel to return   159

Chap. XIII.—The Diabolonians take courage from the departure of Immanuel, and plots are formed in Hell for a counter-revolution in Mansoul. Covetousness, Lasciviousness, and Anger, by changing their names, are introduced into respectable families, where they corrupt their masters, and do incredible mischief. An army of twenty thousand Doubters raised to surprise the town   170

Chap. XIV.—The plot discovered by Mr Prywell. Preparations made for defence. More Diabolonians executed. The army of Doubters approach the town. An assault made upon Ear-gate, which is repelled. The Drummer beats a parley, which is disregarded. Diabolus attempts to deceive by flattery, but is answered by the Lord-Mayor. Jolly and Griggish, two young Diabolonians, executed. Gipe and Rake-all banged. Anything and Loose-foot imprisoned   188

Chap. XV.—The inhabitants of Mansoul make a rash sortie on the enemy by night, but are repulsed with loss. Diabolus makes a desperate attack upon Feel-gate, which, being weak, he forces, and his army of Doubters possess the town and do incredible mischief. The inhabitants sorely aggrieved, determine on a new application to Immanuel, and procure the assistance of the Secretary in preparing the petition, which is presented by Captain Credence. He is favourably received, and appointed lord-lieutenant over all the forces 205

CHAP. XVI.—A new plot is laid to ruin the town by riches and prosperity. Immanuel, according to his promise, appears in the field, to assist the forces of Mansoul, whereby the whole army of Doubters is completely routed. Immanuel enters the town amidst the joyful acclamations of the inhabitants 219

CHAP. XVII.—A new army of Blood-men, or persecutors, attack the town, but are surrounded by the Mansoulians, headed by Faith and Patience. The examination of some of the leaders. Evil-questioning entertains some of the Doubters, but is discovered by Diligence. The principal Doubters tried, convicted, and executed 231

CHAP. XVIII.—More Diabolonians tried and condemned. The work concludes with an admirable speech of Immanuel, reciting his gracious acts, and informing his people of his intention to rebuild the town with the greatest splendour, and recommending a suitable conduct in the mean time 244

THE HOLY WAR.

CHAPTER I.

The original beauty of the town of Mansoul, while under the dominion of SHADDAI. *A dreadful revolution effected in it by the subtlety of* Diabolus. *Captain Resistance, and my Lord Innocency slain.*

IN my travels, as I walked through many regions and countries, it was my chance to arrive at that famous continent of Universe.* A very large and spacious country it is: it lieth between the two poles, and just amidst the four points of the heaven. It is a place well watered, and richly adorned with hills and valleys, bravely situated; and for the most part (at least where I was) very fruitful: also well peopled, and a very sweet air.

Description of the world.

The people are not all of one complexion, nor yet of one language, mode, or way of religion; but differ as much (it is said) as do the planets themselves: some are right, and some are wrong, even as it happeneth to be in lesser regions.†

In this country, as I said, it was my lot to travel; and there travel I did, and that so long, even till I had learned much of their mother-tongue, together with the customs and manners of them among whom I was. And, to speak truth, I was much delighted to see and hear many things which I saw and heard among them: yea, I had, to be sure, even lived and died a native among them (I was so taken with them and their doings,) had not my Master sent for me home to his house, there to do business for him, and to oversee business done.‡

A natural state pleasing to the flesh.

Now there is, in the gallant country of Universe, a fair and delicate town, a corporation called MANSOUL; a town for its building so curious, for its situation so commodious, for its privileges so advantageous (I mean with reference to its original,)

---

* *Universe:* The world at large is here intended, displaying the wisdom, power, and goodness of the great Creator.
† Sin has introduced universal disorder into the world. Its original harmony and beauty are lost.
‡ The author refers to his own experience before his conversion, and his being called by grace to serve the Lord Christ as a minister in his church.

that I may say of it, as was said before of the continent in which it is placed, " There is not its equal under the whole heaven."*

As to the situation of this town, it lieth between the two worlds:

Scriptures. and the first founder and builder of it, so far as by the best and most authentic records I can gather,

The Almighty. was one SHADDAI;† and he built it for his own delight, Gen. i. 26. He made it the mirror and glory of all that he made, even the top-piece, beyond any thing else that he did in that country. Yea, so goodly a town was

Created angels. Mansoul, when first built, that it is said by some, the gods, at the setting up thereof, came down to see it, and sung for joy. And as he made it goodly to behold, so also mighty to have dominion over all the country round about. Yea, all were commanded to acknowledge Mansoul for their metropolitan, all were enjoined to do homage to it. Aye, the town itself had positive commission, and power from her King, to demand service of all, and also to subdue those that any-ways denied it.

There was reared up in the midst of this town, a most famous

The heart. and stately palace: for strength it may be called a castle; for pleasantness, a paradise; for largeness, a place so copious as to contain all the world, Eccles. iii. 11. This place, the King Shaddai intended but for himself alone, and not another with him: partly because of his own delights, and partly because he would not that the terror of strangers

The powers of the soul. should be upon the town. This place Shaddai made also a garrison of; but he committed the keeping of it only to the men of the town.

The walls of the town were well built: yea, so fast and firm

The body. were they knit and compacted together, that, had it not been for the townsmen themselves, they could not have been shaken or broken for ever. For here lay the excellent wisdom of him that built Mansoul, that the walls could never be broken down nor hurt, by the most mighty adverse potentates, unless the townsmen gave consent thereto.‡

---

* By the town of *Mansoul*, as every reader must perceive, is intended *The Soul of Man*; figuratively represented, throughout this work, as a town. Just commendation is here given of it; for the human soul, in its original state, was truly glorious, bearing the holy and happy image of God himself.

† Shaddai. This is a name of God often used in the Old Testament, but translated ALMIGHTY. It is a Hebrew word, signifying *All-sufficient*, or *Almighty*. It is derived from the Hebrew word for *the breast*, which affords nourishment to young creatures; and so intimates, that we derive all our support from God, as the helpless infant from the mother's breast. This name is, in this work, applied to God the Father.

‡ The powers of the soul are very capacious, and the body itself, before the introduction of sin, was firm and strong. Nothing but sin, voluntarily admitted, could have injured either.

This famous town of Mansoul had five gates, at which to come out, and at which to go in; and these were made likewise answerable to the walls, to wit, impregnable, and such as could never be opened nor forced, but by the will and leave of those within. The names of the gates are these: Ear-gate, Eye-gate, Mouth-gate, Nose-gate, and Feel-gate.*

The five senses.

Other things there were that belonged to the town of Mansoul, which, if you adjoin to these, will yet give further demonstration to all, of the glory and strength of the place. It had always a sufficiency of provision within its walls; it had the best, most wholesome and excellent law, that was then extant in the world. There was not a rogue, rascal, or traitorous person then within its walls; they were all true men, and fast joined together; and this, you know, is a great matter. And to all these, it had always, so long as it had the goodness to keep true to Shaddai, the king, his countenance, his protection, and it was his delight, &c.†

The state of Mansoul at first.

Well, upon a time there was one Diabolus, a mighty giant, made an assault upon the famous town of Mansoul, to take it, and make it his own habitation. This giant was king of the Blacks or Negroes, and a most raving prince he was. We will, if you please, first discourse of the original of this Diabolus, and then of his taking of this famous town of Mansoul.‡

Devils the fallen angels.

The origin of Diabolus.

This Diabolus is indeed a great and mighty prince, and yet both poor and beggarly. As to his original, he was at first one of the servants of King Shaddai, by whom he was made, and raised to a most high and mighty place, yea, and was put into such principalities as belonged to the best of his territories and dominions, Isa. xiv. 12. This Diabolus was made son of the morning, and a brave place he had of it: it brought him much glory, and gave him much brightness: an income that might have contented his Luciferian heart, had it not been insatiable, and enlarged as hell itself.

Well, he seeing himself thus exalted to greatness and honour, and raging in his mind for higher state and degree, what doth he but begin to think with himself, how he might be set up as lord over all, and have

Pride kindles in Diabolus.

---

* The five senses are very properly described as so many gates of the city for these are the doors by which good or evil must enter

† God made man upright, and entered into a covenant of life with him, the condition of which was his perfect obedience.

‡ *Diabolus* is the Greek and Latin name for the Devil, and properly signifies the Calumniator or Accuser. The word is used, in Scripture, collective-

the sole power under Shaddai, 2 Pet. ii. 4. Jude 6. (Now that did the king reserve for his Son, yea, and he had already bestowed it upon him.) Wherefore he first consults with himself what had best to be done; and then breaks his mind to some others of his companions, to which they also agreed. So, in fine, they came to this issue, that they should make an attempt upon the King's Son to destroy him, that the inheritance might be theirs. Well, to be short, the treason, as I said, was concluded, the time appointed, the word given, the rebels rendezvoused, and the assault attempted. Now the King and his Son, being all and always eye, could not but discern all passages in his dominions; and he having always a love for his Son, as for himself, could not, at what he saw, but be greatly provoked and offended: wherefore what does he, but takes them in the very nick, and the first trip that they made towards their design, convicts them of the treason, horrid rebellion, and conspiracy that they had devised, and now attempted to put into practice, and casts them altogether out of all places of trust, benefit, honour and preferment: this done, he banishes them the court, turns them down into horrid pits; never more to expect the least favour from his hands, but to abide the judgment that he had appointed, and that for ever and ever.*

Shaddai discovers treason and rebellion among his angels.

Now they being thus cast out of all places of trust, profit and honour, and also knowing that they had lost their Prince's favour for ever, being banished his court and cast down to the horrible pits, you may be sure they would now add to their former pride what malice and rage against Shaddai, and against his Son, they could, 1 Pet. v. 8. Wherefore roving and ranging in much fury from place to place (if perhaps they might find something

---

ly, for the whole body of fallen spirits, whose original state of holiness and happiness the author describes.

* The scripture informs us that the devils were once angels, and that they sinned, (2 Pet. ii. 4.) We are not expressly told what their sin was, yet it may be presumed (from 1 Tim. iii. 6.) that it was pride; and it is generally thought that their pride consisted in opposition to the decree of God concerning his Son Jesus Christ, who was to be lord of the whole creation. (Psalm ii. 6, 7.) Of this, however, we are certain, that "they kept not their first estate;" (Jude ver. 6.)—they did not retain their primitive integrity, but "left their own habitation;" they relinquished, and were, by the righteous judgment of God, cast down from the mansions of bliss and glory which would have been their everlasting habitation had they not sinned; but "God spared them not," for their first sin; he hurled them down, with righteous indignation, into some unknown place of misery, called The Deep and The Bottomless Pit, and has reserved them in chains of darkness, like condemned prisoners, unto the judgment of the great day, when their torment will be completed, and they shall be forever confined to that fire which is prepared for Diabolus and his associates.

that was the King's,) to revenge themselves on him, by spoiling that; at last they happened into this spacious country of Universe, and steered their course towards the town of Mansoul: and considering that the town was one of the chief works and delights of King Shaddai; what do they, but after counsel taken, make an assault upon that. I say, they knew that Mansoul belonged unto Shaddai: for they were there when he built, and beautified it for himself.* So when they had found the place, they shouted horribly for joy, and roared on it like as a lion on its prey; saying, now we have found the prize, and how to be revenged on King Shaddai for what he hath done to us. So they sat down, and called a council of war; and considered with themselves, what ways and methods they had best engage in, for the winning to themselves this famous town of Mansoul; and these four things were then propounded to be considered of.

A council of war held by Diabolus, to consider about winning the town of Mansoul.

First, Whether they had best all of them to show themselves in this design to the town of Mansoul?

Secondly, Whether they had best to go and sit down against Mansoul, in their now ragged and beggarly guise?

Thirdly, Whether they had best to show to Mansoul their intentions, and what design they came about; or whether to assault it with words and ways of deceit?

Fourthly, Whether they had not best give out private orders, to some of their companions, to take the advantage, if they see one or more of the principal townsmen, to shoot them; if thereby they shall judge their cause and design will the better be promoted?

It was answered, to the first of these proposals, in the negative; to wit, that it would not be best that all should show themselves before the town, because the appearance of many of them might alarm and frighten the town; whereas a few, or but one of them, was not so likely to do it. And to cause this advice to take place, it was added further, that if Mansoul was frighted, or did take the alarm, it is impossible, said Diabolus (for he spoke now,) that we should take the town; for that none can enter it

Diabolus gives his advice, which is adopted.

---

* It is supposed that the fall of angels took place after the creation of man, and therefore it seems probable that the angels who fell, as well as those who continued in their integrity, were witnesses of the glory of God in the formation of man. This is thought to be the meaning of Job xxxviii. 7. "the morning stars sang together, and all the sons of God shouted for joy;"—the angels rejoiced at the founding of the earth, extolling the divine glory of its Maker.

without its own consent.* Let therefore but a few, or but one, assault Mansoul, and, in my opinion, said Diabolus, let me be he. Wherefore to this they all agreed: and then to the second proposal they came, namely,

II. Whether they had best to go and sit down before Mansoul in their now ragged and beggarly guise?

To which it was answered also in the negative, By no means; and that because, though the town of Mansoul had been made to know, and to have to do with, before now, things that are invisible; they never did as yet see any of their fellow-creatures in so bad and rascally a condition as they: and this was the advice of the fierce Alecto. Then said Apollyon, the advice is pertinent; for even one of us appearing to them as we are now, must needs both beget and multiply such thoughts in them, as will both put them into a consternation of spirit, and necessitate them to put themselves upon their guard: and if so, said he, then, as Diabolus said but now, it is in vain for us to think of taking the town. Then said that mighty giant Beelzebub, The advice that is already given is safe; for though the men of Mansoul have seen such things as we once were, yet hitherto they did never behold such things as we now are. And it is best, in my opinion, to come upon them in such a guise as is common to, and most familiar among them. To this when they had consented; the next thing to be considered, was, in what shape, hue, or guise, Diabolus had best to show himself, when he went about to make Mansoul his own. Then one said one thing, and another the contrary. At last Lucifer† answered, that, in his opinion, it was best that his lordship should assume the body of one of those creatures that they of the town had dominion over: for, quoth he, those are not only familiar to them, but, being under them,

Alecto.

Apollyon.

Beelzebub's advice.

Lucifer also gives his advice, which is applauded by all.

---

* The will of man, in his original state, was certainly free, which is thus expressed by Milton:
  God made thee perfect, not immutable;
  And good he made thee; but to persevere
  He left it in thy power; ordained thy will
  By nature free......   *Paradise Lost.*

† These names are well chosen: *Apollyon* signifies the Destroyer: *Beelzebub*, the Lord of Flies, an idol of the heathen, and a name used by the Jews for the prince of devils: *Lucifer*, the Morning Star, another name of a fallen angel: *Legion*, a name assumed by the Demoniac, (Mark v. 9. 15);—a battalion of the Roman army, consisting of 4000 or 5000 men. *Alecto*, a feigned being among the heathen, one of the Furies; described by their poets as having her head covered with snakes, and breathing vengeance: *Tisiphone*, another of the Furies.

they will never imagine that any attempt should by them be made upon the town; and, to blind all, let him assume the body of one of those beasts that Mansoul deems to be wiser than any of the rest, Gen. iii. 1. Rev. xx. 1, 2. This advice was applauded of all; so it was determined that the giant Diabolus should assume the dragon; for that he was, in those days, as familiar with the town of Mansoul, as now is the bird with the boy; for nothing that was in its primitive state was at all amazing to them. They then proceeded to the third thing, which was,

III. Whether they had best show their inclinations, or the design of their coming to Mansoul, or no?

This also was answered in the negative, because of the weight that was in their former reasons, to wit, for that Mansoul were a strong people, a strong people in a strong town, whose wall and gates were impregnable (to say nothing of their castles,) nor can they by any means be won but by their own consent. Besides, said Legion, (for he gave answer to this,) a discovery of our intentions may make them send to their King for aid; and if that be done, I know what time of the day it will be with us: therefore let us assault them in all pretended fairness, covering our intentions with all manner of lies, flatteries, delusive words: feigning things that will never be, and promising that to them which they shall never find: this is the way to win Mansoul, and to make them willingly open their gates to us; yea, and desire us also to come in to them.

Legion advises dissimulation and craft.

And the reason why I think that this project will do, is, because the people of Mansoul are now every one simple and innocent: all honest and true: nor do they as yet know what it is to be assaulted with fraud, guile, and hypocrisy. They are strangers to lying and dissembling lips; wherefore we cannot, if thus we be disguised, by them at all be discerned; our lies shall go for true sayings, and our dissimulation for upright dealings. What we promise them, they will in that believe us; especially if in all our lies and feigned words we pretend great ove to them, and that our design is only their advantage and honour. Now there was not one bit of a reply against this, for it went as current down as doth the water down a deep descent: wherefore they go to consider of the last proposal, which was,

IV. Whether they had not best to give out orders to some of their company, to shoot some one or more of the principal of the townsmen; if they judge that their cause might be promoted thereby?

This was carried in the affirmative; and the man that was de-

Of Captain Resistance. signed by this stratagem to be destroyed, was one Mr Resistance, otherwise called Captain Resistance, and a great man in Mansoul this Captain Resistance was; and a man that the giant Diabolus, and his band, more feared, than they feared the whole town of Mansoul besides. Now who should be the actor to do the murder; that was the next: and they appointed one Tisiphone, a fury of the lake, to do it.

The result of their council. Thus they having ended the council of war, rose up, and assayed to do as they had determined:* they marched towards Mansoul, but all in a manner invisible, save only one; nor did he approach the town in his own likeness, but under the shape and in the body of the dragon.

Diabolus marches up to the town. So they drew up, and sat down before Ear-gate; for that was the place of hearing for all without the town, as Eye-gate was the place of perception. So, as I said, he came up with his train to the gate, and laid his ambuscade for Captain Resistance, within bowshot of the town. This done, the giant ascended up close to the gate, and called to the town of Mansoul for audience. Nor took he any with him but one Illpause, who was his orator in all difficult matters. Now, as I said, he being come up to the gate (as the manner of those times was,) sounded his trumpet

The lords of Mansoul appeared. for audience; at which the chief of the town of Mansoul, such as my Lord Innocent, my Lord Will-be-will,† my Lord-mayor, Mr Recorder,‡ and Captain Resistance, came down to the wall, to see who was there, and what was the matter. And my Lord Will-be-will, when he looked over, and saw who stood at the

---

* The enemies of our souls are, in this council, represented as full of all subtlety, agreeably to the scripture account; for Satan is called "the Deceiver, who deceiveth the whole world;" believers are said to be acquainted with his "devices," and are exhorted to "watch and pray, lest they enter into temptation."

It was justly observed, "that none could enter the soul without its own consent." Satan may tempt, but cannot force the soul to sin: but "every man is tempted, when he is drawn away of his own lust, and enticed," James . 4. We are therefore commanded to *resist* the devil, that he may fly from us. To destroy this necessary *resistance*, therefore, must be a great point with the enemy.

† My Lord *Will-be-Will* signifies that power of the mind called the will, by which we determine for or against an action.

‡ The Recorder is *Conscience*. By this faculty we judge of an action as good or bad, according to the light we enjoy, whether of the law of nature only, or of the written law, Rom. ii. 15. Conscience records our actions; and in the great day of judgment, the book of conscience is one of those which shall be opened.

gate, demanded what he was, and wherefore he was come, and why he roused the town of Mansoul with so unusual a sound?'

Diabolus then, as if he had been a lamb, began his oration and said, "Gentlemen of the famous town of Mansoul, I am, as you may perceive, no far dweller from you, but near, and one that is bound by the King to do you homage, and what service I can; wherefore, that I may be faithful to myself and to you, I have somewhat of concern to impart unto you; wherefore grant me your audience, and hear me patiently. And, first, I will assure you, it is not myself but you, not mine but your advantage, that I seek by what I now do; as will full well be made manifest, by that I have opened my mind to you. For, Gentlemen, I am (to tell you the truth) come to show you how you may obtain great and ample deliverance from a bondage that unawares to yourselves you are captivated and enslaved under." At this the town of Mansoul began to prick up its ears. "And what is it, pray? what is it?" thought they. And he said, "I have something to say to you concerning your King, concerning his law, and also touching yourselves. Touching your King, I know he is great and potent; but yet, all that he has said to you is neither true, nor yet for your advantage. 1. It is not true; for that wherewith he hath hitherto awed you, shall not come to pass, though you do the thing he hath forbidden. But if there was danger, what a slavery it is to live always in fear of the greatest of punishments, for doing so small and trivial a thing as eating a little fruit is! 2. Touching his laws, this I say, further, they are both unreasonable, intricate, and intolerable. Unreasonable, as was hinted before, for that the punishment is not proportioned to the offence: there is a great difference and disproportion betwixt the life, and an apple; yet the one must go for the other, by the law of your Shaddai. But it is also intricate, in that he saith, first you may eat of *all*: and yet, after forbids the eating of *one*. And then, in the last place, it must needs be intolerable; forasmuch as that fruit, which you are forbidden to eat of (if you are forbidden any,) is that, and that alone, which is able by your eating, to minister you a good, as yet unknown by you. This is manifest by the very name of the tree, it is called The Tree of Knowledge of Good and Evil: and have you that knowledge as yet? No, no; nor can you conceive how good, how pleasant, and how much to be desired to make one wise, it is, so long as you stand by your King's commandment.

Diabolus's oration.

Mansoul engaged.

Diabolus's subtlety made up of lies.

False reasoning by Diabolus.

Why should you be holden in ignorance and blindness? Why should you not be enlarged in knowledge and understanding? And now, O ye inhabitants of the famous town of Mansoul, to

He holds out a false liberty.
speak more particularly to yourselves, ye are not a free people: ye are kept both in bondage and slavery, and that by a grievous threat, no reason being annexed, but, so I will have it, so it shall be. And is it not grievous to think on, that the very thing you are forbidden to do, might you but do it, would yield you both wisdom and honour? for then your eyes will be opened, and you shall be as gods. Now, since this is thus, quoth he, can you be kept by any prince in more slavery, and in greater bondage than you are under this day? You are made underlings, and are wrapt up in inconveniencies, as I have well made appear: for what bondage greater than to be kept in blindness! Will not reason tell you, that it is better to have eyes, than to be without them? and that to be at liberty, is better than to be shut in a dark and stinking cave."*

And just now, while Diabolus was speaking these words to

Captain Resistance slain.
Mansoul, Tisiphone shot at Captain Resistance, where he stood on the gate, and mortally wounded him in the head: so that he, to the amazement of the townsmen, and the encouragement of Diabolus, fell down dead quite over the wall.† Now when Captain Resistance was dead (and he was the only man of war in the town,) poor Mansoul was wholly left naked of courage, nor had she now any heart to resist: but this was as the devil would have it. Then stood forth that He, Mr Ill-pause, that Diabolus brought with him, who was his orator, and he addressed himself to speak to the town of Mansoul: the tenour of whose speech here follows:

ILL-PAUSE. "Gentlemen," quoth he, "it is my master's

Mr Ill-pause, his speech to the town of Mansoul.
happiness, that he has this day a quiet and teachable auditory; and it is hoped by us, that we shall prevail with you not to cast off good advice: my master has a very great love for you; and although he very well knows that he runs the hazard of the anger of King Shaddai, yet love to you will

---

* This artful speech of Diabolus is founded upon the scriptural account of the first temptation, Gen. iii. 1—4, "and the serpent said unto the woman, yea, hath God said, ye shall not eat," &c. In this passage the prohibition is represented as too strict, as intended to abridge their happiness, and that dis obedience would be attended with no danger, but rather with great advantage. The devil, the father of lies, finding this method so successful, still persists in it. God says—Sinner, thou shalt die; Satan says—Thou shalt not die; which of these ought we to believe?

† Resistance to the suggestions of Satan failed in our first mother. She parleyed with the temptation which she ought to have resisted and rejected

make him do more than that. Nor doth there need that a word more should be spoken to confirm for truth what he hath said; there is not a word but carries with itself evidence in its bowels; the very name of the tree may put an end to all controversy in this matter. I therefore at this time shall only add this advice to you, under and by the leave of my lord (and with that he made Diabolus a very low congee:) consider his words; look on the tree, and the promising fruit thereof; remember also, that yet you know but little, and this is the way to know more: and if your reason be not conquered to accept of such good counsel, you are not the men I took you to be." But when the towns-folk saw that the tree was good for food, and that it was pleasant to the eye, and a tree to be desired to make one wise, they did as old Ill-pause advised, they took and did eat thereof. Now this I should have told you before, that even then, when this Ill-pause was making this speech to the townsmen, my Lord Innocency (whether by a shot from the camp of the giant, or from some qualm that suddenly took him, or whether by the stinking breath of that treacherous villain old Ill-pause, for so I am most apt to think) sunk down in the place where he stood, nor could he be brought to life again.* Thus these two brave men died; brave men I call them, for they were the beauty and glory of Mansoul, so long as they lived therein: nor did there now remain any more a noble spirit in Mansoul; they all fell down and yielded obedience to Diabolus, and became his slaves and vassals, as you shall hear.

Now these being dead, what do the rest of the townsfolk, but as men that had found a fool's paradise, they presently, as afore was hinted, fell to prove the truth of the giant's words: and first, they did as Ill-pause had taught them, they looked, they considered, they were taken with the forbidden

Strong temptation.

My Lord Innocency's death.

The town taken by Diabolus and his bands.

with abhorrence. She *paused:* and it was an *ill-pause.* There was no occasion to pause or ponder on what the Devil had said, for he had given the lie to the God of truth. Whatever contradicts the word of God should be instantly resisted as diabolical.

* The very breath of temptation, received and entertained a single moment, destroyed primitive innocence. When the lies of Satan were admitted, unbelief entered and innocence died. "Thou shalt surely die," said Jehovah. In a spiritual sense, man did indeed die immediately. He died spiritually, he died to God. "Lust conceived, and brought forth sin, and sin when finished, brought forth death," Jam. i. 5. By this one fatal act of disobedience, the whole world was ruined. "By one man sin entered into the world, and death by sin." "By one man's disobedience many were made sinners." "By the offence of one, judgment came upon all men to condemnation. Rom. v. 18, 19.

fruit, "they took thereof, and did eat;"* and having eaten, they became immediately drunken therewith; so they opened the gates, both Ear-gate and Eye-gate, and let in Diabolus with all his bands, quite forgetting their good Shaddai, his law, and the judgment that he had annexed with solemn threatening to the breach thereof.

CHAPTER II.

Diabolus takes possession of the Castle. Mr Understanding, the Lord Mayor, is deposed, and a wall built before his house to darken it. Mr Conscience the Recorder is displaced. My Lord Will-be-will is appointed Governor. The image of Shaddai defaced. A new corporation chosen, and forts erected.

DIABOLUS having now obtained entrance in at the gates of the town, marches up to the middle thereof, to make his conquest as sure as he could; and finding, by this time, the affections of the people warmly inclining to him, he, thinking it was best striking while the iron is hot, made this further deceivable speech unto them, saying, "Alas, my poor Mansoul! I have done thee indeed this service, as to promote thee to honour, and to greaten thy liberty; but alas! alas! poor Mansoul, thou wantest now one to defend thee; for assure thyself, when Shaddai shall hear what is done, he will come; for sorry will he be that thou hast broken his bonds, and cast his cords away from thee. What wilt thou do? Wilt thou, after enlargement, suffer thy privileges to be invaded and taken away? or what wilt thou resolve with thyself?" Then they all with one consent said to this bramble, "Do thou reign over us." So he accepted *Diabolus is entertained for their king.* the motion, and became the king of the town of Mansoul. This being done, the next thing was, to give him possession of the castle, and so of the whole strength of the town. Wherefore into the castle he goes (it was that which Shaddai built in Mansoul, for his own delight and pleasure:) this was now become a den and hold for the giant Diabolus. Now having got possession of *He is possessed of the castle,* this stately palace or castle, what doth he, but make it a garrison for himself, and strengthens and fortifies it with all sorts of provisions against

---

* Milton finely represents the fatal act:
    "So saying, her rash hand in evil hour
    "Forth reaching to the fruit, she pluck'd, she eat:
    "Earth felt the wound, and nature from her seat,
    "Sighing through all her works, gave signs of woe
    "That all was lost."   *Book IX. l. 780.*

and fortifieth it for himself. the king Shaddai, or those that should endeavour the regaining of it to him and his obedience again.*

This done, but not thinking himself yet secure enough, in the next place he bethinks himself of new modelling the town: and so he does, setting up one and putting down another at pleasure. Wherefore my Lord Mayor, whose name was my Lord Understanding, and Mr Recorder, whose name was Mr Conscience, these he put out of place and power.

Diabolus new-models the town.

As for my Lord Mayor, though he was an understanding man, and one too that had complied with the rest of the town of Mansoul in admitting the giant into the town, 2 Cor. x. 4, 5. yet Diabolus thought not fit to let him abide in his former lustre and glory, because he was a seeing man, Eph. iv. 18, 19, wherefore he had darkened him not only by taking from him his office and power, but by building of an high and strong tower, just between the sun's reflection and the windows of my lord's palace; by which means the house, and the whole of his habitation, was made as dark as darkness itself: and thus, being alienated from the light, he became as one that was born blind. To this house my lord was confined, as to a prison; nor might he, upon his parole, go further than within his own bounds. And now, had he had an heart to do for Mansoul, what could he do for it, or wherein could he be profitable to her? So then, so long as Mansoul was under the power and government of Diabolus (and so long it was under him, as it was obedient to him; which was even until by a war it was rescued out of his hand;) so long my Lord Mayor was rather an impediment in, than an advantage to, the famous town of Mansoul.†

The lord Mayor put out of place.

As for Mr Recorder, before the town was taken, he was a man well read in the laws of his king, and also a man of courage and faithfulness to speak truth on every occasion; and he had a tongue as bravely hung, as he had an head filled with judgment.

The recorder put out of place.

---

* The *Heart* of fallen man, signified by the *castle*, is in the possession of Satan; "the strong man armed" keepeth this palace, which was erected for the habitation of God. The powers of the soul are perverted, and made "strong holds" against God, 2 Cor. x. 4. Satan is become "the prince of this world," and powerfully works in the children of disobedience, Eph. ii. Yea, he is called "the god of this world," and is not only obeyed by sinners universally, but, under various forms, is worshipped by many of the heathen.

† The understanding, which was once full of light, is now most miserably darkened by sin and Satan; so that man is "alienated from the life of God, through the ignorance and blindness of his heart." The understanding, which took the lead in the heart, as chief magistrate, is now deposed and the corrupted *will* takes his place.

Now this man, Diabolus could by no means abide, because, though he gave his consent to his coming into the town, yet he could not, by all wiles, trials, stratagems, and devices that he could use, make him his own. True, he was much degenerated from his former king, and also much pleased with the giant's service, and many of his laws. But this would not do, forasmuch as he was not wholly his; he would now and then think upon Shaddai, and have a dread of his law upon him, and then he would speak against Diabolus with a voice as great as when a lion roareth: yea, and would also at certain times, when his fits were upon him (for you must know, that sometimes he had terrible fits,) make the whole town of Mansoul shake with his voice; and therefore the new king of Mansoul could not abide him.*

He sometimes speaks for the first king.

Diabolus therefore feared the Recorder more than any that was left alive in the town of Mansoul, because, as I said, his words did shake the whole town; they were like the rattling of thunder, and also like thunder-claps. Since therefore the giant could not make him wholly his own, what doth he do, but studies all that he could to debauch the old gentleman, and by debauchery, to stupify his mind, and more harden his heart in the ways of vanity. And as he attempted so he accomplished his design: he debauched the man, and by little and little so drew him into sin and wickedness, that at last he was not only debauched as at first, and so by consequence defiled, but was almost (at last, I say) past all conscience of sin. And this was the farthest Diabolus could go. Wherefore he bethinks himself of another project, and that was, to persuade the men of the town that Mr Recorder was mad, and so not to be regarded. And for this he urged his fits, and said, If he be himself, why doth he not do thus always? But, quoth he, all mad folks have their fits, and in them raving language; so hath this old and doating gentleman. Thus by one means or other he quickly got Mansoul to slight, neglect and despise whatever Mr Recorder could say.

He is more debauched than before.

The town taken off from heeding him.

For, besides what you have already heard, Diabolus had a way to make the old gentleman, when he was merry, unsay, and deny what he in his fits had affirmed. And in-

* The office and power of *conscience* (or the old recorder) is beautifully described. He will sometimes speak, yea, roar aloud, testifying for God, and against sin. But it is the interest of Satan to debauch the conscience, and if possible, to silence it; and, if this cannot be done, to represent its faithful remonstrances as the ravings of madness.

deed this was the next way to make himself ridiculous, and to cause that no man should regard him. Also now he never spake freely for king Shaddai, but always by force and constraint. Besides, he would at one time be hot against that, about which at another he would hold his peace, so uneven was he now in his doings. Sometimes he would be as if fast asleep, and again sometimes as dead, even then when the whole town of Mansoul was in her career after vanity, and in her dance after the giant's pipe.

How conscience becomes so ridiculous as with carnal men it is.

Wherefore sometimes, when Mansoul did use to be frighted with the thundering voice of the Recorder that was, and when they did tell Diabolus of it, he would answer, that what the old gentleman said was neither out of love to him, nor pity to them, but of a foolish fondness that he had to be prating; and so would hush, still, and put all to quiet again. And that he might leave no argument unurged that might tend to make them secure, he said, and said it often, Oh Mansoul! consider, that notwithstanding the old gentleman's rage, and the rattle of his high and thundering words, you hear nothing of Shaddai himself, (when liar and deceiver, that he was, every outcry of Mr Recorder against the sin of Mansoul was the voice of God in him to them.) But he goes on, and says, you see that he values not the loss nor rebellion of the town of Mansoul; nor will he trouble himself with calling his town to a reckoning, for their giving themselves to me. He knows, that though you were his, now you are lawfully mine; so leaving us to one another, he hath now shaken his hands of us.

Satanical rhetoric.

Moreover, O Mansoul! quoth he, consider how I have served you, even to the uttermost of my power; and that with the best that I have, could get, or procure for you in all the world: besides, I dare say, that the laws and customs that you now are under, and by which you do homage to me, do yield you more solace and content than did the paradise that at first you possessed. Your liberty also, as yourselves do very well know, has been greatly widened and enlarged by me; whereas I found you a penned up people, I have not laid any restraint upon you: you have no law, statute, or judgment of mine to fright you; I call none of you to account for your doings, except the madman, you know who I mean: I have granted you to live, each man like a prince in his own palace, even with as little control from me as I have from you.

Satan's flatteries.

Conscience.

And thus would Diabolus hush up and quiet the town of

Men sometimes angry with their conscience. Mansoul, when the Recorder that was, did at times molest them; yea, and with such cursed orations as these would set the whole town in a rage and fury against the old gentleman; yea, the rascally crew at some times would be for destroying him. They have often wished, in my hearing, that he had lived a thousand miles off from them; his company, his words, yea, the sight of him, and especially when they remembered how in old times he did use to threaten and condemn them (for all he was now so debauched,) did terrify and afflict them sore.*

But all their wishes were vain; for I don't know how, unless by the power of Shaddai, and his wisdom, he was preserved in being amongst them. Besides his house was as strong as a castle, and stood hard by a strong-hold of the town: moreover, *Ill thoughts. (a) Of fears.* if at any time any of the crew or rabble attempted to make him away, he could pull up the sluices(a) and let in such floods as would drown all round about him.

But to leave Mr Recorder, and to come to my Lord Will-be-will, another of the famous town of Mansoul. *The will* This Will-be-will was as high-born in Mansoul, and was as much, if not more, a freeholder, than many of them were: besides, if I remember my tale aright, he had some privileges peculiar to himself in the famous town of Mansoul. Now, together with these, he was a man of great strength, resolution, and courage, nor in his occasion could any turn him away. But I say, whether he was proud of his estate, privileges, strength or what (but sure it was through pride of something,) he scorns now to be a slave in Mansoul; and therefore resolves to bear office under Diabolus, that he might (such a one as he was) be a petty ruler and governor in Mansoul; and (headstrong man that he was) thus he began betimes; for this man, when Diabolus did make his oration at Ear-gate, was one of the first that was for consenting to his words, and for accepting of his counsel as wholesome, and that was for opening the gate and letting him into the town: wherefore Diabolus had a kindness for him, and for that reason designed him for a place; and perceiving the valour and stoutness of the man, he coveted to have him for one

---

* *Conscience,* in natural men, is very unequal and irregular in his opposition to sin; yet, by fits and starts he will cry out, and so frighten the sinner, that he wishes him "a thousand miles off," so as to give him no disturbance, or prevent his quiet enjoyment of that liberty to sin, which Satan boasts he has granted to Mansoul. Nevertheless the power of conscience cannot be utterly destroyed.

of his great ones, to act and do in matters of the highest concern."

So he sent for him, and talked with him of that secret matter which lay in his breast; but there needed not much persuasion in the case; for as at first he was willing that Diabolus should be let into the town, so now he was as willing to serve him there.

The will takes place under Diabolus.

When the tyrant, therefore, perceived the willingness of my lord to serve him, and that his mind stood bending that way, he forthwith made him captain of the castle governor of the wall, and keeper of the gates of Mansoul: yea, there was a clause in his commission, that nothing without him should be done in all the town of Mansoul: so that now, next to Diabolus himself, who but my Lord Will-be-will in all the town of Mansoul! nor could any thing be now done, but at his will and pleasure, throughout the town of Mansoul, Rom. viii. 7.

Mr Mind, my lord's clerk.

He had also one Mr Mind for his clerk; a man, to speak on, every way like his master; for he and his lord were in principle one, and in practice not far asunder, Eph. ii 2, 3, 4. And now was Mansoul brought under to purposes, and made to fulfil the lusts of the will, and of the mind.†

But it will not be out of my thoughts, what a desperate one this Will-be-will was, when power was put into his hand. First, he flatly denied that he owed any suit or service to his former prince and liege lord. This done, in the next place he took an oath, swore fidelity to his great master Diabolus, and then being stated and settled in his place, office, advancement, and preferment, oh you cannot think, unless you had seen it, the strange work that this workman made in the town of Mansoul.

First, He maligned Mr Recorder to death; he would neither endure to see him, nor hear the words of his mouth, he would shut his eyes when he saw him, and stop his ears when he heard him speak. Also he could not endure that so much as a fragment of the law of Shaddai should be any where seen

The carnal will opposes conscience.

---

* My Lord *Will-be-will.*—The author represents the will as a lord, a person of great consequence in the town, and very justly, for the human will is that power of the soul whereby we choose and determine. It is a governing faculty; and there could be no sin, till the will consented to the temptation. In fallen man the will is not subject to the law of God, but obstinately opposed to it, and therefore a fit deputy for the devil.

† By the *mind*, the author probably designs the judgment, or that faculty by which we distinguish between good and evil, and we are assured by the scriptures that "the carnal mind is enmity against God."

in the town. For example, his clerk, Mr Mind, had some old rents, Nehem. ix. 26, and torn parchments of the law of good Shaddai in his house: but when Will-be-will saw them, he cast them behind his back. True, Mr Recorder had some of the laws in his study; but my lord could by no means come at them: he also thought and said, the windows of my old lord mayor's house were always too light for the profit of the town of Mansoul. The light of a candle he could not endure. Now nothing at all pleased Will-be-will, but what pleased Diabolus his lord.*

Corrupt will loves a dark understanding.

There was no other like him to trumpet about the streets the brave nature, the wise conduct and great glory of the king Diabolus. He would range throughout all the streets of Mansoul, to cry up his illustrious lord; and would make himself even as an abject, among the base and rascally crew, to cry up his valiant prince. And I say, when and wheresoever he found those vassals, he would even make himself as one of them. In all ill courses, he would act without bidding, and do mischief without commandment.

Vain thoughts.

The Lord Will-be-will also had a deputy under him, and his name was Mr Affection: one that was also greatly debauched in his principles, and answered thereto in his life, Rom. i. 25: he was only given to the flesh, and therefore they call him Vile-affection. Now there was he, and one Carnal-lust, the daughter of Mr Mind (like to like, quoth the devil to the collier,) that fell in love and made a match, and were married; and, as I take it, they had several children, as Impudence, Black-mouth, and Hate-reproof. These three were black boys; and besides these three, they had three daughters, as Scorn-truth, Slight-God, and the name of the youngest was Revenge; these were all married in the town, and also begot and yielded many bad brats, too many to be inserted. But to pass by this.†

A match between Vile-affection and Carnal-lust.

When the giant had thus ingarrisoned himself in the town of Mansoul, and had put down and set up whom he thought good, he betakes himself to defacing. Now there was in the market-place of Mansoul, and also upon the gates of the castle, an

---

* Great is the aversion of the carnal mind and will to the Bible. Never was greater hatred to it discovered than in this day! But why do our infidels hate it? The true reason is, "they love darkness rather than light, because their deeds are evil," John iii. 19. The little remaining light of conscience they cannot endure, because it condemns their beloved carnality.

† The affections follow the dictates of the will. The offspring of Vile-affection and Carnal-lust are enumerated: a wretched brood!

image of the blessed king Shaddai; this image was so exactly engraven (and it was engraven in gold) that it did the most resemble Shaddai himself, of any thing that then was extant in the world. This he basely commanded to be defaced, and it was basely done by the hand of Mr No-truth. Now you must know, that as Diabolus had commanded, and that by the hand of Mr No-truth, the image of Shaddai was defaced; he likewise gave order that the same Mr No-truth should set up in its stead, the horrid and formidable image of Diabolus; to the great contempt of the former king, and debasing his town of Mansoul.*

What No-truth did.

Moreover, Diabolus made havock of all remains of the laws and statutes of Shaddai, that could be found in the town of Mansoul; to wit, such as contained either doctrines or morals, with all civil and natural documents: also relative severities he sought to extinguish. To be short, there was nothing of the remains of good in Mansoul, which he and Will-be-will sought not to destroy; for their design was, to turn Mansoul into a brute, and to make it like the sensual sow, by the hands of Mr No-truth.†

All law-books destroyed that could be found.

When he had destroyed what law and good orders he could, then further to effect his design, namely to alienate Mansoul from Shaddai her king, he commands, and they set up his own vain edicts, statutes, and commandments in all places of resort or concourse in Mansoul, 1 John ii. 16, to wit, such as gave liberty "to the lusts of the flesh, the lusts of the eyes, and the pride of life, which are not of Shaddai, but of the world." He encouraged, countenanced, and promoted lasciviousness and all ungodliness there. Yea, much more did Diabolus to encourage wickedness in the town of Mansoul; he promised them peace, content, joy and bliss, in doing his commands, and that they should never be called to an account for their not doing the contrary. And let this serve to give a taste to them that love to hear of what is done beyond their knowledge, afar off in other countries.

The edicts of Diabolus set up.

* God made man in his own holy and beautiful image. Sin has miserably defaced this image of God in the soul, and substituted the horrid and deformed image of the devil. O what a change!

† Satan would obliterate all the commandments of God, prevent the practice of all duty to him or to our neighbour, and makes us merely carnal and brutish. Awfully hath he succeeded, so that man is become that motley monster, "half beast, half devil," as bishop Hall calls him; uniting in himself the sensual appetites of the former, with the diabolical tempers of the latter.

Now Mansoul being wholly at his beck, and brought wholly to his bow, nothing was heard or seen therein but that which tended to set up him.

But now, he having disabled the Lord Mayor and Mr Recorder from bearing any office in Mansoul, and seeing that the town, before he came to it, was the most ancient of corporations in the world; and fearing, if he did not maintain greatness, they at any time should object that he had done them an injury; therefore, I say (that they might see that he did not intend to lessen their grandeur, or to take from them any of their advantageous things) he did chose for them a lord mayor and a recorder to himself; and such as contented them to the heart, and such also as pleased him wondrous well.

They have a new lord mayor and a new recorder.

The name of the mayor that was of Diabolus' making, was the Lord Lustings. A man that had neither eyes nor ears; all that he did, whether as a man or an officer, he did it naturally as doth the beast; and that which made him yet more ignoble, though not to Mansoul, yet to them that beheld, and were grieved for its ruin, was, that he could never favour good but evil.*

The new mayor.

The recorder was one whose name was Forget-good; and a very sorry fellow he was; he could remember nothing but mischief, and to do it with delight.

The new recorder.

He was naturally prone to do things that are hurtful; even hurtful to the town of Mansoul, and to all the dwellers there. These two, therefore, by their power and practice, examples, and smiles upon evil, did much more mischief, and settled the common people in hurtful ways; for who doth not perceive, that when those that sit aloft are vile and corrupt themselves, they corrupt the whole region and country where they are.†

Besides these Diabolus made several burgesses and aldermen in Mansoul; such as out of whom the town, when it needed, might chuse them officers, governors and magistrates; and these are the names of the chief of them: Mr Incredulity, Mr Haughty, Mr Swearing, Mr Whoring, Mr Hardheart, Mr Pitiless, Mr Fury, Mr No-truth, Mr Stand-to-lies, Mr False-

He doth make them new aldermen.

---

* Instead of the *understanding*, which, before the revolution, governed the town, Mr *Lustings* is made lord mayor. This wretch "had neither eyes nor ears." So beastly are carnal lusts, that they pay no regard to reason nor danger, but are hurried on by mere appetite to every fleshy indulgence.

† The *memory* has suffered much by the fall. It is wonderfully tenacious of evil, but is sure to forget every thing that is good.

THE HOLD OF DEFIANCE.   P. 35.

peace, Mr Drunkenness, Mr Cheating, Mr Atheism; thirteen in all. Mr Incredulity is the eldest, and Mr Atheism the youngest of the company.*

There was also an election of common-council-men, and others: as bailiffs, serjeants, constables, &c. but all of them, like those afore-named, being either fathers, brothers, cousins, or nephews, to them, whose names, for brevity-sake, I omit to mention.

He buildeth three strong holds. When the giant had thus far proceeded in his work, in the next place he betook him to build some strong holds in the town; and he built three that seemed to be impregnable. The first he called the hold of Defiance, because it was made to command the whole town, and to keep it from the knowledge of its ancient king. The second he called Midnight hold, because it was built on purpose to keep Mansoul from the true knowledge of itself. The third was called Sweet-sinhold, because by that he fortified Mansoul against all desires of good. The first of these holds stood close by Eye-gate, that the light might as much as possible be darkened there. The second was built hard by the old castle, to the end that that might be made more blind, if possible. And the third stood in the market-place.

He that Diabolus made governor over the first of these, was one Spite-God, a most blasphemous wretch. He came with the whole rabble of them that came against Mansoul at first, and was himself one of themselves. He that was made the governor of Midnight-hold was one Love-no-light, he was also one of them that came first against the town. And he that was made the governor of the hold called Sweet-sin-hold, was one whose name was Love-flesh; he was also a very lewd fellow, but not of that country from whence the others are bound. This fellow could find more sweetness when he was sucking a lust, than he did in the Paradise of God.

Diabolus has made his nest. And now Diabolus thought himself safe; he had taken Mansoul; he had ingarrisoned himself therein; he had put down the old officers, and set up new ones; he had defaced the image of Shaddai, and had set up his own; he had spoiled the old law-books, and had promoted his own vain lies; he had made him new magistrates, and set up new aldermen; he had built his new holds and had manned them for himself. And all this he did to make himself secure,

* A fit set of wretches to govern under *Diabolus!* It is well observed, that of there vile aldermen, *Incredulity* (or unbelief) was the eldest, and *Atheism*, the youngest. Unbelief naturally ends in Atheism.

in case the good Shaddai, or his Son should come to make an incursion upon him*.

CHAPTER III.

Information of the revolution carried to Shaddai. His great resentment on the occasion. His gracious intentions of restoring Mansoul. Some intimation of this published. Care of Diabolus to suppress this information. His stratagems to secure the possession of the town, and prevent its return to Shaddai.

NOW you may well think, that, long before this time, word by some or other could not but be carried to the good king Shaddai, how his Mansoul on the continent of Universe was lost; and that the giant Diabolus, once one of his majesty's servants, had, in rebellion against the king, made sure thereof for himself, and that to a very circumstance.

Tidings carried to the court, of what had happened in Mansoul.

At first, How Diabolus came upon Mansoul, (they being a simple people and innocent) with craft, subtlety, lies, and guile: Item, That he had treacherously slain their right noble and valiant captain, the Captain Resistance, as he stood upon the gate with the rest of the townsmen: Item, How my brave Lord Innocent fell down dead (with grief, some say; or with being poisoned with the stinking breath of one Ill-pause, as say others) at the hearing of his just lord and rightful prince Shaddai so abused by the mouth of so filthy a Diabolonian as that varlet Ill-pause was. The messenger further told, that after this Ill-pause had made a short oration to the townsmen, in behalf of Diabolus his master, the simple town, believing to be true what was said, with one consent did open Ear-gate, the chief gate of the corporation, and did let him with his crew into the possession of the famous town of Mansoul. He further showed how Diabolus had served the Lord-mayor and Mr Recorder, to wit, that he had put them from all place of power and trust. Item, He showed also, that my Lord Will-be-will was turned a very rebel and runnagate, and that so was one Mr Mind, his clerk; and that they two did range and revel it all the town over, and teach the wicked ones their ways. He said moreover, that this Will-be-will was put into great trust, and particularly that Diabolus had put into Will-be-will's hand all

* The revolution is completed. The understanding is darkened; the conscience debauched; the will perverted; the image of God defaced; the law of God suppressed, and beastly lusts triumphant. While the proud sinner defies God, loves midnight darkness, and wallows in sin. What an awful but accurate picture of apostate man! God be merciful to us sinners!

the strong places in Mansoul; and that Mr Affection was made my Lord Will-be-will's deputy, in his most rebellious affairs. Yea, said the messenger, this monster, Lord Will-be-will, has openly disavowed the King Shaddai, and hath given his faith and plighted troth to Diabolus.

Also, said the messenger, besides this, **the new king, or rather rebellious tyrant, over the once famous, but now perishing town of Mansoul, has set up a lord-mayor and recorder of his own.** For mayor he has set up one Mr Lustings; and, for recorder, Mr Forget-good; **two of the vilest of all the town of Mansoul.** This faithful messenger also proceeded, and told what a sort of new burgesses Diabolus had made; also that he had built several strong forts, towers, and strong-holds in Mansoul. He told too, the which I had almost forgot, how Diabolus had put the town of Mansoul into arms, the better to capacitate them, on his behalf, to make resistance against Shaddai their king, should he come to reduce them to their former obedience.

New officers appointed by Diabolus.

Now the tidings-teller did not deliver his relation of things in private, but in open court, the king and his son, high lords, chief captains, and nobles, being all there present to hear. But by that they had heard the whole of the story, it would have amazed one to have seen, had he been there to behold it, what sorrow and grief, and compunction of spirit, there was among all sorts, to think that the famous Mansoul was now taken; only the king and his son foresaw all this long before, yea, and sufficiently provided for the relief of Mansoul, though they told not every body thereof. Yet because they too would have a share in condoling the misery of Mansoul, therefore they also did, and that at a rate of the highest degree, bewail the losing of Mansoul. The king said plainly, that, "it grieved him at the heart," Gen. vi. 5, 6. and you may be sure that his son was not a whit behind him. Thus they gave conviction to all about them, that they had love and compassion for the famous town of Mansoul.*

Grief at court to hear the tidings.

---

* "Known unto God are all things, from the beginning of the world." The fall was foreseen from all eternity. God, in his unsearchable wisdom permitted it, and provided, in the covenant of grace, for the restoration of his people.

Nothing can more awfully bespeak the extreme sinfulness and misery of man, than the words here referred to—"It repented the Lord that he had made man on the earth, and it grieved him at his heart." God's resentment against sin is here expressed after the manner of men, and must not be understood as implying *uneasiness* or *change of mind* in Jehovah, but his just displeasure against sin and sinners, as odious to his holiness, and obnoxious to his justice. He is spoken of as *grieved*, like a person whose kindness has been abused—who has fostered a snake in his bosom which now hisses and

Well, when the king and his son were retired into the privy chamber, they there again consulted about what they had designed before, to wit, That as Mansoul should in time be suffered to be lost; so as certainly it should be recovered again. Recovered, I say, in such a way, as that both the king and his son would get themselves eternal fame and glory thereby. Wherefore, after this consultation, the son of Shaddai (a sweet and comely person, and one that had always great affection for those that were in affliction, but one that had mortal enmity in his heart against Diabolus, because he was designed for it, and because he sought his crown and dignity, Isaiah, xlix. 5. 1 Tim. i. 15. Hos. xiii. 14;) this son of Shaddai, I say, having striken hand with his father, and promised that he would be his servant to recover Mansoul again, stood by his resolution, nor would he repent of the same. The purport of which agreement was this, to wit, That at a certain time, prefixed by both, the king's son should take a journey into the country of Universe, and there in a way of justice and equity, by making amends for the follies of Mansoul, he should lay the foundation of her perfect deliverance from Diabolus, and from his tyranny.*

The secrets of his purpose.

The Son of God.

A brave design set on foot for the town of Mansoul.

Moreover, Immanuel resolved to make, at a time convenient, a war upon the giant Diabolus, (a) even while he was possessed of the town of Mansoul; and that he would fairly, by strength of hand, drive him out of his hold, his nest, and take it to himself, to be his habitation.

(a) *By the Holy Ghost.*

This being now resolved upon, order was given to the Lord Chief Secretary, to draw up a fair record of what was determined, and to cause that it should be published in all the corners of the kingdom of Universe. A short breviat of the contents thereof, you may, if you please, take here as follows:

The Holy Scriptures.

'Let all men know, who are concerned, than the son of Shaddai, the great king, is engaged by covenant to his father, to bring his Mansoul to

The contents.

---

stings. "Doth God thus hate sin, and shall not we hate it? Hath our sin grieved him to the heart, and shall not we be grieved to the heart for it? O that this consideration may humble and shame us, and that we may look upon him whom we have thus grieved and mourn." *Henry.*

* How astonishing is the divine benignity! and who can express it so well as in the words of Immanuel himself (John iii. 6.) *God SO loved the world*—so loved! How much he loved, no tongue can tell, no heart conceive. It is love unsought, unparalleled, free, and everlasting!

him again; yea, and to put Mansoul too, through his love, into a far better and more happy condition than it was in before it was taken by Diabolus."*

These papers, therefore, were published in several places, to the no little molestation of the tyrant Diabolus; for now, thought he, I shall be molested, and my habitation will be taken from me.

But when this matter, I mean this purpose of the king and his son, did at first take air at court, who can tell how the high lords, chief captains and noble princes that were there, were taken with the business! First, They whispered to one another, (a) and after that it began to ring throughout the king's palace, all wondering at the glorious design that between the king and his son was on foot for the miserable town of Mansoul: yea, the courtiers could scarcely do any thing, either for the king, or kingdom, but they would mix, with the doing thereof, a noise of the love of the king and his son, that they had for the town of Mansoul.† Nor could these lords, high captains, and princes, be content to keep this news at court; yea, before the records thereof were perfected, themselves came down and told it in Universe.

(a) Among the angels.

At last it came to the ears, as I said, of Diabolus, to his no little discontent; for you must think it would perplex him to hear of such a design against him. Well, but after a few casts in his mind, he concluded upon these four things: First, That this news, these good tidings (if possible) should be kept from the ears of the town of Mansoul; for, said he, if they should once come to the knowledge that Shaddai, their former king, and Immanuel his son, are contriving good for the town of Mansoul, what can be expected by me, but that Mansoul will revolt from under my hand and government, and return again to him.‡

Diabolus perplexed at the news.

He concluded on several things.

Now to accomplish this his design, he renews his flattery with

---

* Early intimation was given to a lost world of God's gracious design in favour of rebel man; and the Lord designing to make the Scriptures, which are inspired by the Holy Spirit (the Secretary) the instrument in his hands for his recovery, was pleased to publish in them his benevolent purpose.

† Angels desire to pry into the wonders of redemption. They would be astonished at the discovery; as, long after they proved themselves to be, by the chorus they sang at our Saviour's birth—"Glory to God in the highest! on earth, peace! good-will towards men!" These benevolent spirits were also sometimes the messengers of evangelical tidings to the fathers previous to the incarnation of Immanuel.

‡ It is the interest of hell to keep men in ignorance of the gospel, the proper tendency of which is to induce sinners to return to God, 2 Cor. iv. 4.

my Lord Will-be-will, and also gives him strict charge and command, that he should keep watch by day and night at all the gates of the town, especially Ear-gate and Eye-gate: for I hear of a design, quoth he, a design to make us all traitors, and that Mansoul must be reduced to its first bondage again. I hope they are but flying stories, quoth he; however, let no such news by any means be let into Mansoul, lest the people be dejected thereat: I think, my lord, it can be no welcome news to you, I am sure it is none to me: and I think, that at this time it should be all our wisdom and care to nip the head of all such rumors as shall tend to trouble our people; wherefore I desire, my lord, that you will in this matter do as I say. Let there be strong guards daily kept at every gate of the town. Stop also and examine from whence such come, whom you perceive do come from far hither to trade: nor let them by any means be admitted into Mansoul, unless you shall plainly perceive that they are favorers of our excellent government. I command, moreover, said Diabolus, that there be spies continually walking up and down the town of Mansoul; and let them have power to suppress and destroy any that they shall see plotting against us, or that shall prate of what by Shaddai and Immanuel is intended.

First, how to keep the news from Mansoul.

The will engaged against the gospel.—Good thoughts must be kept out of Mansoul.

All good thoughts and words are to be suppressed.

This therefore was accordingly done; my Lord Will-be-will hearkened to his lord and master, went willingly after his commandment, and with all the diligence he could, kept any that would from going out abroad, or that sought to bring these tidings to Mansoul, from coming into the town.

Secondly, This done, in the next place Diabolus, that he might make Mansoul as sure as he could, frames and imposes a new oath and horrible covenant upon the town's folk:

A new oath imposed.

To wit, That they should never desert him, nor his government, nor yet betray him, nor seek to alter his laws: but that they should own, confess, stand by, and acknowledge him for their rightful king, in defiance of any that do, or hereafter shall, by any pretence, law, or title whatsoever, lay claim to the town of Mansoul, Isa. xxviii. 15. thinking belike that Shaddai had not power to absolve them from this covenant with death, and agreement with hell. Nor did the silly Mansoul stick or boggle at all at this most monstrous engagement, but, as if it had been a sprat in the

They take the oath.

mouth of a whale, they swallowed it without any chewing. Were they troubled at it? Nay, they rather bragged and boasted of their so brave fidelity to the tyrant their pretended king; swearing that they would never be changelings, nor forsake their old lord for a new.*

Thus did Diabolus tie poor Mansoul fast; but jealousy that never thinks itself strong enough, put him, in the next place, upon another exploit, which was, yet more, if possible, to debauch this town of Mansoul; wherefore he caused, by the hand of one Mr Filth, an odious, nasty, lascivious piece of beastliness (a) to be drawn up in writing, and set upon the gates: whereby he granted and gave licence to all his true and trusty sons in Mansoul, to do whatsoever their lustful appetites prompted them to do, and that no man was to let, hinder, or control them, upon pain of incurring the displeasure of their prince.†

(a) *Odious atheistical pamphlets, and filthy ballads and romances full of ribaldry.*

Now this he did for these reasons:

1. That the town of Mansoul might be yet made weaker and weaker, and so more unable, should tidings come that their redemption was designed, to believe, hope, or consent to the truth thereof: for reason says, 'the bigger the sinner, the less ground or hope of mercy.'

Reasons for his thus doing.

2. The second reason was, If perhaps Immanuel, the son of Shaddai their king, by seeing the horrible and profane doings of the town of Mansoul, might repent, though entered into a covenant of redeeming them, of pursuing that covenant of their redemption; for he knew that Shaddai was holy, and that his son Immanuel was holy; yea, he knew it by woful experience: for, for the iniquity and sin of Diabolus was he cast from the highest orbs. Wherefore what more rational than for him to conclude, that thus for sin it might fare with Mansoul? But fearing lest also this knot should break, he bethinks himself of another, to wit

---

* Hardened sinners seem to be sworn vassals of Satan, and sometimes make desperate resolutions never to be religious. "We have made a covenant with death, and with hell are we at agreement." Isa. xxviii. 15. Such men " glory in their shame," and determine to be more and more vile.

† The margin informs us what this means. Would to God there were none of these infidel and obscene pamphlets, pictures and songs among us! But they abound; are circulated with diligence, introduced into schools among boys and girls, read with avidity, and they produce the damnable effects which the Devil designs; for the deeper the heart is immersed in sensuality, the less regard will be paid to God and religion; and not unfrequently, a secret despair possesses the sinner, that there is no hope for him, and therefore he may as well enjoy the full pleasures of sin.

Thirdly, To endeavour to possess all hearts in the town of Mansoul, that Shaddai was raising an army, to come to overthrow and utterly to destroy the town of Mansoul (and this he did to forestal any tidings that might come to their ears, of their deliverance;) for, thought he, If I first spread this abroad, the tidings that might come after will be swallowed up of this; for what else will Mansoul say, when they shall hear that they must be delivered, but that the true meaning is, Shaddai intends to destroy them? Wherefore he summons the whole town into the market-place, and there with deceitful tongue thus he addresses himself unto them: "Gentlemen, and my very good friends, you are all, as you know, my legal subjects, and men of the famous town of Mansoul; you know how, from the first day that I have been with you until now, I have behaved myself among you, and what liberty and great privileges you have enjoyed under my government; I hope, to your honour and mine, and also to your content and delight. Now, my famous Mansoul, a noise of trouble there is abroad, of trouble to the town of Mansoul; sorry I am therefore for your sakes. For I received but now by the post, from my Lord Lucifer (and he used to have good intelligence) that your old king Shaddai is raising an army to come against you, to destroy you root and branch ; and this, O Mansoul, is now the cause that at this time I have called you together, namely, to advise what in this juncture is best to be done. For my part, I am but one, and can with ease shift for myself, did I list to seek my own ease, and to leave my Mansoul in all danger, but my heart is so firmly united to you, and so loth am I to leave you, that I am willing to stand and fall with you, to the utmost hazard that shall befal me. What say you, O my Mansoul? will you now desert your old friend; or do you think of standing by me?

The place of hearing and of considering.

Then as one man, with one mouth, they cried out together, "Let him die the death that will not."

Then said Diabolus again, "'Tis in vain for us to hope for quarter, for this King knows not how to show it. True, perhaps he, at his first sitting down before us, will talk of, and pretend to mercy, that thereby with the more ease, and less trouble, he may again make himself the master of Mansoul; whatever therefore he should say, believe not one syllable or tittle of it, for all such language is but to overcome us, and to make us, while we wallow in our blood, the trophies of his merciless victory. My mind is, therefore, that we resolve to the last man to resist him, and not

Very deceiving language.

to believe him on any terms; *for in at that door will come our danger.* But shall we be flattered out of our lives? I hope you know more of the rudiments of politics, than to suffer yourselves to be so pitifully served.

"But suppose he should, if he get us to yield, save some of our lives, or the lives of some of them that are underlings in Mansoul, what help will that be to you that are the chief of the town, especially you whom I have set up, and whose greatness has been procured by you through your faithful sticking to me?

Lying language. And suppose again, that he should give quarter to every one of you, be sure he will bring you into that bondage under which you were captivated before, or a worse, and then what good will your lives do you? Shall you with him live in pleasure, as you do now! No, no, you must be bound by laws that will pinch you, and be made to do that which at present is hateful to you*. I

He is afraid of loosing Mansoul. am for you if you are for me; and it is better to die valiantly than to live like pitiful slaves. But I say, the life of a slave will be accounted a life too good for Mansoul now; blood, blood, nothing but blood, is in every blast of Shaddai's trumpet against poor Mansoul now: pray be concerned, I hear he is coming up, and stand to your arms, that

He puts them upon arming themselves. now, while you have leisure, I may teach you some feats of war. Armour for you I have, and by me it is; yea, and it is sufficient for Mansoul, from top to toe, nor can you be hurt by what his force can do, if you shall keep it well girt and fastened about you: come therefore to my castle and welcome, and harness yourselves for the war. There is helmet, breast-plate, sword, shield, and what not, that you will fight like men.

"1. My helmet, otherwise called an head-piece, is hope of doing well at last, what lives soever you live, Deut.

His helmet. xxix. 19. This is that which they had, who said that 'they should have peace, though they walked in the wickedness of their heart, to add drunkenness to thirst:' a piece of approved armour is this; and whoever has it, and can hold it, so long no arrow, dart, sword, or shield, can hurt him; this therefore keep on, and thou wilt ward off many a blow, my Mansoul.

"2. My breast-plate is a breast-plate of iron, Rev. ix. 9. 1

---

* Carnal men readily believe this lie, and make it one of their apologies for their dislike of religion, that it is destructive of liberty and pleasure. But believers assuredly know that "Christ's yoke is easy and his burden light;" his "service is perfect freedom," and all "his ways are pleasantness and peace."

His breast-plate. had it forged in mine own country, and all my soldiers are armed therewith; in plain language, it is an hard heart, an heart as hard as iron, and as much past feeling as a stone; the which if you get and keep, neither mercy shall win you, nor judgment fright you. This therefore is a piece of armour most necessary for all to put on that hate Shaddai, and that would fight against him under my banner.

"3. My sword is a tongue that is set on fire of hell, Psalm lvii. *His sword.* 4. lxiv. 3. James iii. 6. and that can bend itself to speak evil of Shaddai, his son, his ways, his people; use this, it has been tried a thousand times twice told; whoever hath it, keeps it, and makes use of it as I would have him, can never be conquered by mine enemy.

"4. My shield is unbelief, Job xv. 26. Psalm lxxvi. 3. Mark vi. 5. 6. or calling into question the truth of the word, or all the *His shield.* sayings that speak of the judgment that Shaddai has appointed for wicked men: use this shield; many attempts he has made upon it, and sometimes, 'tis true, it has been bruised; but they that have writ of the wars of Immanuel against my servants, have testified, that "he could do no mighty work there, because of their unbelief." Now, to handle this weapon of mine aright, is, not to believe things because they are true, of what sort, or by whomsoever asserted: if he speaks of judgment, care not for it; if he speaks of mercy, care not for it; if he promises, if he swears that he would do to Mansoul, if it turns, no hurt, but good; regard not what is said, question the truth of all; for this is to wield the shield of unbelief aright, and as my servants ought, and do: and he that does otherwise, loves me not, nor do I count him but an enemy unto me.

"5. Another part or piece, said Diabolus, of mine excellent armour, is "a dumb and prayerless spirit," a spirit that scorns *Another piece* to cry for mercy, let the danger be ever so great; *of armour.* wherefore be you, my Mansoul, sure that you make use of this. What! cry for quarter? Never do that, if you would be mine: I know you stout men; and am sure that I have clad you with that which is armour proof; wherefore to cry to Shaddai for mercy, let that be far from you. Besides all this, I have a maul, firebrands, arrows, and death, all good hand-weapons, and such as will do execution.*

After he had thus furnished his men with armour and arms,

---

* This is a just description of that "whole armour" of the devil, with which mistaken sinners defend themselves against God. Presumption—hardness of heart—a blasphemous tongue—unbelief, and a prayerless spirit. This is Satan's armour, the very reverse of that which God has provided for christian soldiers.

UNBELIEF. *P.* 44.

He backs all with a speech unto them. he addressed himself to them in such like words as these: "Remember, quoth he, that I am your rightful king: and that you have taken an oath, and entered into covenant, to be true to me and to my cause: I say, remember this, and show yourselves stout and valiant men of Mansoul. Remember also the kindness that I have always showed to you, and that without your petition. I have granted to you external things; wherefore the privileges, grants, immunities, profits, and honours, wherewith I have endowed you, do call forth at your hands returns of loyalty, my lion-like men of Mansoul: and what so fit a time to show it, as when others shall seek to take my dominion over you into their own hands? One word more, and I have done: Can we but stand, and overcome this one shock or brunt, I doubt not but in a little time all the world will be ours; and when that day comes, my true hearts, I will make you kings, princes, and captains, and what brave days shall we have then.*

Diabolus having thus armed and fore-armed his servants and vassals in Mansoul, against their goood and lawful king Shaddai, in the next place he doubleth his guards at the gates of the town, and betakes himself to the castle, which was *They of Mansoul show their loyalty to the giant.* his strong hold: his vassals also, to show their wills, and supposed (but ignoble) gallantry, exercise them in their arms every day, and teach one another feats of war, they also defied their enemies, and sung up the praises of their tyrant; they threatened also what men they would be, if ever things should rise so high as a war between Shaddai and their king.

CHAPTER IV.

Shaddai sends an army of forty thousand men to reduce Mansoul, under the command of Boanerges, Conviction, Judgment, and Execution. The captains address themselves the inhabitants in speeches of great energy, but to little purpose, Diabolus, Incredulity, Ill-pause and others interposing to prevent submission. Prejudice defends Ear-gate with a guard of sixty deaf men.

Now all this time the good king, the king Shaddai, was preparing to send an army to recover the town of Mansoul again

---

* Thus Satan deceiveth (almost) the whole world, promising liberty and pleasure, while slavery and destruction are his only aim. Nor need we wonder that he thus assaults us, for he had the presumption to attack our divine Lord in the same manner; "All these things," said he,—all the glories and pleasures of the world—"will I give thee if thou wilt fall down and worship me." None of these things, however, seduced his heart; but alas! how small a portion of wordly good is generally enough to allure us!

from under the tyranny of their pretended king Diabolus: but he thought good, at the first, not to send them by the hand and conduct of brave Immanuel his Son, but under the hand of some of his servants, to see first by them the temper of Mansoul, and whether by them they would be won to the obedience of their king. The army consisted of above forty thousand, all true men; for they came from the king's own court, and were those of his own choosing.

Shaddai prepareth an army for the recovery of Mansoul.

They came up to Mansoul under the conduct of four stout generals, each man being captain of ten thousand men; and these are their names, and their ensigns. The name of the first was Captain Boanerges; the name of the second was Captain Conviction; the name of the third, Captain Judgment; and the name of the fourth was Captain Execution. These were the captains that Shaddai sent to regain Mansoul.

The captains' names.

These four captains (as was said) the king thought fit in the first place to send to Mansoul, to make an attempt upon it; for indeed generally, in all his wars, he did use to place these four captains in the van, for they were very stout and rough-hewn men, Psal. lx. 4. men that were fit to break the ice, and to make their way by dint of sword, and their men were like themselves.

To each of these captains the king gave a banner, that it might be displayed, because of the goodness of his cause, and because of the right that he had to Mansoul.

The king gives them a banner.

First, To Captain Boanerges, for he was the chief, to him, I say, were given ten thousand men: his ensign was Mr Thunder: he bore the black colours, and his scutcheon was the three burning thunderbolts, Mark iii. 17.

The second captain was Captain Conviction; to him were given ten thousand men: his ensign's name was Mr Sorrow; he did bear the pale colours, and his scutcheon was the book of the law wide open, from whence issued a flame of fire, Deut. xxxiii. 2.

The third captain was Captain Judgment; to him were given ten thousand men: his ensign's name was Mr Terror; he bare the red colours, and his scutcheon was a burning fiery furnace, Matt. xiii. 40, 41.

The fourth captain was Captain Execution; to him were given ten thousand men: his ensign was one Mr Justice he also bare the red colours, and his scutcheon was a fruitless tree, with an axe lying at the root thereof, Matt. iii. 10.

The four captains have each ten thousand men under them.
These four captains, as I said, had every one of them under his command ten thousand men, all of good fidelity to the King, and stout at their military actions.*

Well, the captains and their forces, their men and under officers, being had upon a day by Shaddai into the field, and there called over by their names, were then and there put into such harness as became their degree, and that service that now they were going about for their king.

Now when the king had mustered his forces (for it was he that mustered the host to the battle,) he gave unto the captains their several commissions, with charge and commandment, in the audience of all the soldiers, that they should take heed faithfully and courageously to do and execute the same. Their commissions were, for the substance of them, the same in form, though as to name, title, place, and degree of the captains, there might be some, but very small variation: and here let me give you an account of the matter and sum contained in their commission.

A Commission from the great King Shaddai, King of Mansoul, to his trusty and noble Captain, the Captain Boanerges, for making war upon the town of Mansoul.

Commission from the great King Shaddai.
'O thou Boanerges, one of my stout and thundering captains, over one ten thousand of my valiant and faithful servants, Matt. x. 11. Luke x. 5. go thou in my name, with this thy force, to the miserable town of Mansoul, and when thou comest thither, offer them first conditions of peace; and command them, that, casting off the yoke and tyranny of the wicked Diabolus, they return to me, their rightful prince and lord; command them also, that they cleanse themselves from all that is in the town of Man-

---

* In all ages of the world, even those previous to the incarnation of Christ, God has sent messages of mercy to his sinful creatures by his servants, whose various gifts are described by the four captains. *Boanerges* (Mark iii. 17.) signifies the powerful and awakening preaching of the word; *Conviction* means the awful display of the holy law, as at Sinai, with its proper effect on the conscience, convincing of the transgressions committed against it; *Judgment* is designed to show the terror of a sinner, alarmed by the dreadful threatenings of offended justice, and expectation of the great day of accounts; and *Execution* may signify the fulfilment of those threatenings in the final destruction of impenitent and unbelieving sinners, who reject the overtures of mercy in the gospel. These are the instruments which God is pleased generally to employ in convincing and converting sinners, as might be exemplified in the case of the jailer, Acts xvi.; but he sometimes works with equal efficacy by milder means, and at once gently opens the heart to admit Immanuel, as in the instance of Lydia, mentioned in the same

soul, (and look to thyself, that thou have good satisfaction touching the truth of their obedience.) Thus when thou hast commanded them (if they in truth submit thereto,) then do thou to the uttermost of thy power, what in thee lies, to set up for me a garrison in the famous town of Mansoul; nor do thou hurt the least native that moveth or breatheth therein, if they will submit themselves to me, but treat thou such as if they were thy friends or brethren; for all such I love, and they shall be dear unto me; and tell them, that I will take a time to come unto them, and to let them know that I am merciful, 1 Thess. ii. 7—11.

'But if they shall, notwithstanding thy summons, and the producing of my authority, resist, stand out against thee, and rebel; then I do command thee to make use of all thy cunning, power, might, and force, to bring them under by strength of hand. Farewell.

Thus you see the sum of their commissions; for, as I said before, for the substance of them, they were the same that the rest of the noble captains had.

Wherefore they having received each commander his authority at the hand of their king; the day being appointed, and the place of their rendezvous prefixed, each commander appearing in such gallantry as his cause and calling required; so after a new entertainment from Shaddai, with flying colours they set forward to march towards the famous town of Mansoul. Captain Boanerges led the van, Captain Conviction and Captain Judgment made up the main body, and Captain Execution brought up the rear. They then having a great way to go (for the town of Mansoul was far off from the court of Shaddai, Eph. ii. 13, 17.) marched through the regions and countries of many people, not hurting or abusing any, but blessing wherever they came. They also lived upon the king's cost, all the way they went.*

They prepare for a march.

Having travelled thus for many days, at last they came within sight of Mansoul; the which when they saw, the captains could for their hearts do no less for a while than bewail the condition of the town; for they quickly saw that it was prostrate to the will of Diabolus, and to his ways and designs.

Well, to be short, the captains come up before the town,

---

* Fallen man is indeed very far from God and righteousness; but, "in Christ Jesus, they who were sometimes far off, are made nigh by his blood." To effect this, God sends his ministers, who come not on "this warfare at their own charges," but are supported by their divine master, and those whose hearts are affected with the miserable condition of their fellow men.

march up to Ear-gate, and sit down there (for that was the place of hearing.) So when they had pitched their tents, and intrenched themselves, they addressed themselves to make their assault.

Now the townsfolk at first, beholding so gallant a company so bravely accoutred, and so excellently disciplined, having on their glittering armour, and displaying their colours, could not but come out of their houses and gaze. But the cunning fox Diabolus, fearing that the people, after this sight should, on a sudden summons, open the gates to the captains, came down with all haste from the castle, and made them retire into the body of the town; who, when he had them there, made this lying and deceivable speech unto them.*

The world are convinced by the well ordered life of the godly.

"Gentlemen," quoth he, "although you are my trusty and well-beloved friends, yet I cannot but (a little) chide you for your late uncircumspect action, in going out to gaze on that great and mighty force that but yesterday sat down before (and have now intrenched themselves, in order to the maintaining of the siege against) the famous town of Mansoul. Do you know who they are? whence they came? and what is their purpose in sitting down before the town of Mansoul? They are they of whom I told you long ago, that they would come to destroy this town, and against whom I have been at the cost to arm you cap-a-pié for your body, besides great fortifications for your mind. Wherefore then did you not rather, even at the first appearance of them, cry out, Fire the beacons, and give the whole town an alarm concerning them, that we might all have been in a posture of defence, and have been ready to have received them with the highest acts of defiance? then had you showed yourselves men to my liking, whereas by what you have done, you have made me half afraid; I say, half afraid, that when they and we shall come to push a pike, I shall find you want courage to stand it out any longer. Wherefore have I commanded a watch, and that you should double your guards at the gates? Wherefore have I endeavoured to make you as hard as iron; and your hearts as a piece of

Diabolus alienates their minds from them.

Satan greatly afraid of God's ministers, that they will set Mansoul against him.

---

* There is such a beauty and glory in the holy walk of godly ministers and sincere christians, that the world cannot help admiring and commending them; it is therefore the interest of Satan, by all means to prejudice their minds against them, by such abominable lies as those contained in the following speech.

the nether millstone? Was it, think you, that you might show yourselves women; and that you might go out, like a company of innocents, to gaze on your mortal foe? Fie fie, put yourselves into a posture of defence, beat up the drum, gather together in warlike manner, that our foes may know, that before they shall conquer this corporation, there are valiant men in Mansoul.

He stirs them up to bid defiance to the ministers of the word.

'I will leave off now to chide, and will not further rebuke you: but I charge you, that henceforwards you let me see no more of such actions. Let not henceforwards a man of you, without order first obtained from me, so much as show his head over the wall of the town of Mansoul: you have now heard me; do as I have commanded, and you shall cause me that I dwell securely with you, and that as I take care for myself, so for your safety and honour also. Farewell.'*

Now were the townsfolk strangely altered; they were as men striken with a panic fear: they ran to and fro in the streets of the town of Mansoul, crying out, "Help! help! the men that turn the world upside down are come hither."† Nor could any of them be quiet after; but still, as men bereft of wit, they cried out, "The destroyers of our peace and people are come." This went down with Diabolus: Ah quoth he to himself, this I like well, now it is as I would have it, now you show your obedience to your prince; hold you but here, and then let them take the town if they can.

When sinners hearken to Satan, they are set in a rage against godliness.

Well, before the King's forces had set before Mansoul three days, Captain Boanerges commanded his trumpeter to go down to Ear-gate; and there, in the name of the great Shaddai, to summon Mansoul to give audience to the message that he in his master's name was commanded to deliver to them. So the trumpeter, whose name was Take-heed-what-you-hear, went up as he was commanded to Ear-gate, and there sounded

The King's trumpet sounded at Ear-gate.

---

* It is no uncommon thing to find persons severely blamed and threatened by their carnal relations for going to hear a single sermon from a gospel minister. Upon the very approach of a man of God, Satan would have the inhabitants sound the alarm, and treat him as an enemy. With many he obtains his desire; and they will boast that they never entered a place of worship of any other description than that to which their education attached them.

† This was the cry of the ignorant when the apostles preached, and will ever be so, where men are kept by their blind teachers in profound ignorance

They will not hear. his trumpet for a hearing; but there was none that appeared, that gave answer or regard,* for so had Diabolus commanded; so the trumpeter returned to his captain, and told him what he had done, and also how he had sped; whereat the captain was grieved, but bid the trumpeter go to his tent. *A second summons repulsed.* Again Captain Boanerges sendeth his trumpeter to Ear-gate, to sound as before for an hearing; but they again kept close, came not out, nor would they give him an answer, so observant were they of the command of Diabolus their king. Then the captains and other field-officers called a council of war, *A council of war held.* to consider what further was to be done for gaining the town of Mansoul; and, after some close and thorough debate upon the contents of their commissions, they concluded yet to give the town, by the hand of the forenamed trumpeter, another summons to hear: but if that shall be refused, say they, and that the town shall stand it out still, Luke xiv. 23, then they determined, and bid the trumpeter tell them so, that they would endeavour by what means they could to compel them by force to the obedience of their king.

So Captain Boanerges commanded his trumpeter to go up to Ear-gate again, and, in the name of the great king Shaddai, to give it a very loud summons to come down without delay, to Ear-gate, there to give audience to the king's most noble captains. *A third summons.* So the trumpeter went, and did as he was commanded: he went up to Ear-gate, and sounded his trumpet, and gave a third summons to Mansoul, Isa. lviii. 1.† He said, moreover, that if this they should still refuse to do, the captains of his prince would with might come down upon them, and endeavour to reduce them to their obedience by force.

Then stood my Lord-Will-be-will, who was the governor of the town (this Will-be-will was the apostate of whom mention was made before,) and the keeper of the gates of Mansoul. *Lord-Will-be-will's speech to the trumpeter.* He therefore, with big and ruffling words, demanded of the trumpeter who he was, whence he came, and what was the cause of his making so hideous a noise at the gate, and speaking such unsufferable words against the town of Mansoul?

---

* "Faith cometh by hearing." Ministers are therefore to address the outward ear, as the gate that leads to the mind and heart; but alas! too many turn a deaf ear to the messages of heaven.

† "Cry aloud, spare not, lift up thy voice like a trumpet, and show my people their transgression, and the house of Jacob their sins."

The trumpeter. The trumpeter answered, I am servant to the most noble captain, Captain Boanerges, general of the forces of the great king Shaddai, against whom both thyself and the whole town of Mansoul have rebelled, and lift up the heel; and my master the captain hath a special message to this town, and to thee as a member thereof: the which if you of Mansoul shall peaceably hear, so; if not, take what follows.

Will-be-will. Then said the Lord Will-be-will, I will carry the words to my lord, and will know what he will say.*

Trumpeter. But the trumpeter replied, saying, Our message is not to the giant Diabolus, but to the miserable town of Mansoul; nor shall we at all regard what answer by him is made, nor yet by any for him; we are sent to this town, to recover it from under his cruel tyranny, and to persuade it to submit, as in former times it did, to the most excellent King Shaddai.

Will-be-will. Then said the Lord Will-be-will, I will do your errand to the town.

Trumpeter. The trumpeter then replied, Sir, do not deceive us, lest, in so doing you deceive yourselves much more. He added, moreover, For we are resolved, if in peaceable manner, you do not submit yourselves, then to make war upon you, and bring you under by force. And of the truth of what I say, this shall be a sign unto you, you shall see the black flag, with its hot burning thunderbolts, set upon the mount to-morrow, as a token of defiance against your prince, and of our resolution to reduce you to our Lord and rightful King.

The trumpeter returns to the camp. So the said Lord Will-be-will returned from off the wall, and the trumpeter came into the camp. When the trumpeter was come into the camp, the captains and officers of the mighty King Shaddai came together, to know if he had obtained a hearing, and what was the effect of his errand. So the trumpeter told, saying, When I had sounded my trumpet, and called aloud to the town for a hearing, my Lord Will-be-will, the governor of the town, and he that hath charge of the gates, came up, when he heard me sound, and, looking over the wall, he asked me what I was, whence I came, and what was the cause of my making this noise? So I told him my errand, and by whose authority I

* How wretchedly are poor sinners enslaved to the devil, " led captive by him at his will," and not daring, as it were, to listen to God without his leave. But the ministers of the gospel must persist, " whether they will hear or whether they will forbear."

brought it. Then said he, I will tell it the governor, and to Mansoul: and then I returned to my lord.

Then said the brave Boanerges, Let us yet for a while still lie in our trenches, and see what these rebels will do. Now when the time drew nigh that audience by Mansoul must be given to the brave Boanerges and his companions, it was commanded, that all the men of war throughout the whole camp of Shaddai should, as one man, stand to their arms, and make themselves ready, if the town of Mansoul shall hear, to receive it forthwith to mercy; but if not, to force it to a subjection. So the day being come, the trumpeters sounded, and that throughout the whole camp, that the men of war might be in readiness for that which then should be the work of the day. But when they that were in the town of Mansoul heard the sound of the trumpet throughout the camp of Shaddai, and thinking no other but that it must be in order to storming the corporation, they at first were put to great consternation of spirit; but after they were a little settled again, they made what preparation they could for a war, if they did storm; else to secure themselves.

Carnal souls make a wrong interpretation of the design of a gospel ministry.

Well, when the utmost time was come, Boanerges was resolved to hear their answer; wherefore he sent out his trumpeter again to summon Mansoul to a hearing of the message that they had brought from Shaddai: so he went up and sounded, and the townsmen came up, but made Ear-gate as sure as they could, Zech. vii. 11. Now when they were come up to the top of the wall, Captain Boanerges desired to see the lord mayor; but my Lord Incredulity was then lord mayor, for he came in the room of my Lord Lustings: so Incredulity came up and showed himself over the wall. But when the captain Boanerges had set his eyes upon him, he cried out aloud, This is not he; where is my Lord Understanding, the ancient lord mayor of the town of Mansoul? for to him I would deliver my message.*

Boanerges refuses to make Incredulity a judge of what he had to deliver to the famous town of Mansoul.

Then said the Giant (for Diabolus was also come down) to the captain: Mr Captain, you have, by your boldness, given to Mansoul at least four summonses, to subject herself to your king: by whose authority, I know not; nor will I dispute that now. I ask,

* The ministers of Christ wish to address themselves to the understanding, but instead of this Unbelief presents himself. Ear-gate is also secured to prevent a candid attention to the word

therefore, what is the reason of all this ado? or what would you be at, if you know yourselves?

Then Captain Boanerges, whose were the black colour, and whose escutcheon was three burning thunderbolts (taking no notice of the giant, or of his speech) thus addressed himself to the town of Mansoul: Be it known unto you, O unhappy and rebellious Mansoul! that the most gracious king, the great King Shaddai, my master, hath sent me unto you, with commission (and so he showed to the town his broad seal) to reduce you to his obedience. And he hath commanded me, in case you yield upon my summons, to carry it to you as if you were my friends or brethren; but he also hath bid, that if, after summons to submit, you still stand out and rebel, we should endeavour to take you by force.

Boanerges's speech.

Then stood forth Captain Conviction, and said, (his were the pale colours, and for an escutcheon he had the book of the law wide open, &c.) "Hear, O Mansoul: Thou, O Mansoul, wast once famous for innocency, but now thou art degenerated into lies and deceit; Rom. iii. 10—19, 23. chap. xvi. 17, 18. Psalm 1. 21, 22. Thou hast heard what my brother, the Captain Boanerges, hath just now said, and it is your wisdom, and will be our happiness, to stoop to, and accept of, conditions of peace and mercy, when offered; especially when offered by one against whom thou hast rebelled, and one who is of power to tear thee in pieces, for so is Shaddai our king; nor, when he is angry, can any thing stand before him. If you say you have not sinned, or acted rebellion against our king, the whole of your doings, since the day that you cast off his service (and there was the beginning of your sin,) will sufficiently testify against you; what else means your hearkening to the tyrant, and your receiving him for your king? What means else your rejecting the laws of Shaddai, and your obeying Diabolus? Yea, what means this your taking up arms against, and your shutting the gates upon us the faithful servants of your king? Luke xii. 58, 59. Be ruled, then, and accept of my brother's invitation, and overstand not the time of mercy, but agree with thine adversary quickly. Ah, Mansoul! suffer not thyself to be kept from mercy, and to be run into a thousand miseries, by the flattering wiles of Diabolus: perhaps that piece of deceit may attempt to make you believe that we seek our own profit in this our service: but know, it is obedience to our king, and love to your happiness, that is the cause of this undertaking of our's.

Captain Conviction's speech.

He invites them to return to their lawful sovereign.

"Again, I say unto thee, O Mansoul, consider if it be not amazing grace, that Shaddai should so humble himself as he doth, 2 Cor. v. 18—21. Now he, by us, reasons with you, in a way of intreaty and sweet persuasion, that you would subject yourselves to him. Has he that need of you, that we are sure you have of him? No, no; but he is merciful, and will not that Mansoul should die, but turn to him and live."*

Then stood forth **Captain Judgment**, whose were the red colours, and for a scutcheon had the burning fiery furnace; and he said, "O ye inhabitants of the town of Mansoul, that have lived so long in rebellion and acts of treason against the King Shaddai; know, that we come not to-day to this place, in this manner, with our message, of our own minds, or to avenge our own quarrel; it is the king our master that hath sent us to reduce you to your obedience to him; the which if you refuse in a peaceable way to yield, we have commission to compel you thereto. And never think of yourselves, nor yet suffer the tyrant Diabolus to persuade you to think, that our king, by his power, is not able to bring you down, and lay you under his feet: for he is the Former of all things; and if he touches the mountains they smoke. Nor will the gate of the king's clemency stand always open: for the day that shall burn like an oven, is before him; yea, it hasteth greatly, and slumbereth not, Mal. iv. 1. 1 Pet. ii. 3. O Mansoul, is it little in thine eyes, that our king does offer thee mercy, and that after so many provocations? Yea, he still holdeth out his golden sceptre to thee, and will not suffer his gate to be shut against thee: wilt thou provoke him to do it? Consider what I say; to thee it shall be opened no more for ever, Job xxxvi. 14. 18. Ps. ix .7. Isa. lxvi. 15. 'If thou sayest thou shalt not see him, yet judgment is before him; therefore trust thou in him. Yea, because there is wrath, beware lest he take thee away with his stroke; then a great ransom cannot deliver thee. Will he esteem thy riches? No, not gold, nor all the forces of strength. He hath prepared his throne for judgment; for he will come with fire, and with his chariots, like a whirlwind, to render his anger with fury, and rebukes with flames of fire.' Therefore, O Mansoul, take heed, lest, after thou hast fulfilled the judgment of the wicked, justice and judgment should take hold of thee."

Captain Judgment's speech.

* Conviction, whose scutcheon is the book of the law wide open, here addresses Mansoul, declaring their rebellion and transgressions, and tracing them to the original apostacy, charging home their sins upon their conscience. Such addresses as these are likely, under God, to be very useful, accompanied, as this is, with a declaration of the good will which dictates them, and the condescension of grace in sending such messages of mercy.

It is proper to set before sinners "Judgments to come," warning every man against the fearful wrath of God. Thus did the apostle Paul warn and beseech the Ephesians night and day with tears.

Now, while Captain Judgment was making this oration to the town of Mansoul, it was observed by some that Diabolus trembled.* But he proceeded in his speech, and said, "O thou woful town of Mansoul! wilt thou not yet set open the gate to receive us, the deputies of the king, and those that would rejoice to see thee live? Ezek. xxii. 14. 'Can thine heart endure, or can thine hands be strong, in the day that he shall deal in judgment with thee?' I say, canst thou endure to be forced to drink, as one would drink sweet wine, the sea of wrath that our king has prepared for Diabolus and his angles? Consider, betimes consider."

On hearing this speech, Diabolius trembles.

Then stood forth the fourth captain, the noble Captain Execution, and said: "O town of Mansoul, once famous, but now like the fruitless bough; once the delight of the high ones, but now a den for Diabolus: hearken also to me, and to the words that I shall speak to thee in the name of the great Shaddai. Behold, 'the axe is laid to the root of the tree; every tree, therefore, that bringeth not forth good fruit, is hewn down, and cast into the fire.' Matt. iii. 7—10.

Captain Execution's speech.

"Thou, O town of Mansoul, hast hitherto been this fruitless tree; thou bearest nought but thorns and briers, Deut. xxxii. 32. Thy evil fruit forespeaks thee not to be a good tree; thy grapes are grapes of gall, thy clusters are bitter. Thou hast rebelled against thy king; and lo, we, the power and force of Shaddai, are the axe that is laid to thy roots. What sayest thou? Wilt thou turn? I say again, tell me, before the first blow is given, wilt thou turn? Our axe must first be laid *to* thy root, before it be laid *at* thy root: it must first be laid to thy root in a way of threatening, before it is laid at thy root by way of execution; and between these two is required thy repentance, and this is all the time thou hast. What wilt thou do? Wilt thou turn, or shall I smite? If I fetch my blow, Mansoul, down you go: for I have commission to lay my axe *at*, as well as *to*, thy root; nor will any thing, but yielding to our king, prevent doing of execution. What art thou fit for, O Mansoul, if mercy preventeth not, but to be hewn down, and cast into the fire, and burnt?

"O Mansoul! patience and forbearance do not act for ever a year or two, or three, they may; but if thou provoke by a three year's rebellion (and thou hast already done more than this,) then what follows, but 'cut it down?' nay after that, 'thou shalt cut it down.' Luke xiii. 9. And dost thou think that these

---

* So, when Paul reasoned of Righteousness, Temperance, and Judgment to come, Felix trembled. Alas! many tremble who never turn.

are but threatenings, or that our king has not power to execute his words? O Mansoul, thou wilt find in the words of our king, when they are by sinners made little or light of, there is not only threatening, but burning coals of fire.

"Thou hast been a cumber-ground long already, and wilt thou continue so still? Thy sin has brought his army to thy walls, and shall it bring in judgment to do execution to thy town? Thou hast heard what the captains have said, but as yet thou shuttest thy gates: speak out, Mansoul, wilt thou do so still; or wilt thou accept of conditions of peace?"*

These brave speeches of these four noble captains, the town of Mansoul refused to hear; yet a sound thereof did beat against Ear-gate, though the force thereof could not break it open. In fine, the town desired time to prepare their answer to these demands. The captains then told them, that if they would throw out to them one Ill-pause that was in the town, that they might reward him according to his works, then they would give them time to consider; but if they would not cast him to them over the wall of Mansoul, then they would give them none: for, said they, we know, that so long as Ill-pause draws breath in Mansoul, all good considerations will be confounded, and nothing but mischief will come thereon.

Mansoul desires time to make answer.

Upon what conditions the captains would give them time.

Then Diabolus, who was there present, being loth to lose Ill-pause, because he was his orator (and yet be sure he had, could the captains have laid their fingers on him,) was resolved at this instant to give them answer by himself; but then changing his mind, he commanded the then lord-mayor, the Lord Incredulity, to do it; saying, My lord, do you give these renegades an answer, and speak out, that Mansoul may hear and understand you.

Diabolus interrupts them, and sets Incredulity to answer them.

So Incredulity, at Diabolus's command, began and said, "Gentlemen, you have here, as we do behold, to the disturbance of our prince, and molestation of the

His speech.

---

* There is much energy in this speech. In this manner faithful ministers, knowing the terrors of the Lord, should persuade men. These pungent addresses to the conscience are often blessed of God to the conversion of souls. Yet all this, without the power of his spirit, will not prove effectual. Sinners will consult with flesh and blood, and, though partly convinced, will pause and delay, and defer submission to the call of God. The captains therefore require that Ill-pause should be thrown over the wall to them, for indeed, no good will be done in the soul, till this spirit of procrastination be destroyed.

town of Mansoul, encamped against it: but from whence you come, we will not know; and what you are we will not believe. Indeed, you tell us in your terrible speech, that you have this authority from Shaddai; but by what right he commands you to do it, of that we shall be yet ignorant.

"You have also, by the authority aforesaid, summoned this town to desert her lord, and for protection to yield up herself to the great **Shaddai**, your king: flatteringly telling her, that if she will do it, he will pass by; and not charge her with her past offences.

"Further, you have also, to the terror of the town of Mansoul, threatened with great and sore destruction to punish this corporation, if she consent not to do as your wills would have her.

"Now captains, from whencesoever you come, and though your designs be ever so right, yet know ye, that neither my lord Diabolus, nor I his servant Incredulity, nor yet our brave Mansoul, doth regard either your persons, message, or the king that you say hath sent you: his power, his greatness, his vengeance, we fear not; nor will we yield at all to your summons.

The true picture of unbelief.

"As for the war that you threaten to make upon us, we must therein defend ourselves as well as we can: and know ye, that we are not without wherewithal to bid defiance to you. And in short, (for I will not be tedious,) I tell you, that we take you to be some vagabond runagate crew, who, having shaken off all obedience to your king, have gotten together in a tumultuous manner, and are ranging from place to place, to see if, through those flatteries you are skilled to make, on the one side, and threats wherewith you think to fright on the other, you can make some silly town, city, or country, to desert their place, and leave it to you: but Mansoul is none of them.

"To conclude: We dread you not, we fear you not, nor will we obey your summons: our gates we will keep shut against you, our place we will keep you out of; nor will we long thus suffer you to sit down before us. Our people must live in quiet: your appearance doth disturb them, Luke xi. 21, wherefore, arise with bag and baggage, and be gone, or we will let fly from the walls (*a*) against you.'"*

(*a*) *Flesh.*

This oration, made by old Incredulity, was seconded by desperate Will-be-will, in words to this effect:

---

* This is the true language of unbelief. We will not know—we will not believe—we will not submit—we must not be disturbed—therefore ye ministers of Christ be gone or we will persecute you.

"Gentlemen, we have heard your demand, and the noise of your threats, and heard the sound of your summons; but we fear not your force, we regard not your threats, but we will abide as you found us. And we command you, that in three days time you cease to appear in these parts, or you shall know what it is once to dare to offer to rouse the lion Diabolus, when asleep in the town of Mansoul."

The speech of the lord Will-be-will.

The recorder, whose name was Forget-good, he also added as followeth: "Gentlemen, my lords, as you see, have with mild and gentle words answered your rough and angry speeches: they have, moreover, in my hearing, given you leave quietly to depart as you came: wherefore take their kindness, and be gone. We might have come out with force upon you, and have caused you to feel the dint of our swords: but as we love ease and quiet ourselves, so we love not to hurt or molest others."

The speech of Forget-good the recorder.

Then did the town of Mansoul shout for joy; as if by Diabolus and his crew some great advantage had been obtained over the captains. They also rang the bells, and made merry, and danced upon the walls.

The town resolved to withstand the captains.

Diabolus also returned to the castle, and the lord-mayor and recorder to their places; but the Lord Will-be-will took special care that the gates should be secured with double guards, double bolts, and double locks and bars. And that Ear-gate, especially, might be the better looked to (for that was the gate, in at which the king's forces sought most to enter,) the Lord Will-be-will made one old Mr Prejudice (an angry and ill-conditioned fellow) captain of the ward at that gate; and put under his power sixty men, called deaf men; men advantageous for that service, forasmuch as they mattered no words of the captain, nor of the soldiers.*

The band of deaf men set to keep Ear-gate.

---

* How often do poor mistaken sinners rejoice in their sins, and glory in their shame: but small cause for joy have they, who reject the counsel of God against themselves. Miserable is the state of that man, whose prejudices shut his ears against the gospel of salvation, and who is deaf to all the calls of

CHAPTER V.

The captains attack the town, and are violently resisted. They retire to winter quarters. Tradition, Human-wisdom, and Man's Invention taken prisoners. Hostilities renewed. A famine in Mansoul; and a mutiny. The Town sounds a parley. Propositions made and rejected. Lord Understanding and Mr Conscience quarrel with Incredulity. A skirmish ensues, and mischief is done.

NOW when the captains heard the answer of the great ones, and that they could not get a hearing from the old natives of the town, and that Mansoul was resolved to give the king's army battle; they prepared themselves to receive them, and to try it out by the power of the arm. And, first, they made their force more formidable against Ear-gate; for they knew, that unless they could penetrate that, no good could be done upon the town. This done, they put the rest of their men in their places. After which, they gave out the word, which was YE MUST BE BORN AGAIN.* Then they sounded the trumpet: then they in the town made the answer, with shout against shout, charge against charge, and so the battle began. Now they in the town had planted upon Mansoul, over Ear-gate, two great guns, the one called High-mind, and the other Heady. Unto these two guns they trusted much; they were cast in the castle by Diabolus' founder, whose name was Mr Puff-up; and mischievous pieces they were. But so vigilant and watchful were the captains when they saw them, that though sometimes their shot would go by their ears with a whiz, yet they did them no harm. By these two guns, the townsfolk made no question but greatly to annoy the camp of Shaddai, and well enough to secure the gate; but they had not much cause to boast of what execution they did, as from what follows will be gathered.

The captains resolve to give them battle.

The battle begun.

Two guns planted upon Ear-gate.

The famous Mansoul had also some other small pieces in it, of which they made use against the camp of Shaddai.

* The doctrine of the New-Birth should be much insisted upon. Our Lord himself began with it when teaching Nicodemus, John iii. 3. This great truth is often very startling to a carnal mind, and objected to as of old—"How can these things be?" Many would get rid of all its force, by referring it to baptism, and others, with equal ignorance, think it means the resurrection. Much opposition may be expected to this leading truth, as long as men are "*heady* and *high-minded*," which is signified by the two guns mounted upon the wall. From this sort of artillery, however, ministers of the gospel have little to fear, their shots may whiz, but cannot wound.

They from the camp also did as stoutly, and with as much of that as may in truth be called valour, let fly as fast at the town, and at Ear-gate; for they saw, that unless they could break open Ear-gate, it would be but in vain to batter the wall. Now the king's captains had brought with them several slings and two or three battering rams; with their slings, therefore, they battered the houses and people of the town, and with their rams they sought to break Ear-gate open.

The sentence and power of the word.

The camp and the town had several skirmishes and brisk encounters; while the captains, with their engines, made many brave attempts to break open or beat down the tower that was over Ear-gate, and at the said gate to make their entrance: but Mansoul stood it out so lustily, through the rage of Diabolus, the valour of the Lord Will be-will, and the conduct of old Incredulity the mayor, and Mr Forget-good, the recorder, that the charge and expense of that summer's wars (on the king's side) seemed to be almost entirely lost, and the advantage to return to Mansoul: but when the captains saw how it was, they made a fair retreat, and intrenched themselves in their winter-quarters.*

The town stoutly stands out, and the captains return to their winter quarters.

Now in this war, you must needs think there was much loss on both sides, of which be pleased to take this brief account following.

An account of this war, with reference to the loss on both sides.

The king's captains, when they marched from the court to come against Mansoul to war, as they came crossing over the country, they happened to light upon three young men that had a mind to go for soldiers; proper men they were and men of courage (and skill) to appearance. Their names were Mr Tradition, Mr Human Wisdom, and Mr Man's Invention. So they came up to the captains, and proffered their service to Shaddai. The captains then told them of their design, and bid them not to be rash in their offers; but the young men told them, that they had considered the thing before, and that hearing they were upon their march for such a design, came hither on purpose to meet them, that they might be listed under their excellencies. Then Captain Boanerges, for that they were men of courage, listed them into his company, and so away they went to the war.

The three new soldiers.

* How long do sinners, frequently, resist the Holy Ghost in his word. Satan is unwilling to lose his prey, and unbelief is loth to submit. Ministers of the gospel may almost despair of success, yet must they persevere, whether men will bear, or whether they will forbear."

Now when the war was begun, in one of the briskest skirmishes, so it was, that a company of the lord Will-be-will's men sallied out of the sally ports, or posterns of the town, and fell in upon the rear of Captain Boanerges' men, where these three fellows happened to be, so he took them prisoners, and away they carried them into the town; where they had not lain long in durance, but it began to be noised about the streets of the town, what three notable prisoners the Lord Will-be-will's men had taken, and brought in prisoners out of the camp of Shaddai. At length tidings thereof were carried to Diabolus to the castle, to wit, what my Lord Will-be-will's men had done, and whom they had taken prisoners.

They are taken prisoners.

Then Diabolus called for Will-be-will to know the certainty of this matter. So he asked him, and he told him. Then did the giant send for the prisoners, and when they were come, he demanded of them who they were, whence they came, and what they did in the camp of Shaddai? and they told him. Then he sent them into ward again. Not many days after, he sent for them to him again, and then he asked them if they would be willing to serve him against their former captains? They then told him, that they did not so much live by religion, as by the fates of fortune; and that, since his lordship was willing to entertain them, they should be willing to serve him. Now while things were thus in hand, there was one captain Any-thing, a great doer in the town of Mansoul, and to this Captain Any-thing did Diabolus send these men, with a note under his hand, to receive them into his company; the contents of which letter were these:

They are brought before Diabolus, and are content to fight under his banner.

Any-thing.

"Any-thing, my darling, the three men that are the bearers of this letter, have a desire to serve me in the war, nor know I better to whose conduct to commit them, than to thine; receive them therefore in my name, and as need shall require, make use of them against Shaddai and his men. Farewell." So they came, and he received them, and he made two of them sergeants; but he made Mr Man's Invention his armour bearer.* But thus much for this, and now to return to the camp.

He therefore sends them to Captain Any-thing with a letter.

Any-thing receives them into his service.

---

* Tradition, Human Wisdom, and Man's Invention have too often been enlisted into the service of religion, but they never did any good to it. They

They of the camp did also some execution upon the town; for they did beat down the roof of the new lord-mayor's house, and so laid him more open than he was before. They had almost (with a sling) slain my Lord Will-be-will outright; but he made shift to recover again. But they made a notable slaughter among the aldermen, for with only one shot they cut off six of them; to wit, Mr Swearing, Mr Whoring, Mr Fury, Mr Stand-to-lies, Mr Drunkenness, and Mr Cheating.*

The roof of old Incredulity's house beaten down.

Six aldermen slain.

They also dismounted the two great guns that stood upon the tower over Ear-Gate, and laid them flat in the dirt. I told you before, that the king's noble captains had drawn off to their winter quarters, and had there intenched themselves and their carriages, so as with the best advantage to their king, and the greatest annoyance to the enemy, they might give the seasonable and warm alarms to the town of Mansoul. And this design of them did so hit, that I may say they did almost what they would to the molestation of the corporation.

The two great guns dismounted.

For now could not Mansoul sleep securely as before, nor could they now go to their debaucheries with that quietness as in times past: for they had from the camp of Shaddai such frequent warm alarms; yea, alarms upon alarms, first at one gate and then at another, and again at all the gates at once; that they were broken as to former peace: yea, they had their alarms so frequently, and that when the nights were at the longest, the weather coldest, and so consequently the season most unseasonable, that that winter was to the town of Mansoul a winter by itself. Sometimes the trumpets would sound, and sometimes the slings would whirl the stones into the town. Sometimes ten thousand of the king's soldiers would be running round the walls of Mansoul at midnight, shouting, and lifting up their voice for the battle. Sometimes again, some of them in the town would be wounded, and their cry and lamentable voice would be heard, to the great mo-

Continual alarms given to Mansoul.

The effects of convictions, though common, if abiding.

The town much molested.

are not to be depended upon; and are far more in their element when engaged on the contrary side. Let Captain Any-thing have them and welcome; the gospel of Jesus needs not their services.

* Here is some good effect of the preached word: unbelief is, in part, unveiled and discovered; the stubborn will receives a shock, and some gross immoralities are discarded; the guns are also silenced.—"Heady and High mind," that is, pride, is somewhat brought down.

estation of the now languishing town of Mansoul. Yea, so distressed were they with those that laid siege against them, that I dare say Diabolus their king had in these days his rest much broken.

Change of thoughts in Mansoul.
In those days, as I was informed, new thoughts, and thoughts that began to run counter one to another, by degrees possessed the minds of the men of the town of Mansoul. Some would say, "There is no living thus." Others would then reply, "This will be over shortly." Then would a third stand up and answer, "Let us turn to King Shaddai, and so put an end to all these troubles." And a fourth would come in with a fair speech, saying, "I doubt he will not receive us."*

Conscience speaks.
The old gentleman too, the recorder, that was so before Diabolus took Mansoul, he also began to talk aloud, and his words were now to the town of Mansoul as as if they were great claps of thunder. No noise now so terrible to Mansoul as was his, with the noise of the soldiers, and shoutings of the captains.†

A famine in Mansoul.
Also things began to grow scarce in Mansoul; now the things that her soul lusted after departed from her, Luke xv. 14, 15. Upon all her pleasant things there was a blast, and burning instead of beauty. Wrinkles now, and some shows of the shadow of death, were upon the inhabitants of Mansoul. And now, O how glad would Mansoul have been to have enjoyed quietness and satisfaction of mind, though joined with the meanest condition in the world!‡

They are summoned again to yield.
The captains also, in the deep of winter, did send, by the mouth of Boanerges's trumpeter, a summons to Mansoul to yield up herself to the king, the great king Shaddai. They sent it once, and twice, and thrice; not knowing but that at some time there might be in Mansoul some willingness to surrender up

---

* Further degrees of success; the false peace, which before prevailed, is effectually disturbed by abiding convictions. Alarm follows alarm; and some faint inclinations arise towards peace with God; which, however, the sinner begins to fear may not be practicable.

† Conscience, which had long been unfaithful and silent, awakes from his lethargy, and begins to speak, yea, to cry aloud; and conscience has a dreadfull voice, more awful than thunder.

‡ A famine in Mansoul;—the pleasures of sin begin to fail. The case of the prodigal is here referred to; he never thought of returning to his father till he began to be in want. The dreary season of winter adds to the affliction: the summer of gaiety is gone; the winter of affliction succeeds. This affords a favourable opportunity to the ministers of Christ to renew their message, and press home on the mind the great concerns of salvation. But still Satan retains his power through the influence of unbelief.

themselves unto them, might they but have the colour of an invitation to do it under. Yea, so far as I could gather, the town had been surrendered up to them before now, had it not been for the opposition of old Incredulity, and the fickleness of the thoughts of my Lord Will-be-will. Diabolus also began to rave; wherefore Mansoul, as to yielding, was not as yet all of one mind, therefore they still lay distressed under these preplexing fear.

Mansoul in distress.

I told you but now, that they of the king's army had this winter sent three times to Mansoul, to submit herself.

The first time the trumpeter went, he went with words of peace; telling them, that the captains, the noble captains of Shaddai, pitied and bewailed the misery of the now perishing town of Mansoul, and were troubled to see them stand so much in the way of their own deliverance. He said moreover, that the captains bid him tell them, that if now poor Mansoul would humble herself, and turn, her former rebellions and most notorious treasons, should by their merciful king, be forgiven them, yea, and forgotten too. And having bid them beware that they stood not in their own way, that they opposed not themselves, nor made themselves their own losers; he returned again into the camp.

The contents of the first summons.

The second time the trumpeter went, he treated them a little more roughly; for, after sound of trumpet he told them, that their continuing in their rebellion did but chafe and heat the spirit of the captains, and that they were resolved to make a conquest of Mansoul, or lay their bones before the town walls.

The contents of the second summons.

He went again the third time, and dealt with them yet more roughly; telling them, that now, since they had been so horribly profane, he did not know, not certainly know, whether the captains were inclined to mercy or judgment; only, said he, they commanded me to give you a summons to open the gates unto them: so he returned, and went into the camp.

The contents of the third summons.

These three summons, and especially the two last, so distressed the town, that they presently called a consultation, the result of which was this, that my Lord Will-be-will should go up to Eargate, and there, with sound of trumpet, call to the captains of the camp for a parley. Well, the Lord Will-be-will sounded upon the wall; so the captains came up in their harness, with their ten thousands at their feet. The townsmen then told the

The town sounds for a parley.

They propound conditions of agreement. captains that they had heard and considered their summons; and would come to an agreement with them and with their king Shaddai, upon such certain terms, articles, and propositions, as, with and by the order of their prince, they to them were appointed to propound: to wit, they would agree upon these grounds to be one people with them.

1. "If that those of their own company, as the now lord-mayor, and their Mr Forget-good, with their brave Lord Will-be-will, might, under Shaddai, be still the governors of the town, castle, and gates of Mansoul.

First proposition.

2. "Provided that no man, that now served under the great giant Diabolus, be by Shaddai cast out of house, harbour, or the freedom that he hath hitherto enjoyed in the famous town of Mansoul.

Second proposition.

3. "That it shall be granted them, that they of the town of Mansoul enjoy certain of their rights and privileges; to wit, such as have formerly been granted them, and that they have long lived in the enjoyment of, under the reign of their king Diabolus, that now is, and long has been, their only lord and great defender.

Third proposition.

4. "That no new law, officer, or executioner of law or office, shall have any power over them, without their own choice and consent.

Fourth proposition.

"These be our propositions, or conditions of peace; and upon these terms, said they, we will submit to your king."*

But when the captains had heard this weak and feeble offer of the town of Mansoul, and their high and bold demands, they made to them again, by their noble captain, the Captain Boanerges, this speech following:

"O ye inhabitants of the town of Mansoul, when I heard your trumpet sound for a parley with us, I can truly say, I was glad; but when you said you were willing to submit yourselves to our Lord and King, then was I yet more glad: but when, by your silly provisoes and foolish cavils, you laid the stumbling-block of your iniquity before your faces, then was my gladness turned into sorrow, and my hopeful beginnings of your return, into languishing and fainting fears.

Boanerges' answer.

---

* Sinners, when alarmed by fears of hell, are sometimes willing to become religious *externally*, provided they may retain their worldly lusts; they are ready to assume the form of godliness, but dislike its power.

"I count, that old Ill-pause, the ancient enemy of Mansoul, drew up these proposals that now you present us with, as terms of an agreement; but they deserve not to be admitted to sound in the ear of any man that pretends to have service for Shaddai, 2 Tim. ii. 19. We do therefore jointly, and that with the highest disdain, refuse, and **reject** such things, as the greatest of iniquities.

"But, O Mansoul, if you will give yourselves into our hands, or rather into the hands of our king, and will trust him to make such terms with you, and for you, as shall seem good in his eyes (and I dare say, they will be such as you shall find to be most profitable to you,) then we will receive you, and be at peace with you: but if you like not to trust yourselves in the arms of Shaddai our king, then things are but where they were before, and we know also what we have to do."*

Then cried out old Incredulity, the lord-mayor, and said, *Old Incredulity's reply.* "And who, being out of the hands of their enemies, as ye see ye are now, will be so foolish as to put the staff out of their own hands into the hands of they know not who? I, for my part, will never yield to so unlimited a proposition. Do you know the manner and temper of their king? 'Tis said by some, that he will be angry with his subjects, if but the breadth of an hair they chance to step out of the way: and by others, that he requireth of them much more than they can perform. Wherefore it seems, O Mansoul, to be thy wisdom to take good heed what thou dost in this matter; for if you once yield, you give up yourselves to another, and so you are no more you own, wherefore to give up yourselves to an unlimited power, is the greatest folly in the world; for now indeed you may repent; but can never justly complain. But do you indeed know, when you are his, which of you he will kill, and which of you he will save alive? or whether he will not cut off every one of us, and send out of his country another new people, and cause them to inhabit this town?"†

Unbelief never is profitable in talk, but always speaks mischievously.

This speech of the lord-mayor undid all, and threw flat to the ground their hopes of an accord: wherefore the captains returned to their trenches, to their tents, and to their men, as they were; and the mayor to the castle, and to his king.

This speech undid all.

---

* Terms, like those proposed, can never be admitted by Jesus Christ; for it is his will, that "every one who nameth his name must depart from iniquity."

† Unbelief ever suggests hard thoughts of God, and represents his service as an intolerable burden. This is hateful to God, but pleaseth the devil.

Now Diabolus had waited for his return, for he had heard that they had been at their points. So when he was come into the chamber of state, Diabolus saluted him with, "Welcome, my Lord; how went matters betwixt you to day?" Then the Lord Incredulity (with a low congé) told him the whole of the matter, saying, Thus said the captain of Shaddai, and thus and thus said I. The which, as it was told to Diabolus, he was very glad to hear; and said, "My lord-mayor, my faithful Incredulity, I have proved thy fidelity above ten times already, but never found thee false. I do promise thee, if we rub over this brunt, to prefer thee to a place of honour, a place far better than to be lord-mayor of Mansoul: I will make thee my universal deputy; and thou shalt, next to me, have all nations under thy hand; yea, and thou shalt lay hands upon them, that they may not resist thee; nor shall any of our vassals walk more at liberty, but those that shall be content to walk in thy fetters."

But it pleased the devil.

Now came the lord-mayor out from Diabolus, as if he had obtained a favour indeed; wherefore to his habitation he goes in great state, and thinks to feed himself well enough with hopes, until the time come that his greatness should be enlarged.

The lord-mayor in hopes of promotion.

But now, though the lord-mayor and Diabolus did thus well agree, yet this repulse to the brave captains put Mansoul into a mutiny; for while old Incredulity went into the castle, to congratulate with his lord on what had passed, the old lord-mayor, that was so before Diabolus came to the town, to wit, my Lord Understanding, and the old recorder Mr Conscience, getting intelligence of what had passed at Ear-gate (for you must know that they might not be suffered to be at that debate, lest they should then have mutinied for the captains;) but I say, they got intelligence what had passed there, and were much concerned therewith; wherefore they getting some of the town together, began to possess them with the reasonableness of the noble captains' demands, and with the bad consequences that would follow upon the speech of old Incredulity, the lord-mayor; to wit, how little reverence he showed therein, either to the captains, or their king; also how he implicitly charged them with unfaithfulness and treachery: for what less, quoth he, could be made of his words, when he said he would not yield to their proposition? and added, moreover, a supposition that he would destroy us, when before he had sent us word that he would

The understanding and conscience begin to receive conviction, and set the soul in a hubbub.

show us mercy? The multitude, being now possessed with the conviction of the evil old Incredulity had done, began to run together by companies in all places, and in every corner of the streets of Mansoul; and first they began to mutter, then to talk openly; and after that they ran to and fro, and cried as they ran, O the brave captains of Shaddai! Would we were under the government of the captains, and of Shaddai their king!*

A mutiny in Mansoul.

When the lord-mayor had intelligence that Mansoul was in an uproar, down he comes to appease the people, and thought to have quashed their heat with the bigness and show of his countenance. But when they saw him, they came running upon him, and had doubtless done him mischief, had he not betaken himself to his house. However, they strongly assaulted the house where he was, to have pulled it down about his ears: but the place was too strong, so they failed of that. Then he, taking some courage, addressed himself out of a window to the people in this manner.

Incredulity seeks to quiet the people.

"Gentlemen, what is the reason that there is such an uproar here to day?"

Understanding. Then answered my Lord Understanding. "It is even because thou and thy master have carried it not rightly, and as you should, to the captains of Shaddai; for in three things you are faulty: First, in that you would not let Mr Conscience and myself be at the hearing of your discourse. Secondly, in that you propounded such terms of peace to the captains which could by no means be granted, unless they had intended that their Shaddai should have been only a titular prince; and that Mansoul should still have had power, by law, to have lived in all lewdness and vanity before him, and so by consequence Diabolus should still here be king in power, and the other only king in name. Thirdly, for that thou didst thyself, after the captains had showed us upon what conditions they would have received to mercy, even undo all again with thy unsavoury, unseasonable, and ungodly speech."

My Lord Understanding answers him.

Incredulity. When old Incredulity had heard this speech, he cried out, "Treason! treason! to your arms! to your arms! O ye, the trusty friends of Diabolus in Mansoul!"

Sin and the soul at odds.

---

* When the understanding is somewhat enlightened, and the conscience awakened, unbelief is in danger of destruction. There will then be a party in the soul on the Lord's side. This is called a mutiny. A blessed mutiny it is, when unbelief begins to be opposed, and the sweet hope of pardoning mercy cherished; then, as the margin says, "Sin and the soul are at odds."

Understanding. "Sir, you may put upon my words what meaning you please, but I am sure the captains of such an high Lord as theirs is, deserved a better treatment at your hands."

Incredulity. Then said old Incredulity, "This is but little better. But Sir," quoth he, "what I spake, I spake for my prince, for his government, and the quieting of the people, whom, by your unlawful actions, you have this day set to mutiny against us."

They chide on both sides.

Conscience. Then replied the old recorder, whose name was Mr Conscience, and said, "Sir, you ought not thus to retort upon what my Lord Understanding hath said: it is evident enough that he hath spoken the truth, and that you are an enemy to Mansoul; be convinced, then, of the evil of your saucy and malapert language, and of the grief that you have put the captains to; yea, and of the damages that you have done to Mansoul thereby. Had you accepted of the conditions, the sound of the trumpet and the alarm of war had now ceased about the town of Mansoul; but that dreadful sound abides, and your want of wisdom in your speech has been the cause of it."

Mr Conscience reproaches old Incredulity.

Incredulity. Then said old Incredulity, "Sir, if I live, I will do your errand to Diabolus, and there you shall have an answer to your words. Meanwhile we will seek the good of the town, and not ask counsel of you."

Understanding. "Sir, your prince and you are foreigners to Mansoul, and not the natives thereof. And who can tell but that when you have brought us into greater straits (when you also shall see that yourselves can be safe by no other means than by flight,) you may leave us, and shift for yourselves, or set us on fire, and go away in the smoke, or by the light of our burning, and so leave us in our ruins."

Incredulity. "Sir, you forget that you are under a governor, and that you ought to demean yourself like a subject; and know ye, when my lord the king shall hear of this day's work, he will give you but little thanks for your labour."*

Now while these gentlemen were thus in their chiding words, down come from the walls and gates of the town the Lord Will-be will, Mr Prejudice, old Ill-pause, and several of the new made aldermen and burgesses; and they asked the reason of the hubbub and tumult. And with that every man began to tell his own tale, so that nothing

Men of arms come down.

---

* What formidable obstacles lie in the way of a sinner's conversion to God. The understanding and conscience are warmly opposed by unbelief; and indeed, nothing less than almighty grace can ever effect the work.

could be heard distinctly. Then was silence commanded, and the old fox Incredulity began to speak: "My lord," quoth he, "here are a couple of peevish gentlemen, that have, as a fruit of their bad dispositions, and as I fear, through the advice of one Mr Discontent, tumultuously gathered this company against this day; and also attempted to run the town into acts of rebellion against our prince."

A great confusion.   Then stood up all the Diabolonians that were present, and affirmed these things to be true. Now when they that took part with my Lord Understanding, and with Mr Conscience, perceived that they were like to come by the worst, for that force and power was on the other side, they came in for their help and relief; so a great company was on both sides. Then they on Incredulity's side would have had the two old gentlemen presently away to prison; but they on the other side said they should not. Then they began to cry up parties again: The Diabolonians cry up old Incredulity, Forget-good, the new alderman, and their great one Diabolus. and the other party as fast cried up Shaddai, the captains, his

They fall from words to blows.   laws, their mercifulness, and applauded their conditions and ways. Thus the bickerment went a while: at last they passed from words to blows and now there were knocks on both sides. The good old gentleman Mr Conscience was knocked down twice by one of the Diabolonians, whose name was Mr Benumbing. And my Lord Understanding had like to have been slain with an harquebus, but that he that had shot, failed to take his aim aright. Nor did the other side wholly escape: for there was one Mr Rash-head, a Diabolonian, that had his brains beaten out by one Mr Mind, the Lord Will-be-will's servant: and it made me laugh to see how

A hot skirmish.   old Mr Prejudice was kicked and tumbled about in the dirt: for though a while since he was made a captain of the Diabolonians, to the hurt and damage of the town, yet now they had got him under their feet: and I'll assure you, he had, by some of the Lord Understanding's party, his crown cracked to boot. Mr Any-thing also became a brisk man in the broil; but both sides were against him, because he was true to none. Yet he had, for his malapertness, one of his legs broken; and he that did it, wished it had been his neck. Much harm

Harm done on both sides.   more was done on both sides: but this must not be forgotten, it was now a wonder to see my Lord Will-be-will so indifferent as he was; he did not seem to take one side more than another only it was perceived that he smiled to see how old Prejudice was tumbled up and down in the dirt; also when Captain Any-thing came halting up before him, he seemed to take but little notice of him.*

CHAPTER VI.

Lord Understanding and Mr Conscience imprisoned as authors of the riot. The besieging officers apply to Shaddai for relief. Immanuel, the prince, undertakes to conquer Mansoul. Marches with a great army, and invests the town.

The two old gentlemen put in prison, as the authors of the revel-rout.

NOW when the uproar was over, Diabolus sends for my Lord Understanding and Mr Conscience, and claps them both up in prison, as the ringleaders and managers of this most heavy riotous rout in Mansoul. So now the town began to be quiet again, and the prisoners were used hardly; yea, he thought to have destroyed them, but that the present juncture did not serve for that purpose, for that war was in all their gates.†

The captains call a council, and consult what to do.

But let us return to our story: The captains, when they were gone back from the gate, and were come into the camp again, called a council of war, to consult what was further for them to do. Now some said, Let us go presently and fall upon the town, but the greatest part thought, rather better 'twould be to give them another summons to yield; and the reason why they thought this to be best, was, because that, so far as could be perceived, the town of Mansoul now was more inclinable than heretofore. And if, said they, while some of them are in a way of inclination, we should by ruggedness give them distaste, we may set them further from closing with our summons, than we would be willing they should.‡

The result is, they send another trumpeter to summon

Wherefore to this advice they agreed, and called a trumpeter, put words into his mouth, set him his time, and bid him God speed. Well, many hours were not expired, before the trumpeter addressed himself to his journey. Wherefore coming up to

---

* No small advantage is gained when sinful *Rashness* is destroyed, *Prejudice* thrown down into the dirt, and *Indifference* about religion discarded, while the *Will*, that before was wholly on the part of Satan, begins rather to take the other side.

† The efforts of an enlightened understanding and a renewed conscience cannot but be offensive to Satan, as threatening to subvert his authority in the soul, but where the good work of grace is begun they cannot be destroyed

‡ Ministers should deal gently with awakened sinners. Their great master " will not break the bruised reed," nor should they. Roughness of treatment may occasion discouragement; gentleness attracts.

the wall of the town, he steered his course to Eargate; and there sounded, as he was commanded.

the town to yield.

They then that were within, came out to see what was the matter, and the trumpeter made them this speech following:

The summons itself by the trumpeter of king Shaddai.

"O hard-hearted and deplorable town of Mansoul! how long wilt thou love thy simplicity; and ye fools, delight in your scorning? As yet despise you the offers of grace and deliverance? As yet will ye refuse the golden offers of Shaddai? and trust to the lies and falsehood of Diabolus? Think you, when Shaddai shall have conquered you, that the remembrance of these your carriages towards him will yield you peace and comfort? or that by ruffling language you can make him afraid as a grasshopper? Doth he intreat you, for fear of you? Do you think that you are stronger than he? Look to the heavens, and behold and consider the stars, how high are they? Can you stop the sun from running his course, and hinder the moon from giving her light? Can you count the number of the stars, or stop the bottles of heaven? Can you call for the waters of the sea, and cause them to cover the face of the ground? Can you behold every one that is proud, and abase him; and bend their faces in secret? Yet these are some of the works of our king, in whose name, this day, we come up unto you, that you may be brought under his authority. In his name, therefore, I summon you again to yield up yourselves to his captains."*

The town at a stand.

At this summons the Mansoulians seemed to be at a stand, and knew not what answer to make: wherefore Diabolus forthwith appeared, and took upon him to do it himself; and thus he begins, but turns his speech to them of Mansoul.

Diabolus makes a speech to the town, and endeavours to terrify it with the greatness of God.

"Gentlemen," quoth he, "and my faithful subjects, if it is true, what this summoner hath said, concerning the greatness of their king; by his terror you will always be kept in bondage, and so be made to sneak. Yea, how can you now, though he is at a distance, endure to think of such a mighty One? And if not to think of him while at a distance, how can you endure to

---

* The irresistible greatness, the inconceivable glory of God, especially when coupled with the astonishing condescensions of his grace, are considerations of a most awakening kind. It may well put a sinner to a stand when he reflects on the wonderful love of Christ in sending his ambassadors to beseech us in his stead, to be reconciled to God, 2 Cor. 5.

be in his presence? I your prince am familiar with you, and you may play with me as you would with a grasshopper. Consider, therefore, what is for your profit, and remember the immunities that I have granted you.

"Farther, if all be true that this man hath said, how comes it to pass that the subjects of Shaddai are so enslaved in all places where they come? None in the universe so unhappy as they, none so trampled upon as they;

"Consider, my Mansoul; would thou wert as loth to leave me, as I am loth to leave thee. But consider, I say, the ball is yet at my foot: liberty you have, if you know how to use it: yea, a king you have too, if you can tell how to love and obey him."*

Upon this speech, the town of Mansoul again hardened their hearts yet more against the captains of Shaddai. The thoughts of his holiness sunk them in despair; wherefore, after a short consultation, they (of the Diabolonians' party) sent back this word by the trumpeter: That, for their parts they were resolved to stick to their king, but never to yield to Shaddai; so it was but in vain to give them any further summons, for they had rather die upon the place than to yield. And now things seemed to be gone quite back, and Mansoul to be out of reach or call: yet the captains, who knew what their Lord could do, would not be beat out of heart; they therefore sent them another summons, more sharp and severe than the last; but the sooner they were sent to reconcile to Shaddai, the farther off they were, Hos. xi. 2. "As they called them, so they went from them," yea, though they called them to the Most High.

He drives Mansoul into despair.

Mansoul grows worse and worse.

So they ceased to deal any more with them in that way, and inclined to think of another way. The captains, therefore, gathered themselves together, to have free conference among themselves, to know what was yet to be done to gain the town, and deliver it from the tyranny of Diabolus. And one said after this manner, another after that. Then stood up the right noble Captain Conviction, and said, "My brethren, my opinion is this:

The captains leave off to summons, and betake themselves to prayer.

"First, That we continually play our slings into the town,

---

* By the cruel artifices of Satan, the majesty and greatness of God, which should induce them to seek his favour, are made an argument to terrify and alienate the soul from him. God is represented as a cruel tyrant, and his free subjects as miserable slaves. O unhappy men, thus cheated by the grand deceiver!

Captain Conviction's advice. and keep them in a continual alarm, molesting them day and night; by thus doing, we shall stop the growth of their rampant spirits: for a lion may be tamed by continual molestation.

"Secondly, this done, I advise, that, in the next place, we, with one consent, draw up a petition to our Lord Shaddai, by which, after we have showed our king the condition of Mansoul, and of affairs here, and have begged his pardon for our no better success, we will earnestly implore his majesty's **help**; and that he will please to send us more force and power, and some gallant and well-spoken commander to head them, **that so his majesty** may not lose the benefit of these his good beginnings, **but may complete his conquest upon the town of Mansoul.**"*

To this speech of the noble Captain Conviction they as one man consented, and agreed that a petition should forthwith be drawn up, and sent by a fit man away to Shaddai with speed. The contents of the petition were thus:

"Most gracious and glorious King, the Lord of the best world and Builder of the town of Mansoul; we have, dread **Sovereign**, *The petition of the captains to King Shaddai.* at thy command, put our lives in jeopardy, and at thy bidding made war upon the famous town of Mansoul. When we went up against it, we did according to our commission, first offer conditions of peace unto it, Matt. xxii. 5. Prov. i. Zech. vii. 10—13. But they, great king, set light by our counsel, and would none of our reproof. They were for shutting their gates, and so keeping us out of the town: they also mounted their guns, they sallied out upon us, and have done us what damage they could; but we pursued them with alarm upon alarm, requiting them with such retribution as was meet, and have done some execution upon the town.

"Diabolus, Incredulity, and Will-be-will, are the great doers against us: now we are in our winter-quarters, but so as that we do yet with an high hand molest and distress the town.

"Once, as we think, had we had but one substantial friend in the town, such as would have but seconded the sound of our summons as they ought, the people might have yielded themselves: but there were none but enemies there, nor any to speak in **behalf of our** Lord to the town: wherefore, though **we have** done as we could, yet Mansoul abides in **a state of** rebellion against thee.

---

* Preachers of the gospel must be unwearied in their endeavours to save their hearers; but they must *pray* as well as preach, for painful experience and repeated disappointments will convince them that Paul may plant, and Apollos water, but God alone can give the increase. To him therefore they wisely apply for further assistance.

"Now, kings of kings, let it please thee to pardon the unsuccessfulness of thy servants, who have been no more advantageous in so desirable a work as the conquering of Mansoul is; and send, Lord, as we now desire, more forces to Mansoul, that it may be subdued; and a man to head them, that the town may both love and fear.

"We do not thus speak because we are willing to relinquish the war (for we are for laying our bones against the place,) but that the town of Mansoul may be won for thy Majesty. We also pray thy Majesty, for expedition in this matter, that, after conquest, we may be at liberty to be sent about other thy gracious designs. Amen."

Who carried this petition. The petition, thus drawn up, was sent away with haste to the king by the hand of that good man, Mr Love-to-Mansoul.

When this petition was come to the palace of the king, who *To whom it was delivered.* should it be delivered to, but the king's son. So he took it and read it; and because the contents of it pleased him well, he mended it, and also in some things added to the petition himself. So after he had made such amendments and additions as he thought convenient, with his own hands, he carried it unto the king: to whom when he had with obeisance delivered it, he put on authority, and spake to it himself.*

Now the king, at the sight of the petition, was glad; but *The king receives it with gladness.* how much more, think you, when it was seconded by his son! It pleased him also to hear that his servants, who encamped against Mansoul, were so hearty in the work, and so steadfast in their resolves, and that they had already got some ground upon the famous town of Mansoul.

Wherefore the king called to him Immanuel his son, who *The king calls his son, and tells him that he shall go to conquer the town of Mansoul; and he is pleased at it.* said, Here am I, my father. Then said the king, Thou knowest as I do myself, the condition of Mansoul, and what thou hast done to redeem it. Come now therefore, my son, and prepare thyself for the war, for thou shalt go to my camp at Mansoul; thou shalt also there prosper and prevail, and conquer the town of Mansoul.

Then said the king's son, "Thy law is within my heart: I

---

* Jesus Christ is our great advocate above. He receives, amends, and presents our prayers; and those petitions which have the glory of God for their object, cannot but be acceptable to him.

He solaceth himself in the thoughts of his work. delight to do thy will," Heb. x. This is the day that I have longed for, and the work that I have waited for all this while. Grant me therefore what force thou shalt in thy wisdom think meet; and I will go, and will deliver from Diabolus, and from his power, thy perishing town of Mansoul. My heart has been often pained within me, for the miserable town of Mansoul; but now it is rejoiced, but now it is glad; and with that he leaped over the mountains for joy, saying, I have not in my heart thought any thing too dear for Mansoul; the day of vengeance is in mine heart for thee, my Mansoul; and glad am I that thou, my father, hast made me the captain of their salvation, Heb, ii. 10. And I will now begin to plague all that have been a plague to my town of Mansoul, and I will deliver it from their hands.*

When the king's son had said thus to his father, it presently flew like lightning round about at court: yea, it there became the only talk, what Immanuel was to go to do for the famous town of Mansoul. But you cannot think how the courtiers too were taken with this design of the prince; yea, so affected were they with this work, and with the justness of the war, that the highest lord and greatest peer of the kingdom coveted to have commissions under Immanuel, to go and help to recover again to Shaddai that miserable town of Mansoul.†

The highest peers in the kingdom covet to go on this design.

Then was it concluded that some should go and carry tidings to the camp, that Immanuel was to come to recover Mansoul; and that he would bring along with him so mighty, so impregnable a force, that he could not be resisted. But oh! how ready were the high ones at court to run like lacquies to carry these tidings to the camp that was at Mansoul!

Now when the captains perceived that the king would send Immanuel his son, and that it also delighted the son to be sent on this errand by the great Shaddai his father; they also, to show how they were pleased at the thoughts of his coming, gave a shout that made the earth rend at the sound thereof; yea, the mountains answered the echo, and Diabolus himself tottered and shook.

The camp shout for joy, when they hear the tidings.

* The salvation of souls is "the pleasure of the Lord," and it shall prosper in his hands. How does this bespeak the infinite value of an immortal spirit, and how should it engage all the people of God to seek, not only their own personal salvation, but that also of their fellow sinners throughout the world.

† Angels are "ministering spirits to the heirs of salvation," and glad they are to be employed in promoting their eternal welfare

Now you must know, that though the town of Mansoul itself was not much, if at all, concerned with the project (for, alas for them! they were wofully besotted, for they chiefly regarded their pleasure and lusts;) yet Diabolus their governor was, for he had his spies continually abroad, who brought him intelligence of all things; and they told him what was doing at court against him, and that Immanuel would certainly come shortly with a power to invade him. Nor was there any man in court, nor peer of the kingdom, that Diabolus so feared, as he feared this prince: for, if you remember, I showed you before, that Diabolus had felt the weight of his hand already; so that since it was he that was to come, this made him sore afraid.

Diabolus afraid at the news of his coming.

Well, you see how I have told you that the king's son was engaged to come from the court to save Mansoul, and that his father had made him captain of the forces; the time therefore for his setting forth being now expired, he addressed himself for the march; and taking with him, for his power, five noble captains and their forces.

The prince addresses himself for his journey.

1. The first was that famous captain, the noble Captain Credence; his were the red colours, and Mr Promise bare them, John i. 29. Eph. vi. 16: and for an escutcheon he had the holy lamb and golden shield; and he had ten thousand men at his feet.

2. The second was that famous captain, the Captain Good Hope; his were the blue colours, Heb. vi. 19. His standard-bearer was Mr Expectation; and for an escutcheon he had three golden anchors; and he had ten thousand men at his feet.

3. The third was that valiant captain, the Captain Charity, 1 Cor. xiii. His standard-bearer was Mr Pitiful; his were the green colours, and for his escutcheon he had three naked orphans embraced in the bosom; and he had ten thousand at his feet.

4. The fourth was that gallant commander, the Captain Innocent, Matt. x. 16. His standard-bearer was Mr Harmless; his were the white colours, and for his escutcheon he had three golden doves.

5. The fifth was that truly loyal and well-beloved captain, the Captain Patience: his standard-bearer was Mr Sufferlong; his were the black colours, and for an escutcheon he had three arrows through a golden heart.

These were Immanuel's captains, these their standard-bearers, their colours and escutcheons, and these the men under their command, Heb. vi. 21. So, as was said, the brave prince

Faith and Patience do the work.

took his march, to go to the town of Mansoul. Captain Credence led the van, and Captain Patience brought up the rear. So the other three, with their men, made up the main body. The prince himself rode in his chariot at the head of them.*

But when they set out for their march, oh how the trumpets sounded, their armour glittered, and how the colours waved in the wind! The prince's armour was all gold, and it shone like the sun in the firmament. The captains' armour was of proof, and was in appearance like the glittering stars. There were also some from the court that rode reformades,† for the love that they had to the king Shaddai, and for the happy deliverance of the town of Mansoul.

Their march towards Mansoul.

Immanuel also, when he had thus set forwards to go to recover the town of Mansoul, took with him, at the command of his father, fifty-four battering rams, and twelve slings to whirl stones withal. Every one of these was made of pure gold; and these they carried with them in the heart and body of their army, all along as they went to Mansoul.‡

The holy Bible, containing 66 books.

So they marched till they came within less than a league of the town; and there they lay till the first four captains came thither to acquaint them with matters. Then they took their journey to go to the town of Mansoul, and unto Mansoul they came; but when the old soldiers that were in the camp saw that they had new forces to join with, they again gave such a shout before the walls of Mansoul, that it put Diabolus into another fright. So they sat down before the town, not now as the other four captains did, to wit, against the gates of Mansoul only, but they environed it round on every side, and beset it behind and before; so that now let Mansoul look which way it would, it saw force and

The forces joined with rejoicing.

Mansoul beleaguered round.

---

* When Jesus girds his sword upon his thigh to effect the conquest of the human soul, he comes gloriously attended with those heavenly graces—faith hope, love, innocence, and patience. Faith leads the van; patience brings up the rear. Jesus himself, the captain of our salvation, heads the noble army, and conducts the holy war. "Ride prosperously, gracious majesty, because of truth, meekness, and righteousness, and thy right hand shall teach thee terrible things," Ps. xlv. 4.

† Reformades, an old word signifying Volunteers: the angels are intended, because "ministering spirits," who delight to explore the wonders of redemption, and to serve the heirs of salvation.

‡ The several books of the Old and New Testament, in number 66, are here compared to military engines, such as were formerly used to batter walls and gates. These are the proper weapons of the holy war, and they are, indeed, mighty through God to the pulling down the strong holds of the devil.

power lie in siege against it. Beside, there were mounts cast

Mounts cast up against it. up against it; the Mount Gracious was on the one side, and Mount Justice on the other.

Farther, there were several small banks and advance grounds, as Plain-truth-hill, and No-sin-banks, where many of the slings were placed against the town. Upon Mount Gracious were planted four, and upon Mount Justice were planted as many: and the rest were conveniently placed in several parts round about the town. Five of the best battering rams, that is, of the biggest of them, were placed upon Mount **Hearken,** a mount cast up hard by Ear-gate, with intent to break that open.

Now when the town of Mansoul saw the multitude, and the

The heart of Mansoul begins to fail. soldiers that were come up against the place, and the rams and slings, and the mounts on which they were planted; together with the glittering of the armour, and the waving of their colours; they were forced to shift and shift, and again to shift their thoughts; but they hardly changed for thoughts more stout, but rather for thoughts more faint; for though before they thought themselves sufficiently guarded, yet, now they began to think that no man knew what would be their hap or lot.*

When the good prince Immanuel had thus beleaguered Man-

The white flag hung out. soul, in the first place he hangs out the white flag, which he caused to be set among the golden slings that were planted upon Mount Gracious. And this he did for two reasons: 1. To give notice to Mansoul, that he could and would yet be gracious, if they turned to him. 2. And that he might leave them the more without excuse, should he destroy them, they continuing in their rebellion.

So the white flag, with the three golden doves on it, was hung out for two days together, to give them time and space to consider. But they, as was hinted before, as if they were unconcerned, made no reply to the favourable signal of the prince.

Then he commanded and they set the red flag upon that

The red flag hung out. mount called Justice. It was the red flag of Captain Judgment, whose escutcheon was the burning fiery furnace: also this stood waving before

---

* Thus the soul which the Lord designs to save is surrounded on all sides, Grace and justice, plain truth, and opposition to sin, are visible on every hand. Thus many searchings of heart are excited, men's hearts failing for fear, not knowing what the end of these things will be. But the white flag sufficiently intimates the merciful designs of Immanuel, so, in preaching the gospel, mercy is the prominent object.

them in the wind for several days together. But look how they carried it under the white flag, when that was hung out, so did they also when the red one was; and yet he took no advantage of them.

Then he commanded again that his servants should hang out *The black flag hung out.* the black flag of Defiance against them, whose escutcheon was the three burning thunderbolts. But as unconcerned was Mansoul at this, as at those that went before. But when the prince saw that neither mercy nor judgment, nor execution of judgment, would or could come near the heart of Mansoul, he was touched with much compunction, and said, Surely this strange carriage of the town of Mansoul doth rather arise from ignorance of the manner and feats of war, than from a secret defiance of us, and abhorrence *Christ makes not war as the world does.* of their own lives; or, if they know the manner of the war of their own, yet not the rites and ceremonies of the wars in which we are concerned, when I make wars upon mine enemy Diabolus.

Therefore he sent to the town of Mansoul, to let them know what he meant by those signs and ceremonies of the flag; and *He sends to know if they would have mercy or judgment.* also to know of them which of the things they will chuse, whether grace and mercy, or judgment, and the execution of judgment. All this while they kept the gates shut as fast as they could. Their guards were also doubled, and their watch made as strong as they could. Diabolus also plucked up what heart he could, to encourage the town to make resistance.*

The townsmen also made answer to the prince's messenger, in substance, according to that which follows:

The townsfolk's answer. "Great Sir, as to what, by your messenger, you have signified to us, whether we will accept your mercy, or fall by your justice; we are bound, by the law and custom of this place, and can give you no positive answer: for it is against the law, government, and the prerogative royal of our king, to make either peace or war

---

* Neither *mercy* nor *judgment* impresses the stony heart of man: even the black flag of *defiance* occasions no concern. O how do poor sinners heap up unto themselves wrath against the day of wrath, by thus despising the riches of his patience, forbearance and long suffering. Rom. ii. How graciously candid is the allowance made for their possible ignorance, like that of the suffering Saviour when nailed to the cross: "Father, forgive them, for they know not what they do." The meaning therefore of these flags is explained; thus must ministers deal with poor sinners, giving them " line upon line, precept upon precept." But without divine grace all is in vain, Satan will still foment the spirit of resistance.

without him. But this we will do, we will petition that our prince will come down to the wall, and there give you such a treatment as he shall think fit and profitable for us."

When the good prince Immanuel heard this answer, and saw the slavery and bondage of the people, and how contented they were to abide in the chains of the tyrant Diabolus, it grieved him at the heart. And indeed, when at any time he perceived that any were contented with the slavery of the giant, he would be affected with it.*

Immanuel grieved at the folly of Mansoul.

But to return again to our purpose. After the town had carried this news to Diabolus, and had told him, moreover, that the prince, that lay in the leaguer without the wall, waited upon them for an answer, he refused, and huffed as well as he could, but in heart he was afraid.

Diabolus afraid.

Then said he, "I will go down to the gates myself, and give him such an answer as I think fit. So he went down to Mouth-gate, and there addressed himself to speak to Immanuel (but in such language as the town understood not,) the contents whereof were as follow:

"O thou great Immanuel, lord of the world, I know thee that thou art the son of the great Shaddai! Wherefore art thou come to torment me, and to cast me out of my possession? This town of Mansoul, as thou very well knowest, is mine by right of conquest; I won it in the open field: and 'shall the prey be taken from the mighty, or the lawful captive delivered?' 2. This town of Mansoul is mine also by their subjection. They have opened the gates of their town unto me, they have sworn fidelity to me, and have openly chosen me to be their king. They have also given their castle(*a*) into my hands; they have also put the whole strength of Mansoul under me.

The speech of Diabolus to the prince.

(a) Heart.

"Moreover, this town of Mansoul hath disavowed thee. yea, they have cast thy law, thy name, thy image, and all that is thine, behind their back; and have accepted, and set up in their room, my law, my name, my image, and all that ever is mine. Ask else thy captains, and they will tell thee, that Mansoul hath, in answer to all their summons, shown love and loyalty to me; but always disdain, despite, contempt, and scorn to thee and thine. Now, thou who art the just one and the holy (and shouldst do no iniquity,) depart then, I pray thee, from me, and leave me to my just inheritance peaceably."

* Pitiable indeed is the bondage of sinners:—"they are led captive by him at his will."

This oration was made in the language of Diabolus himself; for although he can to every man speak in their language (else he could not tempt them as he does,) yet he has a language proper to himself, and it is the language of the infernal cave or black pit.

Wherefore the town of Mansoul (poor hearts!) understood him not: nor did they see how he crouched and cringed while he stood before Immanuel their prince. Yea, they all this while took him to be one of that power and force that by no means could be resisted: wherefore, while he was thus intreating that he might have yet his residence there, and that Immanuel would not take it from him by force, the inhabitants boasted even of his valour, saying, Who is able to make war with him?*

Diabolus unable to stand in the presence of Immanuel.

Well, when this pretended king had made an end of what he would say, Immanuel the golden prince stood up, and spake; the contents of whose words follow:

"Thou deceiving one, said he, I have in my father's name, in my own name, and on the behalf and for the good of this wretched town of Mansoul, somewhat to say unto thee. Thou pretendest a right, a lawful right, to the deplorable town of Mansoul, when it is most apparent to all my father's court, that the entrance which thou hast obtained in at the gates of Mansoul was through thy lies and falsehood: thou belyedst my father, thou belyedst his law, and so deceivedst the people of Mansoul. Thou pretendest that the people have accepted thee for their king, their captain, and right liege lord, but that also was by the exercise of deceit and guile. Now if lying, wiliness, sinful craft, and all manner of horrible hypocrisy, will go, in my father's court (in which court thou must be tried) for equity and right, then will I confess unto thee, that thou hast made a lawful conquest. But alas! what thief, what tyrant, what devil, is there, that may not conquer after this sort? But I can make it appear, O Diabolus, that thou, in all thy pretences to a conquest of Mansoul, hast nothing of truth to say. Thinkest thou this to be right, that thou didst put the lie upon my father, and madest him (to Mansoul) the greatest deluder in the world? And what sayest thou to thy perverting, knowingly, the right purport and intent of the law? Was it good also that thou madest

Immanuel's speech to Diabolus.

The craft and subtlety of Diabolus exposed by Immanuel.

---

* Deceived mortals understand not the real designs of the enemy, who first allures to sin, and then becomes an accuser.

a prey of the innocency and simplicity of the now miserable town of Mansoul? Yea, thou didst overcome Mansoul, by promising to them happiness in their transgressions against my father's law, when thou knewest, and couldst not but know, hadst thou consulted nothing but thy own experience, that that was the way to undo them. Thou hast also thyself (O thou master of enmity!) of spite defaced my father's image in Mansoul, and set up thy own in its place; to the great contempt of my father, the heightening of thy sin and to the intolerable damage of the perishing town of Mansoul.

His enmity to Shaddai.

"Thou hast moreover (as if all these were but little things with thee) not only deluded and undone this place, but by thy lies, and fraudulent carriage, has set them against their own deliverance. How hast thou stirred them up against my father's captains, and made them to fight against those that were sent of him to deliver them from their bondage! All these things, and very many more, thou hast done against thy light, and in contempt of my father, and his law: yea, and with design to bring under his displeasure for ever the miserable town of Mansoul. I am therefore come to revenge the wrong that thou hast done to my father, and to deal with thee for the blasphemies wherewith thou hast made poor Mansoul blaspheme his name: yea, upon thy head, thou prince of the infernal cave, will I require it.

"As for myself, O Diabolus, I am come against thee by lawful power; and to take, by strength of hands, this town of Mansoul out of thy burning fingers; for this town of Mansoul is mine, O Diabolus, and that by undoubted right, as all shall see that will diligently search the most ancient and most authentic records, and I will plead my title to it to the confusion of thy face.

"First, For the town of Mansoul, my father built and fashioned it with his hands. The palace also, that is in the midst of the town, he built for his own delight. This town of Mansoul, therefore, is my father's, and that by the best of titles; and he that gainsays the truth of this, must lie against his soul.

The town of Mansoul is the right of Shaddai who built it.

"Secondly, O thou master of the lie, this town of Mansoul is mine:

"1. For that I am my father's heir, his first-born, and the only delight of his heart, Heb. i. 2. John xv. 16. I am, therefore, come up against thee in mine own right, even to recover mine own inheritance out of thine hands.

"2. But further, as I have a right and title to Mansoul by

Also the inheritance of his son Immanuel. being my father's heir, so I have also by my father's donation, John xvii. His it was, and he gave it me: nor have I at any time offended my father, that he should take it from me, and give it to thee, Isa. l. 1. Nor have I been forced, by playing the bankrupt, to sell or set to sale to thee my beloved town of Mansoul. Mansoul is my desire, my delight, and the joy of my heart. But,

"Mansoul is mine by right of purchase. I have bought it, O Diabolus, I have bought it for myself. Now since it was my father's and mine, as I was his heir, and since also I have made it mine by virtue of a great purchase, it followeth, that by all lawful right the town of Mansoul is mine; and that thou art an *Diabolus an usurper and tyrant.* usurper, tyrant, and traitor, in thy holding possession thereof. Now the cause of my purchasing it was this: Mansoul had trespassed against my father. Now my father had said, that in the day that they broke his law, they should die: now it is more possible for heaven and earth to pass away, than for my father to break his word, Matt. v. 18. Wherefore when Mansoul had sinned indeed by hearkening to thy lie, I put in and became a surety to my father, body for body, and soul for soul, that I *O sweet prince Immanuel!* would make amends for Mansoul's transgressions: and my father accepted thereof. So when the time appointed was come, I gave body for body, soul for soul, life for life, blood for blood, and so redeemed my beloved Mansoul.

"4. Nor did I this by halves; my father's love and justice, that were both concerned in the threatening upon transgression, are both now satisfied, and very well content that Mansoul should be delivered.

"5. Nor am I come out this day against thee, but by commandment from my father; 'twas he that said unto me, Go down and deliver Mansoul.

Immanuel commissioned by his father. "Wherefore be it known unto thee, O thou fountain of deceit, and be it also known to the foolish town of Mansoul, that I am not come against thee this day without my father.

"And now, said the golden-headed prince, I have a word to the town of Mansoul (but so soon as mention was made, that he had a word to speak to the besotted town of Mansoul, the gates were double-guarded, and all men commanded not to give him audience;) so he proceeded and said, O unhappy town of Mansoul, I cannot but be touched with pity and compassion

8

Immanuel's address to the town of Mansoul.

for thee. Thou has accepted of Diabolus for thy king, and art become a nurse and minister of Diabolonians against thy sovereign Lord. Thy gates thou hast opened to him, but hast shut them fast against me; thou hast given him a hearing, but hast stopt thine ears to my cry. he brought to thee thy destruction, and thou didst receive both him and it; I am come to thee bringing **salvation, but thou regardest me not.** Besides, thou hast with sacrilegious hands taken thyself, with all that was mine in thee, and hast given all to my foe, and to the greatest enemy my father has. You have bowed and subjected yourselves to him, you have vowed and sworn yourselves to be his. Poor Mansoul! what shall I do unto thee? Shall I save thee? Shall I destroy thee? What shall I do unto thee? Shall I fall upon thee, and grind thee to powder; or make thee a monument of the richest grace? What shall I do unto thee? Hearken therefore, thou town of Mansoul, hearken to my word, and thou shalt live. I am merciful, Mansoul, and thou shalt find me so: shut me not out of thy gates, Cant. v. 2.

"O Mansoul, neither is my commission or inclination at all to do thee hurt: why flyest thou so fast from thy friend, and stickest so close to thine enemy? Indeed I would have thee, because it becomes thee, to be sorry for thy sin: but do not despair of life: this great **force is not to hurt thee, but to deliver thee from thy bondage, and to reduce thee to thy obedience.**

"My commission indeed is, to make war upon Diabolus thy king, and upon all Diabolonians with him, for he is the strong man armed that keeps the house: but I will have him out; his spoils I must divide, his armour I must take from him, his hold I must cast him out of, and must make it an habitation for myself. And this, O Mansoul, shall Diabolus know, when he shall be made to follow me in chains, and when Mansoul shall rejoice to see it too.

Immanuel's commission is to make war upon Diabolus and to save Mansoul.

"I could, would I now put forth my might, cause that forthwith he should leave you, and depart; but I have it in my heart so to deal with him, as that the justice of the war, that I shall make upon him, may be seen and acknowledged by all. He hath taken Mansoul by fraud, and keeps it by violence and deceit; and I will make him bare and naked in the eyes of all observers. All my words are true: I am mighty to save, and will deliver my Mansoul out of his hand."*

Conclusion of Immanuel's speech.

---

* In this speech of Immanuel, the true character of Satan is drawn, and he is represented, as in the sacred scriptures, a liar, a deceiver, a blasphemer, an

This speech was intended chiefly for Mansoul, but Mansoul would not have the hearing of it. They shut up Ear-Gate, they barricadoed it up, they kept it locked and bolted, they set a guard thereat, and commanded that no Mansoulian should go out to him, nor that any from the camp should be admitted into the town; all this they did, so horribly had Diabolus inchanted them to do, and to seek to do for him, against their rightful lord and prince; wherefore no man, nor voice, nor sound of man that belonged to the glorious host, was to come into the town.*

CHAPTER VII.

Immanuel prepares to make war upon Mansoul. Diabolus sends Mr Loth-to-stoop with proposals for accommodating the difference. His dishonourable proposals are rejected by Immanuel. Again he proposes to be Immanuel's Deputy, and turn reformer; this proposal also rejected. New preparations for battle. A violent assault upon Ear-gate with the Battering Rams. The gate broken to pieces; the troops enter the Town; take possession of Mr Conscience's house. Several Diabolonians are killed.

WHEN Immanuel saw that Mansoul was thus involved in sin, he called his army together, (since now all his words were despised,) and gave out a commandment throughout all his hosts, to be ready against the time appointed. Now forasmuch as there was no way lawfully to take the town of Mansoul, but to get in by the gates, and at Ear-gate as the chief, therefore he commanded his captains and commanders to bring their rams, their slings, and their men, and place them at Eye-gate and Ear-gate, in order to his taking the town.

Immanul prepares to make war upon Mansoul.

When Immanuel had put all things in readiness to bid Diabolus battle, he sent again to know of the town of Mansoul, if in peaceable manner they would yield themselves; or whether they were yet resolved to put him to try the utmost extremity? They then, together with Diabolus the king, called a council of war, and resolved upon certain propositions that should be

usurper, the malicious enemy of God and man; while Immanuel claims the human soul as his own, his workmanship, his delight, his inheritance, his purchase.

That part of the speech which is directed to Mansoul, contains the charming substance of the gospel of grace, the merciful design of Christ in his approaches to the soul, which is not to destroy but to save. How well does his gracious address deserve the most cordial acceptation: but, mark the sequel!

* Infatuated sinners! rejecting the counsel of God against themselves Reader, is this thy picture?—pause and examine. Remember, "faith cometh by hearing." "Hear, then, and your soul shall live."

offered Immanuel, if he will accept thereof: so they agreed; and then the next was, who should be sent on this errand. Now there was in the town of Mansoul an old man, a Diabolonian, and his name was Mr Loth-to-stoop; a stiff man in his way, and a great doer for Diabolus; him therefore they sent, and put into his mouth what he should say. So he went, and came to the camp to Immanuel; and when he was come, a time was appointed to give him audience. So at the time he came; and after a Diabolonian ceremony or two, he thus began, and said, Tim. i. 16. "Great Sir, that it may be known unto all men, how good-natured a prince my master is, he hath sent me to tell your lordship, that he is very willing, rather than go to war, to deliver up into your hands one half of the town of Mansoul. I am therefore to know if your Mightiness will accept of this proposition?"

Diabolus sends by the hand of his servant Mr Loth-to-stoop, and by him he propounds conditions of peace.

Diabolus wishes to retain the half of Mansoul.

Then said Immanuel, "The whole is mine by gift and purchase, therefore I will never lose one half."

Then said Mr Loth-to-stoop, "Sir, my master hath said, that he will be content that you shall be the nominal and titular lord of all, if he may possess but a part," Luke xiii. 25.

And will allow Immanuel to be called Lord of all.

Then Immanuel answered, "The whole is mine really, not in name and word only; wherefore I will be the sole lord and possessor of all, or of none at all, in Mansoul."

Then Mr Loth-to-stoop said again, "Sir, behold the condescension of my master! He says, that he will be content if he may but have assigned to him some place in Mansoul, as a place to live privately in, and you shall be lord of all the rest." Acts v. 1—5.

Mark this.

Then said the Golden Prince, "All that the Father giveth me, shall come to me; and of all that he hath given me I will lose nothing, no not the least corner in Mansoul to dwell in, I will have it all to myself."

Then Loth-to-stoop said again, "But, Sir, suppose that my Lord should resign the whole town to you only with this proviso, that he sometimes, when he comes into this country, may, for old acquaintance sake, be entertained as a wayfaring man for two days, or ten days, or a month, or so; may not this small matter be granted?"

Mark this well.

Then said Immanuel, "No. He came as a wayfaring man

to David, nor did he stay long with him, and yet it had like to have cost David his soul, 2 Sam. xii. 1—5. I will not consent that he ever should have any harbour more there."

Then said Mr Loth-to-stoop, "Sir, you seem to be very hard. *Sin and carnal lust.* Suppose my master should yield to all that your lordship hath said, provided that his friends and kindred in Mansoul may have liberty to trade in the town, and to enjoy their present dwellings; may not that be granted, Sir?"

Then said Immanuel, "No; that is contrary to my Father's will, Rom. vi. 13. Col. iii. 5. Gal. v. 24. For all, and all manner of Diabolonians that now are, or that at any time shall be found in Mansoul, shall not only lose their lands and liberties, but also their lives."

Then said Mr Loth-to-stoop again, "But, Sir, may not my master and great lord, by letters, by passengers, by *Mark this.* accidental opportunities, and the like, maintain, if he shall deliver up all unto thee, some kind of old friendship with Mansoul?" John x. 8.

Immanuel answered, "No, by no means; forasmuch as any such fellowship, friendship, intimacy, or acquaintance, in what way, sort, or mode soever maintained, will tend to the corrupting of Mansoul, the alienating of their affections from me, and the endangering their peace with my Father."

Mr Loth-to-stoop yet added further, saying, "But, great Sir, since my master hath many friends, and those *Mark this.* that are dear to him in Mansoul, Rom. vi. 12, 13. may he not, if he depart from them, even of his bounty and good nature, bestow upon them, as he sees fit, some tokens of his love and kindness, that he had for them, to *Delight in the* the end that Mansoul, when he is gone, may look *recollection of* upon such tokens of kindness once received from *past sins.* their old friend, and remember him who was once their king, and the merry times that they sometimes enjoyed one with another while he and they lived in peace together?"

Then said Immanuel, "No; for if Mansoul come to be mine, I shall not admit of, nor consent that there should be the least scrap, shred, or dust of Diabolus left behind, as tokens or gifts bestowed upon any in Mansoul, thereby to call to remembrance the horrible communion that was betwixt them and him."

"Well, sir, said Mr Loth-to-stoop, I have one thing more to propound, and then I am got to the end of my com-
Mark this. mission; 2 Kings i. 3, 6, 7. Suppose that when my

master is gone from Mansoul, any that yet shall live in the town, shall have such business of high concerns to do, that, if they be neglected, the party shall be undone: and suppose, Sir, that nobody can help, in that case, so well as my master and lord; may not now my master be sent for upon so urgent an occasion as this? Or if he may not be admitted into the town, may not he and the persons concerned meet in some of the villages near Mansoul, and there lay their heads together, and there consult together?"

This was the last of those ensnaring propositions that Mr Loth-to-stoop had to propound to Immanuel on behalf of his master Diabolus: but Immanuel would not grant it; for he said, "There can be no case, or thing, or matter fall out in Mansoul, when thy master shall be gone, that may not be solved by my Father, 1 Sam. xxviii. 15. Besides, it will be a great disparagement to my Father's wisdom and skill, to admit any from Mansoul to go out to Diabolus for advice, when they are bid before, in every thing, by prayer and supplication, to let their requests be made known to my Father, 2 Kings i. 2, 3. Further, this, should it be granted, would be to grant that a door should be set open for Diabolonians in Mansoul, to hatch and plot and bring to pass treasonable designs, to the grief of my Father and me, and to the utter destruction of Mansoul."*

All the propositions of Loth-to-stoop in behalf of Diabolus rejected.

When Mr Loth-to-stoop had heard this answer, he took his leave of Immanuel, and departed, saying, that he would carry word to his master concerning this whole affair. So he departed, and came to Diabolus in Mansoul, and told him the whole of the matter; and how Immanuel would not admit, no not by any means, that he,

Loth-to-stoop departs.

---

* The proud heart of man is *loth to stoop* to that absolute and entire obedience to Christ which he justly requires. There are many who would call themselves Christians on some of the conditions here proposed. They would resign half their hearts to Christ, and so serve two masters. Or, they would allow him to be titular lord, a lord in name, but not in authority. Others would serve Jesus, in general, if permitted to enjoy the pleasures of sin occasionally. Others would submit to become religious yet entertain some darling lusts; or maintain correspondence and friendship with Satan; or take delight in the recollection of their pleasant sins. But all this *partial* and *conditional* submission is rejected; Christ will have all the heart or none. To be only "almost a Christian" is to be no Christian at all. The author, wishing to impress these things on the mind of the reader, has repeatedly said in the margin—*mark this*. They do indeed deserve remark, and let every reader consider whether he is offering some of these conditions, or whether he is saying

"Take my whole heart, and let it be
Forever closed to all but thee."

when he was once gone out, should ever have any thing more to do either in, or with any that are of, the town of Mansoul. When Mansoul and Diabolus had heard this relation of things, they with one consent concluded to use their best endeavours to keep Immanuel out of Mansoul; and sent old Ill-pause, of whom you have heard before, to tell the Prince and his captains so. So the old gentleman came up to the top of Ear-gate, and called to the camp for a hearing; who, when they gave audience, he said, "I have in commandment from my high lord to bid you tell it to your prince Immanuel, that Mansoul, and their king, are resolved to stand or fall together, and that it is in vain for your prince to think of ever having Mansoul in his hand, unless he can take it by force." So some went and told Immanuel what old Ill-pause, a Diabolonian in Mansoul, had said. Then said the prince, "I must try the power of my sword, Eph. vi. 17. for I will not (for all the rebellions and repulses that Mansoul has made against me) raise my siege and depart, but will assuredly take my Mansoul, and deliver it from her enemy And with that he gave out a commandment, that Captain Boanerges, Captain Conviction, Captain Judgment, and Captain Execution, should march forthwith up to Ear-gate, with trumpets sounding, colours flying, and with shouting for the battle. Also he would that Captain Credence should join himself in with them: Immanuel moreover gave orders that Captain Good-Hope and Captain Charity should draw themselves up before Eye-gate. He bid also that the rest of his captains and their men should place themselves to the best of their advantage against the enemy, round about the town; and all was done as he commanded. Then he bid that the word should be given forth, and the word was at that time *Immanuel.* Then was an alarm sounded, and the battering rams were played, and the slings whirled stones into the town amain; and thus the battle began. Now Diabolus himself managed the townsmen in the war, and that at every gate; wherefore their resistance was the more forcible, hellish, and offensive to Immanuel. Thus was the good prince engaged and entertained by Diabolus and Mansoul for several days together; and a sight worth seeing it was, to behold how the captains of Shaddai behaved themselves in the war.

A speech of old Ill-pause to the camp.

They must fight. Preparations for the battle.

And first for Captain Boanerges (not to undervalue the rest,) he made three most fierce assaults, one after another, upon Ear-gate, to the shaking of the posts thereof. Captain Conviction also made

Boanerges plays the man.

up as fast with Boanerges as possibly he could; and both discerning that the gate began to yield, they commanded that the rams should still be played against it. Now Captain Conviction going up very near to the gate, was with great force driven back, and received three wounds in his mouth; and those that rode reformades (a) went about to encourage the captains.

Conviction wounded. (a) Angels.

For the valour of the two captains made mention of before, the prince sent for them to his pavilion; and commanded that awhile they should rest themselves, and that with somewhat they should be refreshed. Care was also taken for Captain Conviction, that he should be healed of his wounds; the prince also gav them a chain of gold, and bid them yet be of good courage.

Nor did Captain Good-hope nor Captain Charity come behind in this most desperate fight, for they too so behaved themselves at Eye-gate that they had almost broken it quite open. These had also a reward from their prince, as also had the rest of the captains, because they did valiantly round about the town.*

Good-hope and Charity play the man at Eye-gate

In this engagement, several of the officers of Diabolus were slain, and some of the townsmen wounded, for among the officers there was one Captain Boasting slain. This Boasting thought that nobody could have shaken the post of Ear-gate, nor have shaken the heart of Diabolus. Next to him there was one Captain Secure slain; this Secure used to say, that the blind and lame in Mansoul were able to keep the gates of the town against Immanuel's army, 2 Sam. v. 6. This Captain Secure did Captain Conviction cleave down the head with a two-handed sword, when he himself received three wounds in the mouth.

Captain Boasting slain.

Captain Secure slain.

Besides, there was one Captain Bragman, a very desperate fellow, and he was captain over a band of those that threw fire-brands, arrows, and death; he also received, by the hand of Captain Good-hope at Eye-gate, a mortal wound in the breast.

Captain Bragman slain.

---

* The soul of man is assaulted by the ear. Boanerges, a faithful preacher of the gospel, boldly perseveres in declaring the truth of God, seconded by Conviction; who is here said to be wounded; or, in other words—that conviction which was occasioned by the word of God, is resisted and driven back by the reluctant sinner, yet unwilling to yield to its dictates. Hope and charity, those amiable graces, present themselves to the eye of the world in order to allure their souls.

There was moreover one Mr Feeling, but he was no captain,
Mr Feeling hurt. but a great stickler to encourage Mansoul to rebellion; he received a wound in the eye by the hand of one of Boanerges' soldiers, and had by the captain himself been slain, but that he made a sudden retreat.

But I never saw Will-be-will so daunted in all my life; he *Will-be-will hurt.* was not able to do as he was wont; and some say he also received a wound in the leg, and that some of the men in the prince's army had certainly seen him limp as he afterwards walked on the wall.

I shall not give you a particular account of the names of the soldiers that were maimed, wounded, and slain: for when they saw that the posts of Ear-gate shook, and Eye-gate was well nigh-broken quite open; and also that their captains were slain; this took away the hearts of many of the Diabolonians, so that they fell also by the force of the shot that were sent by the golden slings into the midst of the town of Mansoul.

Love-no-good wounded. Of the townsmen, there was one Love-no-good; he was a townsman, but a Diabolonian; he also received his mortal wound in Mansoul, but he died not very soon.

Mr Ill-pause also, who came along with Diabolus when at first he attempted the taking of Mansoul, received a grievous *Ill-pause wounded.* wound in the head; some say that his brain-pan was cracked; this I have taken notice of, that he was never after this able to do that mischief to Mansoul as he had done in times past. Also old Prejudice and Mr Anything fled.*

Now when the battle was over, the prince commanded that *The white flag hung out again.* yet once more the white flag should be set upon Mount Gracious, in sight of the town of Mansoul; to show that yet Immanuel had grace for the wretched town of Mansoul.

When Diabolus saw the white flag hung out again, and knowing *Diabolus's new prank.* that it was not for him, but Mansoul, he cast in his mind to play another prank, to wit, to see if Immanuel would raise his siege to be gone, upon promise of reformation. So he went down to the gate one

---

* Success now begins to crown these efforts of the gospel ministry. The sinner no longer boasts of his fancied virtue, strength and goodness; sin is no more *bragged* of, and gloried in; the word is now *felt* as well as heard; and even the stubborn *will* of man begins to bend. These and other enemies of Christ are obliged to submit to the victorious weapons of his grace. In this state of things, the display of the white flag, or pardoning mercy, is peculiarly reasonable.

evening, a good while after the sun was gone down, and called to speak with Immanuel; who presently came down to the gate, and Diabolus saith unto him:

His speech to Immanuel. "Forasmuch as thou makest it appear by the white flag, that thou art wholly given to peace and quiet; I thought meet to acquaint thee, that we are ready to accept thereof upon terms which thou mayest admit.

"I know that thou art given to devotion, and that holiness pleases thee; yea, that thy great end in making a war upon Mansoul, is, that it may be an holy habitation. Well, draw off thy forces from the town, and I will bend Mansoul to thy bow.

"First, I will lay down all acts of hostility against thee, and will be willing to become thy deputy; and will, as I have formerly been against thee, now serve thee in the town of Mansoul. And more particularly.

Diabolus would be Immanuel's deputy, "1. I will persuade Mansoul to receive thee for their lord; and I know that they will do it sooner, when they shall understand that I am thy deputy.

"2. I will show them wherein they have erred, and that transgression stands in the way to life.

"3. I will show them the holy law unto which they must conform, even that which they have broken.

"4. I will press upon them the necessity of a reformation, according to law.

and would turn reformer. "5. And moreover, that none of these things may fail, I myself, at my own proper cost and charge, will set up and maintain a sufficient ministry, besides lectures, in Mansoul.

"6. Thou shalt receive, as a token of our subjection to thee, continually, year by year, what thou shalt think fit to lay and levy upon us, in token of such subjection."*

Then said Immanuel to him, "O full of deceit, how moveable are thy ways! How often hast thou changed and re-changed, if so be thou mightest still keep possession of my Mansoul! though, as has been plainly declared before, I am the right heir there-

Immanuel's answer to Diabolus.

---

* It is by no means uncommon for persons under severe convictions of sin, and awful fears of hell, to determine on reformation, or mending their lives. This is agreeable to the first covenant, the terms of which are, "do, and live;" but not according to the new covenant of grace, which says—"believe and live." St Paul speaks with the most poignant grief of his countrymen the Jews, that, though they followed after righteousness, they could not attain it, because they sought it by the works of the law, and that through ignorance of the righteousness of Christ, they went about to establish their own righteousness. See Romans 9th and 10th chapters. Such is the vain attempt of many convinced sinners, who are willing to be reformed, but not to be justified and saved by grace.

of. Often hast thou made thy proposals already, nor is this last a whit better than they, 2 Cor. xi. 14. And failing to deceive when thou showedst thyself in thy black, thou hast now transformed thyself into an angel of light, and wouldst, to deceive, be now as a minister of righteousness.

"But know thou, O Diabolus, that nothing must be regarded that thou canst propound, for nothing is done by thee but to deceive; thou neither has conscience to God, nor love to the town of Mansoul; whence, then, should these thy sayings arise, but from sinful craft and deceit? He that can list and will propound what he pleases, and that therewith he may destroy them that believe him, is to be abandoned, with all that he shall say. But if righteousness be such a beauty-spot in thine eyes now, how is it that wickedness was so closely stuck to by thee before? But this by the bye.

Diabolus has no conscience to God, nor love to Mansoul.

"Thou talkest now of a reformation in Mansoul, and that thou thyself, if I please, wilt be at the head of that reformation; all the while knowing, that the greatest proficiency that man can make in the law, and the righteousness thereof, will amount to no more, for the taking away of the curse from Mansoul, than just nothing at all; for a law being broken by Mansoul, that had before, upon a supposition of the breach thereof, a curse pronounced against him for it of God, can never, by his obeying the law, deliver himself therefrom. (To say nothing of what a reformation is like to be set up in Mansoul when the devil is become the corrector of vice). Thou knowest that all that thou hast now said in this matter is nothing but guile and deceit; and as it was the first, so it is the last card that thou hast to play. Many there be that discern thee, when thou showest them thy cloven foot; but in thy white, thy light, and in thy transformation, thou art seen but of a few. But thou shalt not do thus with my Mansoul, O Diabolus, for I do still love my Mansoul.

He knows that that will do no good, which yet he propounds for the health of Mansoul.

"Besides, I am not come to put Mansoul upon works to live thereby; should I do so, I should be like unto thee; but I am come, that by me, and by what I have and shall do for Mansoul, they may be reconciled to my father, though by their sin they have provoked him to anger, and though by the law they cannot obtain mercy.

"Thou talkest of subjecting this town to good, when none desireth it at thy hands. I am sent by my father to possess it myself, and to guide it, by the skilfulness of my hands, into such a conformity to him as shall be pleasing in his sight. I will therefore possess it myself; I will dispossess and cast thee out: I will set up mine own standard in the midst of them; I will also govern them by new laws, new officers, new motives, and new ways; yea, I will pull down this town, and build it again, and it shall be as though it had not been, and it shall be the glory of the whole universe."*

All things must be new in Mansoul.

When Diabolus heard this, and perceived that he was discovered in all his deceits, he was confounded, and utterly put to a nonplus; but having in himself the fountain of iniquity, rage, and malice against both Shaddai and his Son, and the beloved town of Mansoul, what doth he but strengthen himself what he could to give fresh battle to the noble prince Immanuel. So then, now we must have another fight before the town of Mansoul is taken. Come up then to the mountains, you that love to see military actions, and behold by both sides how the fatal blow is given; while one seeks to hold, and the other seeks to make himself master of, the famous town of Mansoul.

Diabolus confounded.

New preparations for fight.

Diabolus therefore withdrew himself from the walls to his fort that was in the heart of the town of Mansoul; Immanuel also returned to the camp; and both of them, after their divers ways, put themselves into a posture fit to give battle one to another.

Diabolus, as filled with despair of retaining in his hands the famous town of Mansoul, resolved to do what mischief he could (if indeed he could do any) to the army of the prince, and to the famous town of Mansoul; for alas! it was not the happiness of the silly town of Mansoul that was designed by Diabolus, but the utter ruin and overthrow thereof, as now is enough in view, Mark xxvi. 27. Wherefore he commands his officers that they should then, when they saw they could hold the town no longer, do it

Diabolus despairs of holding Mansoul, and therefore contrives to do it what mischief he can.

---

* In this excellent answer of Immanuel we learn, that no self-righteous attempts to justify the soul by its reformation only will be accepted. To persuade convinced sinners to rest in this, to the neglect of Christ and his righteousness, is a dangerous artifice of the devil, who thus "transforms himself into an angel of light," 2 Cor. xi. 14. The sinner, having once broken the law, and thereby incurred "the curse of the law," Gal. iii. 10, can derive no help from the law; but must look to Christ the law fulfiller, for righteousness and reconciliation with God. A man may talk much of reforming his life, and say a great deal about good works, yet remain a subject of Satan's kingdom. We are not Christians till we are in Christ, by believing in him for salvation; and when we are so, we become new creatures: our state is new, being justified by grace; and our disposition is new also, being born again of the Spirit.

what harm and mischief they could, rending and tearing men, women, and children; for said he, we had better quite demolish the place, and leave it a ruinous heap, than that it should be an habitation for Immanuel.*

Immanuel again, knowing that the next battle would issue in his being made master of the place, gave out a royal commandment to all his officers, high captains, and men of war, to be sure to show themselves men of war against Diabolus and all Diabolonians; but favourable, merciful, and meek to the old inhabitants of Mansoul. Bend therefore, said the noble prince, the hottest front of the battle against Diabolus and his men.

The battle joined, and they fight on both sides fiercely.

So the day being come, the command was given, and the prince's men stood bravely to their arms; nor did, as before, bend their forces against Ear-gate and Eye-gate. The word was then MANSOUL IS WON: so they made their assault upon the town. Diabolus also, as fast as he could, with the main of his power, made resistance from within, and his high lords and chief captains for a time fought very cruelly against the prince's army.

Ear-gate broke open.

But, after three or four notable charges by the prince and his noble captains, Ear-gate was broken open, and the bars and bolts, wherewith it was used to be fast shut up against the prince, were broken into a thousand pieces.

The prince's standard set up, and the slings are played still at the castle.

Then did the prince's trumpets sound, the captains shout, the town shake, and Diabolus retreat to his hold.† Well, when the prince's forces had broke open the gate, himself came up, and did set up his throne in it; also he set his standard near it, upon a mount that his men had before cast up to place the mighty slings thereon. The mount was called Mount Hearwell; there therefore the prince abode, to wit, hard by the going in at the gate.

* When Satan can no longer maintain his dominion in the soul, he will endeavour to disturb and distress it by temptations to despair, or to abominable vices, or by stirring up persecution against the struggling sinner; so, when a poor creature was approaching to Christ for cure—"as he was yet a coming the devil threw him down and tear him." Luke ix. 42.

† Thus was the promise fulfilled, Isa. xxix. 18. In that day the deaf shall hear the words of the book;" and xxx. 18, " the ears of the deaf shall be opened." It is a glorious event, when the soul is made sincerely willing to listen to the word of God, when it truly says " speak Lord, for thy servant heareth;" for the way is strait, as the author observes, from Ear-gate to the Recorder's house, that is, to the conscience; and from thence to the Castle, that is, the heart. The importance of opening Ear-gate may be learned from that frequent expression in our Lord's discourses—" he that hath an ear to hear, let him hear." May God bestow the " hearing ear" upon every reader.

He commanded also that the golden slings should yet be played upon the town, especially against the castle, because for shelter thither was Diabolus retreated. Now from Ear-gate the street was strait, even to the house of him who was the recorder before Diabolus took the town; and hard by his house stood the castle, which Diabolus for a long time had made his irksome den. The captains therefore quickly cleared the street by the use of their slings, so that way was made up to the heart of the town. Then the prince commanded that Captain Boanerges, Captain Conviction, and Captain Judgment, should forthwith march up the town to the old gentleman's gate.

Conscience.

Then did the captains in most warlike manner enter into the town of Mansoul, and, marching in with flying colours,

They go to the Recorder's house.

they came up to the Recorder's house (and that was almost as strong as the castle.) Battering-rams they took also with them, to plant against the castle gates. When they were come to the house of Mr Conscience, they knocked and demanded entrance. Now the old gentleman, not knowing as yet fully their design, kept his gates shut all the time of this fight. Wherefore Boanerges

They demand entrance.

demanded entrance at his gates; and no man making answer, he gave it one stroke with the head of a ram, and this made the old gentleman shake, and his house tremble and totter. Then came Mr Recorder down to the gate, and as well as he could, with quivering lips, he asked who was there? Boanerges answered, "We are the captains and commanders of the great Shaddai, and of the blessed Immanuel his son, and we demand possession of your house for the use of our noble prince." And with that the battering-ram gave the gate another shake: this made the old gentleman tremble the more, yet durst he not but open the gate; then the

They go in.

king's forces marched in, namely the three brave captains mentioned before. Now the recorder's house, was a place of much convenience for Immanuel, not only because it was near and fronted the castle, the den where now

They keep themselves reservedly from the recorder.

Diabolus was; for he was now afraid to come out of his hold. As for Mr Recorder, the captains carried it very reservedly to him: as yet he knew nothing of the great designs of Immanuel; so that he did not know what judgment to make, nor

His house the seat of war.

what would be the end of such thundering beginnings.* It was noised in the town, how the recorder's house was possessed, his rooms taken

---

* The conscience submits and trembles. When the soul listens to the threatenings of the holy law, conscience cannot but fear and quake, and till

up, and his palace made the seat of war; and no sooner was i noised abroad, but they took the alarm as warmly, and gave it out to others of his friends; and as, you know, a little snow-ball loses nothing by rolling, so in little time the whole town was possessed, that they must expect nothing from the prince but destruction; and the ground of the business was this, the recorder trembled, and the captains carried it strangely to him: so many came to see; but when they with their own eyes beheld the captains in the palace, and their battering-rams ever played at the castle-gates to beat them down, they were rivetted in their fears, and it made them as in amaze. And, as I said, the man of the house would increase all this; for whoever came to him, or discoursed with him, nothing would he talk of, tell them, or hear, but that death and destruction now attended Mansoul.

The office of Conscience, when he is awakened.

"For (quoth the old gentleman) you are all of you sensible that we have all been traitors to that once despised, but now famously victorious and glorious Prince Immanuel; for he now, as you see, doth not only lie in close siege about us, but hath forced his entrance in at our gates: moreover, Diabolus flies before him; and he hath, as you behold, made of my house a garrison against the castle, where he is. I for my part have transgressed greatly, and he that is clean it is well for him. But, I say, I have transgressed greatly, in keeping silence, when I should have spoken; and in perverting justice, when I should have executed the same. True, I have suffered something at the hands of Diabolus, for taking part with the laws of King Shaddai, but that, alas! what will that do! Will that make compensation for the rebellions and treasons that I have done, and have suffered, without gain-saying, to be committed in the town of Mansoul? O I tremble to think what will be the end of this so dreadful and so direful a beginning!*

Now while these brave captains were thus busy in the house of the old recorder, Captain Execution was as busy in other parts of the town, in securing the back streets and the walls. He also hunted the Lord Will-be-will, sorely, and suffered him not to rest in any corner. He pursued so hard, that he drove

The brave exploits of Captain Execution.

---

further enlightened with the knowledge of the gospel, and the gracious design of God by his gospel, can think and talk of nothing but "death and destruction."

† Conscience, when awakened, will open his mouth in humble confession of past offences, of rebellion again t God, lamenting especially his having kept silence when he ought to have spoken.

his men from him, and made him glad to thrust his head into a hole. Also this mighty warrior cut three of Lord Will-be-will's officers down to the ground; one was old Mr Prejudice, he that had his crown cracked in the mutiny: this man was made, by my Lord Will-be-will, keeper of Ear-gate, and fell by the hand of Captain Execution. There was one Mr Backward-to-all-but-naught, and he also was one of the Lord Will-be-will's officers, and was the captain of the two guns that once were mounted on the top of Ear-gate; he also was cut down to the ground by the hands of Captain Execution. Besides these two there was another, a third, and his name was Captain Treacherous, a vile man this was, but one that Will-be-will put a great deal of confidence in; but him also did this Captain Execution cut down to the ground with the rest. He also made a very great slaughter among my Lord Will-be-will's soldiers, killing many that were stout and sturdy, and wounding many that for Diabolus were nimble and active. But all these were Diabolonians; there was not a man, a native of Mansoul, hurt.

Old Prejudice slain.

Other feats of war were likewise performed by other of the captains, as at Eye-gate, where Captain Good-hope and Captain Charity had a charge, was great execution done; for Captain Good-hope, with his own hands, slew one Captain Blindfold, the keeper of that gate: this Blindfold was captain of a thousand men, and they were they that fought with mauls; he also pursued his men, slew many, and wounded more, and made the rest hide their heads in corners.

Captain Good-hope slays Captain Blindfold,

There was also at that gate Mr Ill-pause, of whom you have heard before; he was an old man, and had a beard that reached down to his girdle; the same was he that was orator to Diabolus: he did much mischief in the town of Mansoul, and fell by the hands of Captain Good-hope.

and old Ill-pause.

What shall I say? The Diabolonians in these days lay dead in every corner, though too many were yet alive in Mansoul.*

---

* The work of conversion proceeds. The carnal *will* is pursued, and gets no rest. *Prejudice*, who once kept Ear-gate barred against Christ, and who was wounded before, is now utterly slain. *Aversion* to good, *Treachery*, *Blindness*, and especially old *Ill-pause*, who was for deferring every thing good to an hereafter—all these were destroyed; but remember, all these were Diabolonians, not one native power of the soul was injured.

CHAPTER VIII.

A conference of the principal inhabitants, who agree to petition the Prince for their lives. The Castle Gate broke open. Immanuel marches into Mansoul. Diabolus is made prisoner, and bound in chains. The inhabitants greatly distressed; petition again and again. At length a free pardon is obtained and universal joy succeeds.

NOW the old recorder, and my Lord Understanding, with some others of the chief of the town, to wit, such as knew they must stand or fall with the famous town of **Mansoul**, came together upon a day, and, after consultation had, jointly agreed to draw up a petition, and send it to Immanuel, now while he sat in the gate of Mansoul. So they drew up their petition to Immanuel, the contents whereof were these; "That they, the old inhabitants of the deplorable town of Mansoul, confessed their sin, and were sorry that they had offended his princely majesty, and prayed that he would spare their lives."*

The old townsmen meet and consult.

The town petition, and are answered with silence.

Unto this petition he gave no answer at all, and that troubled them yet so much the more. Now all this while the captains that were in the recorder's house were playing with the battering-rams at the gates of the castle to beat them down. So after some time, labour, and travail, the gate of the castle that was called Impregnable was beaten open, and broken into several splinters, and so a way was made to go into the hold in which Diabolus had hid himself. Then were tidings sent down to Ear-gate, for Immanuel still abode there, to let him know that a way was made in at the gates of the castle of Mansoul. But O how the trumpets at the tidings sounded throughout the prince's camp, for that now the war was so near an end, and Mansoul itself of being set free!†

The castle gate broke open.

Then the prince arose from the place where he was, and took with him such of his men of war as were fittest for the expedition, and marched up the streets of Mansoul to the old recorder's house.

Immanuel marches into Mansoul.

---

* No sooner does Christ come to a person by converting grace than he begins to pray. "Behold he prayeth!" was Christ's own remark concerning converted Saul, Acts ix. But the praying soul may fear for a time that the Lord does not hear. He may defer his answer, but the christian cannot pray in vain.

† At length the Castle of the heart is taken. That heart yields to God which was before deemed *impregnable*, and indeed was so to any other power than that of invincible grace Then indeed there is joy in heaven

Now the prince himself was clad all in armour of gold, and so he marched up the town, with his standard borne before him; but he kept his countenance much reserved all the way as he went, so that the people could not tell how to gather to themselves love or hatred by his looks. Now as he marched up the street, the townsfolk came out at every door to see, and could not but be taken with his person, and the glory thereof, but wondered at the reservedness of his countenance; for as yet he spake more to them by his actions and works, than he did by words or smiles. But alas poor Mansoul (as in such cases all are apt to do) interpreted the carriage of Immanuel to them, as did Joseph's brethren his to them, even all the quite contrary way: for, thought they, if Immanuel loved us, he would show it to us by word and carriage; but none of these he does, therefore Immanuel hates us. Now if Immanuel hates us, Mansoul shall be slain, then Mansoul shall become a dunghill. They knew that they had transgressed his law, and that against him they had been in league with Diabolus his enemy. They also knew that Prince Immanuel knew all this; for they were convinced that he was an angel of God, to know all things that are done in the earth. And this made them think that their condition was miserable, and that the good prince would make them desolate.*

Immanuel marches through Mansoul.

How they interpreted Immanuel's carriage.

And, thought they, what time so fit to do this in as now, when he has the bridle of Mansoul in his hand? And this I took special notice of, that the inhabitants, notwithstanding all this, could not, no, they could not, when they saw him march through the town, but cringe, bow, bend, and were ready to lick the dust off his feet: they also wished a thousand times over, that he would become their prince and captain, and would become their protector. They would also talk one to another of the comeliness of his person, and how much for glory and valour he outstript the great ones of the world. But, poor hearts! as to themselves, their thoughts would change, and go upon all manner of extremes. Yea, through the working of them backward and forward, Mansoul became as a ball tossed, and as a rolling thing before a whirlwind.

Now when he was come to the castle gates, he commanded

---

* Jesus Christ is truly glorious; the chief among ten thousand, and altogether lovely; but converted sinners do not always enjoy great comfort at first. Sense of sin, and fear of his resentment may keep them low: yet they cannot but admire Immanuel, and heartily desire he may be the lord of their hearts.

He comes to the castle, and commands Diabolus to surrender himself.
Diabolus to appear, and to surrender himself into his hands. But, oh how loth was the beast to appear! How he stuck at it, how he shrunk! How he cringed! Yet now he came to the prince. Then Immanuel commanded, and they took Diabolus and bound him fast in chains, the better to reserve him to the judgment that he had appointed for him. But Diabolus stood up to intreat for himself, that Immanuel would not send him into the deep, but suffer him to depart out of Mansoul in peace.

He is taken and bound in chains.
When Immanuel had taken him and bound him in chains, he led him into the market-place, and there before Mansoul stripped him of his armour which he boasted so much of before. This now was one of the acts of triumph of Immanuel over his enemy: and all the while the giant was stripping, the trumpets of the Golden Prince sounded amain; the captains also shouted, and the soldiers sang for joy. Then was Mansoul called upon to behold Immanuel's triumph over him in whom they had so much trusted, and of whom they had so much boasted in the days when he flattered them.

Mansoul must behold it.

He is bound to his chariot wheels.
Thus having made Diabolus naked in the eyes of Mansoul and before the commanders of the prince, in the next place he commands that Diabolus should be bound with chains to his chariot wheels, Eph. iv. Then leaving some of his forces, to wit, Captain Boanerges and Captain Conviction, a guard for the castle gates, that resistance might be made on his behalf (if any that heretofore followed Diabolus should make an attempt to possess it) he rode in triumph over him quite through the town of Mansoul, and so out at and before the gate called Eye-gate, to the plain were his camp lay.

The prince rides in triumph over him in the sight of Mansoul.

But you cannot think, unless you had been there (as I was) what a shout there was in Immanuel's camp, when they saw the tyrant bound by the hand of their noble prince, and tied to his chariot-wheels. And they said, He hath led captivity captive, and hath spoiled principalities and powers: Diabolus is subjected to the power of the sword, and made the object of all derision.

They sing.

The reformades's joy.
Those also that rode reformades, and that came down to see the battle, shouted with that greatness of voice, and sung with such melodious notes, that they caused them that dwelt in the highest orbs to open

their windows, put out their heads, and look down to see the cause of that glory, Luke xv. 7. 10.

The men of Mansoul taken with Immanuel. The townsmen also, so many of them as beheld this sight, were as it were astonished, while they looked betwixt the earth and the heavens. True, they could not tell what would be the issue of things as to them, all things being done in such excellent methods; and I cannot tell how, but things in the management of them seemed to cast a smile towards the town; so that their eyes, their heads, their hearts, and their minds, and all that they had, were taken and held while they observed Immanuel's order.

Diabolus cast out. So when the brave prince had finished this part of his triumph over Diabolus his foe, he turned him up in the midst of his contempt and shame, having given him a charge no more to be a possessor of Mansoul. Then went he from Immanuel, and out of the midst of his camp, to inherit the parched places in a salt land, seeking rest, but finding none. Matt. xii. 34.*

The carriage of Boanerges and Captain Conviction crushes the spirit of Mansoul. Now Captain Boanerges and Captain Conviction were both of them men of very great majesty; their faces were like the faces of lions, and their words like the roaring of the seas; and they still quartered in Mr Conscience's house, of whom mention was made before. When, therefore, the high and mighty prince had thus far finished his triumph over Diabolus, the townsmen had more leisure to view and behold the actions of their noble captains. But the captains carried it with that terror and dread in all they did (and you may be sure they had private instructions so to do,) that they kept the town under continual heartaching, and caused (in their apprehension) the well-being of Mansoul for the future to stand in doubt before them, so that for some considerable time they neither knew what rest, or ease, or peace, or hope meant.

The prince commands, and the captains put the three chief of Mansoul in ward. Nor did the prince himself as yet abide in the town of Mansoul, but in his royal pavilion in the camp, and in the midst of his father's forces. So at a time convenient he sent special orders to Captain Boanerges, to summons Mansoul, the whole of the townsmen, into the castle-yard, and then there, before their faces to take my

---

* When the soul submits to Jesus, Satan is bound; he shall not rule in the heart any more. Rebel he may, but not reign. He is a chained enemy, and "God shall bruise Satan under our feet shortly." Now Satan is stripped of all that armour in which he trusted, and the Lord Jesus is evidently triumphant. O what a glorious season was that when he ascended up on high

Lord Understanding, Mr Conscience, and that notable one the Lord Will-be-will, and put them all three in ward, and that they should set a strong guard upon them there, until his pleasure concerning them was further known. Which orders, when the captains had put them in execution, made no small addition to the fears of the town of Mansoul: for now, to their thinking, were their former fears of the ruin of Mansoul confirmed. Now what death they should die, and how long

Mansoul greatly distressed. they should be in dying, was that which most perplexed their heads and hearts; yea, they were afraid that Immanuel would command them all into the deep, the place that the prince Diabolus was afraid of; for they had deserved it. Also to die by the sword in the face of the town, and in the open way of disgrace, from the hand of so good and so holy a prince, that, too, troubled them sore: the town was also greatly troubled for the men committed to ward, for that they were their stay and their guide; and for that they believed, that if those men were cut off, their execution would be but the beginning of the ruin of the town of Mansoul.*

Wherefore what do they, but together with the men in prison,

They send a petition to Immanuel by the hand of Mr Wood-live. draw up a petition to the prince, and sent it to Immanuel by the hand of Mr Would-live. So he went, and came to the prince's quarters, and presented the petition; the sum of which was this: "Great and wonderful potentate, victor over Diabolus, and conqueror of the town of Mansoul: we, the miserable inhabitants of that most woful corporation, humbly beg that we may find favour in thy sight, and remember not against us our former transgressions, nor yet the sins of the chief of our town, but spare us according to the greatness of thy mercy, and let us not die, but live in thy sight; so shall we be willing to be thy servants, and, if thou shalt think fit, to gather our meat under thy table. Amen."

So the petitioner went, as was said, with his petition to the

They are answered with silence. prince; and the prince took it at his hand, but sent him away with silence. This still afflicted the town of Mansoul; but yet con-

---

leading captivity captive! Then the angels (here called reformades) rejoiced and shouted, and so we are assured they now do; for " There is joy in the presence of the angels of God over one sinner that repenteth."

* It is no uncommon thing for convinced sinners, before they obtain clear views of the gospel, to remain under considerable terror and alarm. They feel themselves continually condemned by the faithful preaching of the word. The understanding, the conscience and the will may be in a state of bondage, and the whole soul by terrified with fears of death and damnation. But all this will end well—will issue in fervent prayer and happy peace.

sidering that now they must either petition or die (for now they could not do any thing else) therefore they consulted again, and sent another petition, which was much after the form and method of the former.

When the petition was drawn up, by whom should they send it was the next question; for they would not send it by him by whom they sent the first; (for they thought that the prince had taken some offence at the manner of his deportment before him) so they attempted to make Captain Conviction their messenger with it; but he said, that he neither durst nor would petition Immanuel for traitors, nor be to the prince an advocate for rebels. Yet withal, said he, our prince is good, and you may adventure to send it by the hand of one of your town; provided he went with a rope about his head, and pleaded nothing but mercy.

They petition again.

They cannot tell by whom to send it.

Well, they made, through fear, their delays as long as they could, and longer than delays were good; but fearing at last the danger of them, they thought, but with many a fainting in their minds, to send their petition by Mr Desires-awake; so they sent for Mr Desires-awake. Now he dwelt in a very mean cottage in Mansoul; and he came at his neighbours' request. So they told him what they had done, and what they would do concerning petitioning, and that they desired of him that he would go therewith to the prince. Then said Mr Desires-awake, Why should not I do the best I can to save so famous a town as Mansoul from destruction? They therefore delivered the petition to him, and told him how he must address himself to the prince, and wished him ten thousand good speeds. So he came to the prince's pavilion, as the first, and asked to speak with his majesty; so word was carried to Immanuel, and the prince came out to the man. When Mr Desires-awake saw the prince, he fell flat with his face to the ground, and cried out, O that Mansoul might live before thee! and with that he presented the petition. The which when the prince had read, he turned away for a while, and wept; but, refraining himself, he turned again to the man (who all this while lay crying at his feet as at first,) and said to him, Go thy way to thy place, and I will consider of thy requests.*

Mr Desires-awake goes with the petition.

His entertainment.

Now you may think that they of Mansoul that had sent him,

---

* We must pray and pray again. We must pray in humility, confessing our desert of punishment, as it were with ropes about our necks. The petition is sent by Mr Desires-awake. The desires of an awakened soul are vented in prayer, and these move the compassionate heart of Jesus.

what with guilt, and what with fear, lest their petition should be rejected, could not but look with many a longing look, and that too with strange workings of heart, to see what would become of their petition. At last they saw their messenger coming back; so when he was come, they asked him how he fared? what Immanuel said? and what was become of the petition? But he told them he would be silent till he came to the prison to my lord-mayor, my Lord Will-be-will, and Mr Recorder. So he went forwards towards the prison-house; where the men of Mansoul lay bound. But, O! what a multitude flocked after, to hear what the messenger said. So when he was come, and had showed himself at the gate of the prison, my lord-mayor himself looked as white as a clout, the recorder also quaked; but they asked, and said, Come, good sir, what did the great prince say to you? Then said Mr Desires-awake, When I came to my lord's pavilion, I called, and he came forth; so I fell prostrate at his feet, and delivered to him my petition (for the greatness of his person, and the glory of his countenance, would not suffer me to stand upon my legs). Now as he received the petition, I cried, O that Mansoul might live before thee! So when for a while he had looked thereon, he turned about, and said to his servant, Go thy way to thy place again, and I will consider of thy requests. The messenger added, moreover, and said, The prince to whom you sent me, is such a one for beauty and glory, that whoso sees him, must love and fear him: I for my part can do no less; but I know not what will be the end of these things.

His return and answer to them that sent him.

Mansoul confounded at the answer.

At this answer they were all at a stand, both they in prison, and they that followed the messenger thither to hear the news; nor knew they what, or what manner of interpretation to put upon what the prince had said. Now when the prison was cleared of the throng, the prisoners began to comment among themselves upon Immanuel's words. My lord-mayor said, that the answer did not look with a rugged face; but Will-be-will said it betokeneth evil; and the recorder, that it was a messenger of death. Now they that were left, and that stood behind, and so could not so well hear what the prisoners said, some of them catched hold of one piece of a sentence, and some on a bit of another; some took hold of what the messenger said, and some of the prisoners' judgment thereon, so none had a right understanding of things; but you cannot imagine what work these people made, and what confusion there was in Mansoul.

The prisoners' judgment upon the prince's answer.

Misgiving thoughts breed confusion in Mansoul.

For presently they that had heard what was said flew about the town, one crying one thing, and another quite the contrary, and both were sure enough they told true, for they heard, they said, with their ears what was said, and therefore could not be deceived. One would say, "We must all be killed;" another would say, "We must all be saved;" and a third would say, "That the prince would not be concerned with Mansoul;" and a fourth, "That the prisoners must be suddenly put to death:" and, as I said, every one stood to it, that he told his tale the rightest, and that all others but he were out. Wherefore Mansoul had now molestation upon molestation, nor could any man know on what to rest the sole of his foot; for one would go by now, and, as he went, if he heard his neighbour tell his tale, to be sure he would tell the quite contrary, and both would stand in it that he told the truth. Nay, some of them had got this story by the end, "That the prince intended to put Mansoul to the sword." And now it began to be dark; wherefore poor Mansoul was in a sad perplexity all that night, until the next morning.*

Mansoul in perplexity.

But so far as I could gather by the best information I could get, all this hubbub came through the words that the recorder said, when he told them, that in his judgment the prince's answer was a messenger of death. 'Twas this that fired the town, and that began the fright in Mansoul; for Mansoul in former times used to count that Mr Recorder was a seer, that his sentence was equal to the best of oracles; and thus was Mansoul a terror to itself.

What will not guilt do.

And now they began to feel the effects of stubborn rebellion, and unlawful resistance against their prince. I say, now they began to feel the effects thereof by guilt and fear, that now had swallowed them up; and who more involved in the one, but they that were most in the other, to wit, the chief of the town of Mansoul?

They resolve to petition again.

Their petition.

To be brief; when the fame of the fright was out of the town, and the prisoners had a little recovered themselves, they take to themselves some heart, and think to petition the prince again for life. So they drew up a third petition, the contents whereof were these:

"Prince Immanuel the Great, Lord of all worlds, and Master

---

* How anxious the praying soul to know whether he shall succeed or not Perplexity and fear may greatly prevail for a season, till the truths of the gospel be clearly understood and cordially believed. But this state of fear discovers what an evil and bitter thing it is to sin against God. Thus sin is embittered, and Christ rendered more precious.

of mercy, we, thy poor, wretched, miserable, dying town of Mansoul, do confess unto thy great and glorious Majesty, that we have sinned against thy Father and Thee; and are no more worthy to be called thy Mansoul, but rather to be cast into the pit. If thou wilt slay us, we have deserved it. If thou wilt condemn us to the deep; we cannot but say thou art righteous. We cannot complain, whatever thou dost, or however thou carriest it towards us! But oh! let mercy reign, and let it be extended to us! O let mercy take hold upon us, and free us from our transgressions, and we will sing of thy mercy, and of thy judgments! Amen."

This petition, when drawn up, was designed to be sent to the prince as the first; but who should carry it, that was the question. Some said let him do it that went with the first; but others thought good not to do that, and that because he sped no better. Now there was an old man in the town, and his name was Mr Good-deed; a man that bare only the name, but had nothing of the nature of the thing. Some were for sending him; but the recorder was by no means for that: for, said he, we now stand in need of, and are pleading for mercy, wherefore, to send our petition by a man of his name, will seem to cross the petition itself, should we make Mr Good-deed our messenger, when our petition cries for mercy.

Prayer attended with difficulty.

Old Good-deed propounded as a fit person to carry the petition.

The old recorder opposes it, and he is rejected.

Besides, quoth the old gentleman, should the prince now, as he receives the petition, ask him, and say, What is thy name? (and nobody knows but he will) and he should say, Old Good-deed; what think you would Immanuel say but this, Ay, is Old Good-deed yet alive in Mansoul? then let old Good-deed save you from your distresses. And if he says so, I am sure we are lost, nor can a thousand of old Good-deeds save Mansoul.*

After the recorder had given in his reasons, why old Good-leed should not go with this petition to Immanuel, the rest of

---

* Still the spirit of prayer prevails in Mansoul; for "men ought always to pray and not to faint." And it is observable how these petitions improve from time to time. How much more light and humility appear in the third petition than in the first. It was also wisely determined not to send Mr Good-leed with it, for this would contradict the prayer of the petition, which was for mercy, not reward; and yet how absurd is the conduct of some, whose only hope of mercy is on account of their good deeds; it is a sense of our bad deeds, not our good ones, that will make us seek in earnest for mercy. If we plead good works, may not the Lord say—Let good works save them—What need of my grace, for if righteousess can be obtained by the law, grace is frustrated, and the death of Christ a needless thing.

the prisoners and chiefs of Mansoul opposed it also; and so old Good-deed was laid aside, and they agreed to send Mr Desires-awake again. Accordingly they sent for him, and desired that he would a second time go with their petition to the prince; and he readily told them he would: but they bid him, that in any wise he should take heed that in no word or carriage he gave offence to the prince; for by doing so, for aught we can tell, said they, you may bring Mansoul into utter destruction.

Now Mr Desires-awake, when he saw that he must go on this errand, besought that they would grant that Mr Wet-eyes might go with him. Now this Wet-eyes was a near neighbour of Mr Desires, a poor man, a man of broken spirit, yet one that could speak well to a petition. So they granted that he should go with him. Wherefore they address themselves to their business: Mr Desires put a rope upon his head, and Mr Wet-eyes went with his hands wringing together. Thus they went to the prince's pavilion.*

Mr Desires-awake goes again, and takes one Wet-eyes with him.

Now when they went to petition this third time, they were not without thoughts that by often coming they might be a burden to the prince, wherefore when they were come to the door of his pavilion, they first made their apology for themselves, and for their coming to trouble Immanuel so often; and they said, that they came not hither to-day for that they delighted to hear themselves talk, but for that necessity caused them to come to his Majesty; they could, they said, have no rest day nor night because of their transgressions against Shaddai and Immanuel his son. They also thought that some misbehaviour of Mr Desires-awake, the last time, might give some disgust to his Highness, and so caused that he returned from so merciful a prince empty, and without countenance. So when they had made this apology, Mr Desires-awake cast himself prostrate upon the ground, as at the first, at the feet of the mighty prince, saying, Oh that Mansoul might live before thee! so he delivered his petition. The prince, when he had read the petition, turned aside awhile as before; and, coming again to the place where the petitioner lay on the ground, he demanded what his name was, and of what esteem in the account of Mansoul, for that he, above all the multitude of Mansoul, should be sent to him on such an errand? Then said the man to the prince, O let

Their apology for their coming again.

The prince talketh with them.

---

* Mr Wet-eyes, the son of Repentance, was a very proper man to accompany Mr Desires: our desires after mercy should be joined with a broken and a contrite spirit, for to such persons will the Lord look with a benignant eye.

not my lord be angry; and why inquirest thou after the name of such a dead dog as I am? Pass by, I pray thee, and take no notice of whom I am, because there is, as thou very well knowest, so great a disproportion between me and thee. Why the townsman chose to send me on this errand to my lord, is best known to themselves; but it could not be for that they had thought I had favour with my lord. For my part, I am out of charity with myself: who then should be in love with me? Yet live I would, and so would I that my townsmen should; and because both they and myself are guilty of great transgressions, therefore they have sent me, and I am come in their names to beg of my lord for mercy. Let it please thee therefore to incline to mercy; but ask not what thy servants are.

Mr Desire's free speech to his prince.

Then said the prince, And what is he that is become thy companion in this so weighty a matter? So Mr Desires told Immanuel, that he was a poor neighbour of his, and one of his most intimate associates; and his name, said he, may it please your most excellent Majesty, is Wet-eyes, of the town of Mansoul. I know that there are many of that name that are naught: but I hope it will be no offence to my lord, that I have brought my poor neighbour with me.

Then Mr Wet-eyes fell on his face to the ground; and made this apology for coming with his neighbour to his lord.

"O my lord," quoth he, "what I am, I know not myself, nor whether my name be feigned or true, especially when I begin to think what some have said, namely, that this name was given me, because Mr Repentance was my father. Good men have had bad children, and the sincere do oftentimes beget hypocrites. My mother also called me by this name from my cradle; whether because of the moistness of my brain, or the softness of my heart, I cannot tell. I see dirt in my own tears, and filthiness in the bottom of my prayers.* But I pray thee, (and all this while the gentleman wept,) that thou wouldst not remember against us our transgressions, nor take offence at the unqualifiedness of thy servants, but mercifully pass by the sin of Mansoul, and refrain from the glorifying of thy grace no longer."

Mr Wet-eyes' apology for coming with his neighbour.

So at his bidding they arose, and both stood trembling before him, and he spake to them to this purpose:

---

* Humble souls will acknowledge with good **Bishop Beveridge**, that "their repentance needs to be repented of, their tears want washing, and the very washing of their tears needs still to be washed over again with the blood of their Redeemer."

"The town of Mansoul hath grievously rebelled against my father, in that they have rejected him from being their king, and chose for themselves, for their captain, a liar, a murderer, and a runagate slave. For this Diabolus, your pretended prince, though once so highly accounted of by you, made rebellion against my father and me, even in our palace and highest court there, thinking to become a prince and a king. But being timely discovered and apprehended, and for his wickedness bound in chains, and separated to the pit with those that were his companions, he offered himself to you, and you have received him.

The prince's answer.

The original of Diabolus.

"Now this is, and for a long time hath been, an high affront to my father; wherefore my father sent to you a powerful army to reduce you to your obedience. But you know how those men, their captains and their counsels, were esteemed of you, and what they received at your hand. You rebelled against them, you shut your gates upon them, you bid them battle; you fought them, and fought for Diabolus against them. So they went to my father for more power; and I, with my men, am come to subdue you. But as you treated the servants, so you treated their lord: You stood up in hostile manner against me, you shut up your gates against me, you turned a deaf ear to me, and resisted as long as you could; but now I have made a conquest of you. Did you cry to me for mercy so long as you had hopes that you might prevail against me? But now I have taken the town, you cry; but why did you not cry before, when the white flag of my mercy, the red flag of justice, and the black flag that threatened execution were set up to cite you to it? Now I have conquered your Diabolus, you come to me for favour; but why did you not help me against the mighty? Yet I will consider your petition, and will answer it so as will be for my glory.

Mansoul's rebellion.

"Go, bid Captain Boanerges and Captain Conviction bring the prisoners out to me into the camp to-morrow; and say you to Captain Judgment and Captain Execution, Stay in the castle, and take good heed to yourselves that you keep all quiet in Mansoul until you shall hear further from me." And with that he turned himself from them, and went into his royal pavilion.*

The prisoners ordered out into the camp.

---

* This answer of Immanuel was intended to deepen their sense of sin, and make them reflect with pain and shame on their former transgressions, and of their contempt of mercy, until the Lord arrested them in their mad career. Thus, the law enters that sin may abound—that it may appear exceeding sinful, and render the grace of God infinitely precious.

So the petitioners, having received this answer from the prince, returned, as at the first, to go to their companions again. But they had not gone far but thoughts began to work in their minds, that no mercy as yet was intended by the prince to Mansoul: so they went to the place where the prisoners lay bound; but these workings of mind, about what would become of Mansoul, had such strong power over them, that by that they were come unto them that sent them, they were scarce able to deliver their message.

But they came at length to the gates of the town, (now the townsmen were waiting with eagerness for their return,) where many met them, to know what answer was given to the petition. Then they cried out to those that were sent, What news from the prince? And what hath Immanuel said? But they said, that they must (as afore) go up to the prison, and there deliver their message. So away they went to the prison, with a multitude(*a*) at their heels. Now when they were come to the gates of the prison, they told the first part of Immanuel's speech to the prisoners;

(*a*) *Inquisitive thoughts.*

to wit, how he reflected upon their disloyalty to his father and himself, and how they had chosen and closed with Diabolus and fought for him, hearkened to him, and been ruled by him: but had despised him and his men. This made the prisoners look pale; but the messengers proceeded, and said, He the prince said moreover, that yet he would consider your petition, and give such answer thereto as will stand with his glory. And as these words were spoken, Mr Wet-eyes gave a great sigh. At this they were all of them struck into their dumps, and could not tell what to say: fear also possessed them in marvellous manner, and death seemed to sit upon some of their eye-brows. Now there was in the company a notable sharp-witted fellow, a man of mean estate, and his name was old Inquisitive; this man asked the petitioners if they had told out every whit of what Immanuel said. And they answered, Verily no. Then said Inquisitive, I thought so indeed. Pray what was it more that he said unto you? Then they paused awhile, but at last they brought out all, saying, The prince ordered us to bid Captain Boanerges and Captain Conviction bring the prisoners down to him to-morrow; and that Captain Judgment and Captain Execution should take charge of the castle and town till they should hear further from him. They said also, that when the prince had commanded

The messengers in telling their tale frighten the prisoners.

Old Inquisitive.

them so to do, he immediately turned his back upon them, and went into his royal pavilion.

But oh! how this return, and especially this last clause of it, that the prisoners must go out to the prince into the camp, brake all their loins in pieces! Wherefore with one voice they set up a cry which reached up to the heavens. This done, each of the three prepared himself to die (and the Recorder(*a*) said unto them, This was the thing that I feared) for they concluded, that to-morrow, by that the sun went down, they should be tumbled out of the world. The whole town also counted of no other, but that in their time and order they must all drink of the same cup. Wherefore the town of Mansoul spent that night in mourning, and sackloth and ashes. The prisoners also, when the time was come to go down before the prince, dressed themselves in mourning attire, with ropes upon their heads. The whole town of Mansoul also showed themselves upon the wall, and clad in mourning weeds, if perhaps the prince with the sight thereof might be moved with compassion. But, Oh, how the busy-bodies, that were in the town of Mansoul, now concerned themselves. They ran here and there through the streets of the town by companies, crying out as they ran in tumultuous wise, one after one manner, and another the quite contrary, to the almost utter distraction of Mansoul.*

(*a*) *Conscience.*

Vain thoughts.

Well, the time is come that the prisoners must go down to the camp, and appear before the prince. And thus was the manner of their going down: Captain Boanerges went with a guard before them, and Captain Conviction came behind, and the prisoners went bound in chains in the midst; so I say, the prisoners went in the midst, and the guard went with flying colours behind and before, but the prisoners went with drooping spirits. Or more particularly, thus:

The prisoners had to trial.

The prisoners went down all in mourning: they put ropes upon themselves, they went on smiting themselves on their breasts, but durst not lift up their eyes to heaven. Thus they went out at the gate of Mansoul till they came into the midst of the prince's army, the sight and glory of which greatly heightened their affliction. Nor could they now longer forbear but cry out aloud, O unhappy men; O wretched Mansoul! Their chains still mixing their

How they went.

* The godly sorrow that now prevailed in Mansoul, was only a prelude to joy unspeakable and full of glory. This sort of "weeping may endure for a night, but joy cometh in the morning." These poor prisoners "went forth weeping, bearing precious seed, but were soon to return with joy, bringing their sheaves with them."

dolorous notes with the cries of the prisoners, made the noise more lamentable.

So when they were come to the door of the prince's pavilion, they cast themselves prostrate upon the place: then one went and told the Lord, that the prisoners were come down. The prince then ascended a throne of state, and sent for the prisoners in; who, when they came, trembled before him; also they covered their faces with shame. Now as they drew near the place where he sat, they threw themselves down before him. Then said the prince to the Captain Boanerges, Bid the prisoners stand upon their feet. Then they stood trembling before him; and he said, Are you the men that heretofore were the servants of Shaddai? And they said Yes, Lord, yes. Then said the prince again, Are you the men that suffered yourselves to be corrupted and defiled by that abominable one Diabolus? And they said, We did more than suffer it, Lord; for we chose it of our mind. The prince asked further, saying, Could you have been content that your slavery should have continued under his tyranny as long as you had lived? Then said the prisoners, Yes, Lord, yes; for his ways were pleasing to our flesh, and we were grown aliens to a better state. And did you, said he, when I came against this town of Mansoul, heartily wish that I might not have the victory over you? Yes, Lord, yes, said they. Then said the prince, And what punishment is it, think you, that you deserve at my hands, for these and other your high and mighty sins? And they said, Both death and the deep, Lord; for we have deserved no less. He asked again, if they had aught to say for themselves, why the sentence, which they confessed they had deserved, should not be passed upon them? And they said, We can say nothing, Lord; thou art just, for we have sinned. Then said the prince, And for what are these ropes on your heads? The prisoners answered, The ropes(*a*) are to lead us withal to the place of execution, if mercy be not pleasing in thy sight, Prov. v. 22. So he further asked If all the men in the town of Mansoul were in this confession, as they? And they answered, All the natives,(*b*) Lord: but for the Diabolonians,(*c*) that came into our town when the tyrant got possession of us, we can say nothing for them.

They fell down prostrate before him.

They are upon their trial.

They condemn themselves.

(*a*) Sins.

Powers of d.
Corruptions and lusts.

Then the prince commanded that an herald should be called; and that he should in the midst and throughout the camp of Immanuel proclaim, and that with the sound of trumpet, that the

A victory proclaimed.

prince, the son of Shaddai, had in his father's name, and for his father's glory, gotten a perfect conquest and victory over Mansoul; and that the prisoners should follow him, and say Amen. So this was done as he had commanded.*

Joy for the victory.

And presently the music that was in the upper region sounded melodiously. The captains that were in the camp shouted, and the soldiers sung songs of triumph to the prince, the colours waved in the wind, and great joy was every where, only it was wanting as yet in the hearts of the men of Mansoul.

They are pardoned, which is commanded to be proclaimed to-morrow in Mansoul.

Then the prince called to the prisoners to come and stand again before him, and they came and stood trembling. And he said unto them, The sins, trespasses, and iniquities, that you, with the whole town of Mansoul, have from time to time committed against my father and me, I have power and commandment from my father to forgive to the town of Mansoul, and do forgive you accordingly. And having so said, he gave them written in parchment, and sealed with seven seals, a large and general pardon, commanding my lord-mayor, Lord Will-be-will, and Mr Recorder, to proclaim, and cause it to be proclaimed to-morrow, by that the sun is up, throughout the whole town of Mansoul.

Their rags are taken from them.

Moreover, the prince stripped the prisoners of their mourning weeds, and gave them beauty for ashes, the oil of joy for mourning, and the garment of praise for the spirit of heaviness, Isa. lxi. 3.

A strange alteration.

Then he gave to each of the three, jewels of gold and precious stones; and took away their ropes and put chains of gold about their necks, and ear-rings in their ears. Now the prisoners, when they heard the gracious words of Prince Immanuel, and had beheld all that was done unto them, fainted almost quite away; for the grace, the benefit, the pardon, was sudden, glorious, and so big, that they

---

* The questions proposed by Immanuel were well formed to bring out that clear and full confession of sin, and the desert of it, which appears in the answers. Their language is that of truly humbled and penitent souls. Happy is the reader who makes their words really his own. This is the Lord's doing and a certain taken for good. They who thus " confess and forsake their sin shall find mercy," and in this case, God is faithful to his promise, and just to his Son, to forgive all our sins.

When the soul is brought into this state, the design of God in those convictions which seemed so terrific is answered, the work is done, and it may be truly said, that " Jesus hath obtained a perfect conquest and victory over Mansoul." Heaven and earth resound with joy on this event.

were not able, without staggering, to stand up under it. Yea, my Lord Will-be-will swooned out-right, but the prince stept to him, put his everlasting arms under him, embraced him, kissed him, and bid him be of good cheer, for all should be performed according to his word. He also kissed, embraced, and smiled upon the other two that were Will-be-will's companions, saying, Take these as further tokens of my love, favour, and compassion to you; and I charge you that you Mr Recorder tell the town of Mansoul, what you have heard and seen.

Then were their fetters broken to pieces before their faces, *Their guilt.* and cast into the air, and their steps were enlarged under them. Then they fell at the feet of the prince, kissed them, and wetted them with tears; they also cried out with a mighty strong voice, saying, "Blessed be the glory of the Lord from this place!" So they were bid rise up, and go to the town and tell Mansoul what the prince had *They are sent home with pipe and tabor.* done. He commanded also, that one with pipe and tabor should go and play before them all the way into the town of Mansoul. Then was fulfilled what they never looked for, and they were made to possess what they never dreamt of.* The prince *Captain Credence guards them home.* also called for the noble Captain Credence, and commanded that he and some of his officers should march before the noblemen of Mansoul, with flying colours into the town. He gave also unto *When faith and pardon meet together, judgment and execution depart from the heart.* Captain Credence a charge, that about the time that the Recorder read the general pardon in the town of Mansoul, that at that very time he should with flying colours march in at Eye-gate, with his ten thousand at his feet; and that he should so go until he came by the high street of the town, up to the castle-gates; and that himself should take possession thereof against his Lord came thither. He commanded moreover, that he should bid Captain Judgment and Captain Execution leave the strong-hold to him, and withdraw from Mansoul, and return into the camp with speed unto the prince.

* What a change is effected! "When the Lord turned again the captivity of Zion, we were like them that dream. Then was our mouth filled with laughter, and our tongue with singing: then said they among the heathen, the Lord hath done great things for them. The Lord hath done great things for us, wherefore we are glad." "Who is like unto thee, pardoning iniquity, transgression, and sin?" "Blessed is he whose transgression is forgiven, whose sin is covered. Blessed is the man unto whom the Lord imputeth not iniquity; blessed is the man unto whom God imputeth righteousness without works." Rom. iv. 6.

And now was the town of Mansoul also delivered from the terror of the first four captains and their men.*

CHAPTER IX.

The liberated prisoners return to Mansoul, where they are received with the utmost demonstrations of joy. At the request of the inhabitants Immanuel consents to reside in the town. He makes a public triumphal entry. The town is new modelled, and the image of Shaddai erected.

WELL, I told you before how the prisoners were entertained by the noble prince Immanuel, and how they behaved themselves before him, and how he sent them away to their home with pipe and tabor going before them. And now you must think that those of the town, that had all this while waited to hear of their death, could not but be exercised with sadness of mind, and with thoughts that pricked like thorns. Nor could their thoughts be kept to any one point; the wind blew them all this while at great uncertainties, yea, their hearts were like a balance that had been disquieted with a shaking hand. But at last, as they, with many a long look, looked over the wall of Mansoul, they thought they saw some return to the town; and thought again, who should they be too, who should they be? At last they discerned that they were the prisoners: but can you imagine how their hearts were surprised with wonder, especially when they perceived also in what equipage, and with what honour they were sent home! They went down to the camp in black, but they came back to the town in white; they went down to the camp in ropes, they came in chains of gold; they went down to the camp with feet in fetters, but came back with their steps enlarged under them; they went to the camp looking for death, but came back from thence with assurance of life; they went down to the camp with heavy hearts, but came back with pipe and tabor playing before them. As soon as they came to Eye-gate, the poor and tottering town of Mansoul adventured to give a shout: and they gave such a shout as made the captains in the prince's army leap at the sound thereof. Alas for

The town of Mansoul in suspense concerning the fate of the prisoners.

A strange alteration.

The prisoners return to Eye-gate, and are received with a shout.

* "There is no condemnation to them that are in Christ Jesus." The four captains no longer denounce the wrath of God: the end of their ministry is accomplished; the town is therefore relieved from the terror that their awful speeches occasioned, or as it is expressed in the margin "when faith and pardon meet together, judgment and execution depart from the heart."

them, poor hearts! who could blame them?* since their dead friends were come to life again; for it was to them as life from the dead, to see the ancients of the town of Mansoul shine in such splendour. They looked for nothing but the axe and the block; but behold joy and gladness, comfort and consolation, and such melodious notes attending them, that was sufficient to make a sick man well, Isa. xxxiii. 24. So when they came up, they saluted each other: Welcome, welcome, and blessed be he that spared you! They added also, We see it is well with you; but how must it go with the town of Mansoul? And will it go well with the town of Mansoul? said they. Then answered them the Recorder and my Lord-mayor: Oh! tidings! glad tidings! good tidings of good, and of great joy to poor Mansoul! Then they gave another shout that made the earth ring again. After this, they inquired yet more particularly how things went in the camp, and what message they had from Immanuel to the town. So they told them all passages that had happened to them at the camp, and every thing that the prince did to them. This made Mansoul wonder at the wisdom and grace of the prince Immanuel: then they told them what they had received at his hands for the whole town of Mansoul, and the Recorder delivered it in these words: "Pardon, pardon for Mansoul; and this shall Mansoul know to-morrow." Then he commanded, and they went and summoned Mansoul to meet together in the market-place to-morrow, there to hear their general pardon read.

O the joy! pardon for sin.

But who can think what a turn, what a change, what an alteration this hint of things made in the countenance of the town of Mansoul! No man of Mansoul could sleep that night for joy; in every house there was joy and music, singing and making merry: telling and hearing of Immanuel's happiness, was then all that Mansoul had to do: and this was the burden of all their song, Oh more of this at the rising of the sun! more of this to morrow! Who thought yesterday, one would say, that this day would have been such a day to us! And who thought, that saw our prisoners go down in irons, that they should have returned in chains of gold! Yea, they that judged themselves, as they went to be judged of their judge, were by his mouth acquitted; not

Town-talk of the King's mercy.

---

* Who, indeed, can blame the holy joy of pardoned souls. When the Philipian jailor believed "he rejoiced with all his house;" and when Samaria received the gospel, "there was great joy in that city." The author refers to Isa. xxxiii. 24. "The inhabitants shall not say I am sick; the people that dwell therein shall be forgiven their iniquity:"—as if nothing could be complained of, if pardon be obtained.

for that they were innocent, but of the prince's mercy, and sent home with pipe and tabor. But is this the common custom of princes? Do they use to show such kind of favours to traitors? No! this 's only peculiar to Shaddai, and unto Immanuel his son.*

And of his son Immanuel.

Now morning drew on apace; wherefore the Lord-mayor, the lord Will-be-will, and Mr Recorder, came down to the market-place, at the time that the prince had appointed, where the town-folk were waiting for them: and when they came, they came in that attire and in that glory which the prince had put them into the day before, and the street was 'lightened with their glory: so the Mayor, Recorder, and my lord Will-be-will, drew down to Mouth-gate, which was at the lower end of the market-place, because that of old time was the place where they used to read public matters: thither therefore they came in their robes, and their tabor went before them. Now the eagerness of the people to know the full matter was great.

Then the Recorder stood up upon his feet, and, first beckoning with his hand for silence, he read out with a loud voice the pardon. But when he came to these words, "The Lord, the Lord God is merciful and gracious, pardoning iniquity, transgressions, and sins;" and to them, "all manner of sin and blasphemy shall be forgiven," &c. Exod. xxxiv. Mark iii. they could not forbear leaping for joy: for this you must know, that there was conjoined herewith every man's name in Mansoul, also the seals of the pardon made a brave show.†

The manner of reading the pardon.

When the Recorder had made an end of reading the pardon, the townsmen ran upon the walls of the town, leaped thereon for joy, and bowing themselves seven times with their faces towards Immanuel's pavilion shouted aloud for joy, and said, "Let Immanuel live for ever!"

How they tread upon the flesh.

Then order was given to the young men in Mansoul, that

---

* Pardoned sinners will ever magnify the exceeding riches of divine grace; it cannot but appear marvellous beyond expression; in vain the labouring soul attempts to measure the breadth, the length, the depth, and the height of the love of Christ, it surpasses knowledge. "Is this the manner of man, O Lord!" and what more can we say?

† Believers are said to be "sealed to the day of redemption,"—"sealed with the Holy Spirit;" the Spirit is himself the seal. "God's sealing of believers (saith Dr Owen) is his gracious communication of the Holy Ghost unto them, so to act his divine power in them, as to enable them unto all the duties of their holy calling, evidencing them to be accepted with him, both to themselves and others, and asserting their preservation to eternal salvation. The *effects* of this sealing, are, gracious operations of the Spirit in and upon believers; but the sealing itself is, the communication of the Spirit unto them."

Lively and warm thoughts. they should ring the bells for joy; so the bells rung, the people sung, and the music played in every house in Mansoul.

When the prince had sent home the three prisoners of Mansoul with joy, and pipe and tabor, he commanded his captains, with all the field officers and soldiers, throughout his army, to be ready on the morning that the Recorder should read the pardon in Mansoul, to do his further pleasure. So the morning, as I have showed, being come, just as the Recorder had made an end of reading the pardon, Immanuel commanded that all the trumpets in the camp should sound, that the colours should be displayed, half of them upon Mount Gracious, and half of them upon Mount Justice. He commanded also, that all the captains should show themselves in their complete harness, and that the soldiers should shout for joy. Nor was Captain Credence, though in the castle, silent on such a day, but he from the top of the hold showed himself with the sound of trumpet to Mansoul, and to the prince's camp.

The carriage of the camp.

Faith will not be silent when Mansoul is saved.

Thus have I shown you the manner and way that Immanuel took to recover the town of Mansoul from under the hand and power of the tyrant Diabolus.

Now when the prince had completed these outward ceremonies of his joy, he again commanded that his captains and soldiers should show unto Mansoul some feats of war. So they presently addressed themselves to this work. But oh! with what agility, nimbleness, dexterity, and bravery, did these military men discover their skill in feats of war to the now gazing town of Mansoul! They marched, they countermarched, they opened to the right and left, they divided and subdivided, they closed, they wheeled, made good their front and rear with their right and left wings, and twenty things more, with that aptness, and then were all as they were again, that they took, yea ravished, the hearts that were in Mansoul to behold it. But add to this, the handling of their arms, the managing of their weapons of war, were marvellous taking to Mansoul and me.*

The prince displays his graces before Mansoul.

They are ravished at the sight of them.

When this action was over, the whole town of Mansoul came out as one man to the prince in the camp, to praise him, and

* "The prince displays his graces;"—they are shown the use of them in that warfare which must now begin; Faith, or Credence, shows himself from the castle, the heart, where he has now taken his residence, that Christ may dwell in the heart by faith.

thank him for his abundant favour, and to beg that it would please his Grace to come unto Mansoul with his men, and there to take up their quarters for ever. And this they did in the most humble manner, bowing themselves seven times to the ground before him. Then said he, "All peace be to you:" So the town came nigh, and touched with the hand the top of his golden sceptre; and they said, Oh! that the prince Immanuel, with his captains and men of war, would dwell in Mansoul for ever; and that his battering rams and slings might be lodged in her, for the use and service of the prince, and for the help and strength of Mansoul! for, said they, we have room for thee, we have room for thy men, we have also room for thy weapons of war, and a place to make a magazine for thy carriages. Do it, Immanuel, and thou shalt be king and captain in Mansoul for ever: yea, govern thou also according to all the desire of thy soul, and make thou governors and princes under thee of thy captains and men of war, and we will become thy servants, and thy laws shall be our direction.

They beg that the prince and his men would dwell with them for ever.

Say and hold to it, Mansoul.

They added moreover and prayed his Majesty to consider thereof; for, said they, if now, after all this grace bestowed upon us thy miserable town of Mansoul, thou shouldst withdraw, thou and thy captains from us, the town of Mansoul will die. Yea said they, our blessed Immanuel, if thou shouldst depart from us now, after thou hast done so much good for us, and showed so much mercy unto us, what will follow, but that our joy will be as if it had not been; and our enemies will a second time come upon us with more rage than at the first? Wherefore we beseech thee, O thou the desire of our eyes, and the strength and life of our poor town, accept of this motion that now we have made unto our Lord, and come and dwell in the midst of us, and let us be thy people. Besides, Lord, we do not know but that to this day many Diabolonians may be yet lurking in the town of Mansoul; and they will betray us, when thou shalt leave us, into the hands of Diabolus again, and who knows what designs, plots, and contrivances, have passed betwixt them about these things already? Loth we are to fall again into his horrible hands. Wherefore let it please thee to accept of our palace for thy place of residence, and of the houses of the best men in our town for the reception of thy soldiers, and their furniture.*

Their fears.

---

* Converted souls will most sincerely and earnestly desire the constant residence of Christ with them as their king and captain. This is always the language of first love; but let the caution in the margin be noticed, "Say, and hold to it, Mansoul." Happy are they who continue in this good mind all their days. But the sequel of the story will show how changeable a creature is man

The prince's question to Mansoul. Then said the prince, if I come to your town, will you suffer me further to prosecute that which is in my heart against mine enemies and your's? yea, will you help me in such undertakings?

Their answer. They answered, We know not what we shall do; we did not think once that we should have been such traitors to Shaddai as we have proved to be. What then shall we say to our Lord? Let him put no trust in his saints; let the prince dwell in our castle, and make of our town a garrison; let him set his noble captains and war-like soldiers over us; yea, let him conquer us with his love, and overcome us, and help us, as he did that morning our pardon was read unto us, we shall comply with this our Lord and with his ways, and fall in with his word against the mighty.

One word more, and thy servants have done, and in this will trouble our Lord no more. We know not the depth of the wisdom of thee our prince. Who could have thought, that had been ruled by his reason, that so much sweet as we now enjoy should have come out of those bitter trials wherewith we were tried at the first! But, Lord, let light go before, and let love come after: yea, take us by the hand, and lead *They pray to be directed by Immanuel.* us by thy counsels; and let this always abide upon us, that all things shall be for the best for thy servants, and come to our Mansoul, do as it pleaseth thee: Or, Lord, come to our Mansoul, and do what thou wilt, so thou keepest us from sinning, and makest us serviceable to thy Majesty.*

Then said the prince to the town of Mansoul again, Go, return to your houses in peace. I will willingly in *He consents to dwell in Mansoul, and promises to come in to-morrow.* this comply with your desires: I will remove my royal pavilion; I will draw up my forces before Eye-gate to-morrow, and so will march forwards into the town of Mansoul; I will possess myself of your castle of Mansoul, and will set my soldiers over you; yea, I will yet do things in Mansoul that cannot be paralleled in any nation, country, or kingdom under heaven.

Then did the men of Mansoul give a shout, and return into their houses in peace; they also told to their kindred and friends the good that Immanuel had promised to Mansoul. And to-

---

* Holy jealousy well becomes us. However sincerely we resolve upon obedience to the Lord, we must remember that our hearts are treacherous, and that "without him we can do nothing." To be kept from sin, and made serviceable to Christ, is, however, the prevailing desire of ever Christian.

morrow, said they, he will march into our town, and take up his dwelling, he and his men, in Mansoul.*

Then went out the inhabitants of the town of Mansoul with haste to the green trees, and to the meadows, to gather boughs and flowers, therewith to strew the streets against their prince the son of Shaddai should come; they also made garlands and other fine works, to betoken how joyful they were and should be to receive their Immanuel into Mansoul; yea, they strewed the street quite from Eye-gate to the Castle-gate, the place where the prince should be. They also prepared for his coming what music the town of Mansoul could afford, that they might play before him to the place of his habitation.

Mansoul's preparation for his reception.

So at the time appointed he makes his approach to Mansoul, and the gates were set open for him; there also the ancients and elders of Mansoul met him, to salute him with a thousand welcomes. Then he arose and entered Mansoul, he and all his servants. The elders of Mansoul also went dancing before him, till he came to the castle-gates. And this was the manner of his going up thither: he was clad in his golden armour, he rode in his royal chariot, the trumpets sounded about him, the colours were displayed, his ten thousands went up at his feet, and the elders of Mansoul danced before him. And now were the walls of the famous town of Mansoul filled with the tramplings of the inhabitants thereof, who went up thither to view the approach of the blessed prince and his royal army. Also, the casements, windows, balconies, and tops of the houses, were all now filled with persons of all sorts, to behold how their town was to be filled with good.

He enters the town of Mansoul, and how.

Now when he was come so far into the town as the Recorder's house, he commanded that one should go to Captain Credence, to know whether the castle of Mansoul was prepared to entertain his royal presence (for the preparation of that was left to that captain) and word was brought that it was, Acts xv. 9. Then was Captain Credence commanded also to come forth with his power to meet the prince; which was done as he had commanded, and he conducted him into the castle, Eph. iii. 17. This done, the prince that night lodged in the castle with his captains and men of war, to the joy of the town of Mansoul.†

---

* Well may the soul rejoice that Jesus consents and promises to come and dwell within. "If any man love me, he will keep my words, and my Father will love him, and we will come unto him, and make our abode with him." John xiv. 23.

† Captain Credence was to prepare the castle for Immanuel, in scripture words—"purifying their heart by faith." Acts xv. 9.

Now the next care of the townsfolk was how the captains and soldiers of the prince's army should be quartered among them; and the care was, not how they should shift their hands of them, but how they should fill their houses with them: for every man in Mansoul now had that esteem of Immanuel and his men, that nothing grieved them more, than because they were not enlarged enough, every one of them, to receive the whole army of the prince; yea, they counted it their glory to be waiting upon them, and would in those days run at their bidding like lacqueys. At last they came to this result

The townsmen covet who shall have most of the soldiers belonging to the prince.

1. That Captain Innocency should quarter at Mr Reason's.

How they were quartered in the town of Mansoul.

2. That Captain Patience should quarter at Mr Mind's. This Mr Mind was formerly the lord Will-be-will's clerk in the time of the rebellion.

3. It was ordered that Captain Charity should quarter in Mr Affection's house.

4. That Captain Good-hope should quarter at my lord-mayor's. Now for the house of the Recorder, himself desired, because his house was next to the castle, and because from him it was ordered by the prince, that, if need be, the alarm should be given to Mansoul: it was, I say, desired by him that Captain Boanerges and Captain Conviction should take up their quarters with him, even they and all their men.

5. As for Captain Judgment and Captain Execution, my lord Will-be-will took them and their men to him, because he was to rule under the prince for the good of the town of Mansoul now, as he had done before under the tyrant Diabolus for the hurt and damage thereof. Rom. vi. 19. Eph. iii. 17.

6. And throughout the rest of the town were quartered the rest of Immanuel forces; but Captain Credence, with his men, abode still in the castle. So the prince, his captains, and his soldiers, were lodged in the town of Mansoul.*

Now the ancients and elders of the town of Mansoul thought that they never should have enough of the prince Immanuel; his person, his actions, his words, and behaviour, were so pleasing, so taking, so desirable to them. Wherefore they prayed him, that though the castle of Mansoul was his place of residence (and they desired that he might dwell there for ever) yet that he would often visit the streets, houses, and peo-

Mansoul inflamed with their prince Immanuel.

---

* Much judgment is displayed in this distribution of the soldiers, particularly in quartering Boanerges and Conviction in the house of Conscience.

ple of Mansoul; for, said they, dread sovereign! thy presence, thy looks, thy smiles, thy words, are the life, strength, and sinews of the town of Mansoul.

Besides this, they craved that they might have, without difficulty or interruption, continual access unto him; so for that very purpose he commanded that the gates should stand open, that they might there see the manner of his doings, the fortifications of the place, and the royal mansion house of the prince.

They have access unto him.

When he spake, they all stopped their mouths, and gave audience; and when he walked, it was their delight to imitate him in his goings.

They learn of him.

Now upon a time Immanuel made a feast for the town of Mansoul; and upon the feasting day, the townsfolk were come to the castle to partake of his banquet. And he feasted them with all manner of outlandish food; food that grew not in the fields of Mansoul, nor in all the whole kingdom of Universe. It was food that came from his father's court, and so there was dish after dish set before them, and they were commanded freely to eat. But still, when a fresh dish was set before them, they would, whisperingly say to each other, "What is it?" for they wist not what to call it, Exod. xvi. 15. They drank also of the water that was made wine; and were very merry with him. There was music also all the while at the table, and man did eat angels' food, and had honey given him out of the rock; so Mansoul did eat the food that was peculiar to the court, yea, they had now thereof to the full. Psalm lxxviii. 24, 25.

Promise after promise.

Brave entertainment.

I must not forget to tell you, that at this table there were musicians, so they were not those of the country, nor yet of the town of Mansoul; but they were the masters of the songs that were sung at the court of Shaddai.*

Now after the feast was over, Immanuel was for entertaining the town with some curious riddles of secrets drawn up by his father's secretary, by the wisdom and skill of Shaddai; the like to these there are not in any kingdom.

Riddles.

The riddles were made upon king Shaddai himself, and upon Immanuel his son, and upon his wars and doings with Mansoul. Immanuel also expounded unto them some of those riddles himself; but oh

The holy scriptures.

---

* This is the gospel-feast—a feast of fat things—meat indeed, and drink indeed! not the produce of nature, but imported from heaven. The music also is heavenly; not the song of frothy vanity, but such as saints and angels sing before the throne; the word of Christ, in psalms, hymns, and spiritual songs.

how they were lightened! They saw what they never saw before; they could not have thought that such rarities could have been couched in so few and such ordinary words. I told you before, whom these riddles did concern; and as they were opened, the people evidently saw it was so. Yea, they gathered, that the things themselves were a kind of portraiture, and that of Immanuel himself; for when they read in the scheme where the riddles were writ, and looked in the face of the prince, things looked so like one to the other, that Mansoul could not forbear but say, This is the Lamb, this is the sacrifice, this is the rock, this is the red cow, this is the door, and this is the way; with a great many other things more.*

And thus he dismissed the town of Mansoul. But can you imagine how the people of the corporation were taken with his entertainment? Oh, they were transported with joy, they were drowned with wonder, while they saw, and understood, and considered what their Immanuel entertained them withal, and what mysteries he opened to them; and when they were at home in their houses, and in their most retired places, they could not but sing of him and of his actions. Yea, so taken were the townsmen now with their prince, that they would sing of him in their sleep.

The end of the banquet.

Now it was in the heart of the prince Immanuel to new-model the town of Mansoul, and to put it into such a condition as might be most pleasing to him, and that might best stand with the profit and security of the now flourishing town of Mansoul. He provided also against insurrections at home, and invasions abroad: such love had he for the famous town of Mansoul.†

Mansoul must be new-modelled.

Wherefore he first of all commanded, that the great slings, that were brought from his father's court when he came to the town of Mansoul, should be mounted, some upon the battlements of the castle, some upon the towers; for there were towers in the town of Mansoul, towers new built by Immanuel since he came thither. There was also an instrument invented by Immanuel, that was to throw stones, from the castle of Mansoul, out at Mouth-gate; an instrument that could not be resisted, nor that could miss of execution; wherefore, for the

The instruments of war mounted.

A nameless terrible instrument in Mansoul.

---

* The riddles seem to refer chiefly to the types of Christ, which abound in the scriptures, which are full of divine entertainment to gracious and enlightened souls. The very portraiture of Jesus is seen in them; meditation on these adds greatly to the delight of the gospel feast.

† The soul of man, when converted to God, "must be new-modelled," "old things must pass away, all things be made new."

wonderful exploits that it did when used, it went without a name; and it was committed to the care of, and to be managed by, that brave captain, the Captain Credence, in case of war.*

This done, Immanuel called the Lord Will-be-will to him, and gave him in commandment to take care of the gates, the wall and towers in Mansoul: also the prince gave him the militia into his hand, and a special charge to withstand all insurrections and tumults that might be made in Mansoul, against the peace of our lord the king, and the peace and tranquillity of the town of Mansoul. He also gave him in commission, that if he found any of the Diabolonians lurking in any corner of the famous town of Mansoul, he should forthwith apprehend them and slay them, or commit them to safe custody, that they may be proceeded against according to law.

Will-be-will promoted.

Then he called unto him the Lord Understanding, who was the old lord-mayor, he that was put out of place when Diabolus took the town, and put him into his former office again, and it became his place for his life time. He bid him also build it in fashion like a tower for a defence. He bid him also read in the revelations of mysteries all the days of his life, that he might know how to perform his office aright.

My lord-mayor put into place.

He also made Mr Knowledge the recorder, not of contempt to old Mr Conscience, who had been recorder before; but for that it was in his princely mind to confer upon Mr Conscience another employ; of which he told the old gentleman he should know more hereafter.

Mr Knowledge made recorder.

Then he commanded that the image of Diabolus should be taken down from the place where it was set up; and that they should utterly destroy it, beating it into powder, and casting it into the wind, without the town-wall; and that the image of Shaddai his father should be set up again, with his own, upon the castle-gates; and that it should be more fairly drawn that ever, forasmuch as both his father and himself were come to Mansoul in more grace and mercy than heretofore, Rev. xxii. 4. He would also that his name should be done on the best of gold, for the honour of Mansoul.†

The image of the prince and his father set up in Mansoul.

---

* This nameless engine, placed at mouth-gate, is prayer; its power is wonderful beyond description, and therefore it went without a name; no name can sufficiently describe the use and power of prayer. Matt. xxi. 22.

† The understanding is re-instated in its proper and original office as chief magistrate of the town, and for his direction, is ordered to study the scriptures, for it is thus the understanding must be informed. Knowledge, the knowledge of God in Christ, is to bear sway, another office being appointed for Mr Conscience; the image of Satan is now to be utterly destroyed, and that of God renewed in the soul.

CHAPTER X.

The strong holds of Diabolus destroyed. Incredulity, Lustings, Forget-good, and other Diabolonians apprehended, brought to trial, convicted, and executed, to the great joy of Mansoul.

AFTER this was done, Immanuel gave out a commandment, which was, that those three greatest Diabolonians should be apprehended, namely, the two late lord-mayors, to wit, Mr Incredulity and Mr Lustings, and Mr Forget-good the recorder. Besides these, there were some of them that Diabolus made burgesses and aldermen in Mansoul, that were committed to ward by the hand of the now valiant and now right noble, the brave Lord Will-be-will.

Some Diabolonians committed to prison under the hand of Mr Trueman the keeper.

And these were their names: Alderman Atheism, Alderman Hard-heart, and Alderman False-peace. The burgesses were, Mr No-truth, Mr Pitiless, Mr Haughty, with the like. These were committed to close custody; and the goaler's name was Mr Trueman: this Trueman was one of those that Immanuel brought with him from his Father's court, when at first he made a war upon Diabolus in the town of Mansoul.

After this, the prince gave a charge that the three strong holds which at the command of Diabolus the Diabolonians built in Mansoul, should be demolished and utterly pulled down; of which holds, and their names, with their captains and governors, you read a little before; but this was long in doing, because of the largeness of the places, and because the stones, the timber, the iron, and all the rubbish, were to be carried without the town.*

Diabolus's strong holds pulled down.

When this was done, the prince gave orders that the lord-mayor and aldermen of Mansoul should call a court of judicature for the trial and execution of the Diabolonians in the corporation, now under the care of Mr Trueman the gaoler.

A court to be called to try the Diabolonians.

Now when the time was come, and the court set, commandment was sent to Mr Trueman the gaoler, to bring the prisoners down to the bar. Then were the prisoners brought down, pinioned and chained together, as the custom of the town of Mansoul

The prisoners brought to the bar.

---

* When grace begins to reign, we must mortify the flesh, with its affections and lusts. Jesus Christ came to destroy the works of the devil, and to pull down his strong holds. But, truly, this is a work of time and immense labour.

was. So when they were presented before the lord-mayor, the recorder, and the rest of the honourable bench; first, the jury was empannelled, and then the witnesses sworn. The names of the jury were these: Mr Belief, Mr Truehart, Mr Upright, Mr Hate-bad, Mr Love-good, Mr See-truth, Mr Heavenly-Mind, Mr Moderate, Mr Thankful, Mr Good-work, Mr Zeal-for-God, and Mr Humble. The names of the witnesses were, Mr Know-all, Mr Tell-true, Mr Hate-lies, with my Lord Will-be-will, and his man, if need were.*

The jury empannelled, and witnesses sworn.

So the prisoners were set to the bar. Then said Mr Do-right, (for he was the town-clerk) Set Atheism to the bar, gaoler. So he was set to the bar. Then said the clerk, Atheism hold up thy hand. Thou art here indicted by the name of Atheism (an intruder upon the town of Mansoul) for that thou hast perniciously and doutishly taught and maintained, that there is no God, and so no heed to be taken to religion. This thou hast done against the being, honour, and glory of the king, and against the peace and safety of the town of Mansoul. What sayest thou? art thou guilty of this indictment, or not?

Do-right the clerk.
Atheism set to the bar.
His indictment.

Atheism. Not guilty.

Crier. Call Mr Know-all, Mr Tell-true, and Mr Hate-lies, into the court.

So they were called, and they appeared.

Clerk. Then said the clerk, You, the witnesses for the king, look upon the prisoner at the bar; do you know him?

Know-all. Then said Mr Know-all, Yes, my lord, we know him; his name is Atheism, he has been a very pestilent fellow for many years in the miserable town of Mansoul.

Clerk. You are sure you know him?

Know-all. Know him! Yes, my lord. I have heretofore too often been in his company to be at this time ignorant of him. He is a Diabolonian, the son of a Diabolonian; I knew his grandfather and his father.

Mr Know-all's evidence against Atheism.

Clerk. Well said: he standeth here indicted by the name of Atheism, &c. and is charged, that he hath maintained, and taught that there is no God, and so no heed to be taken to any religion. What say you, the king's witnesses, to this? is he guilty, or not?

Know-all. My lord, I and he were once in Villains-lane to-

---

* A very good jury indeed!—" honest men and true," who will give a faithful verdict for God against sin.

gether, and he at that time talked briskly of divers opinions; and then and there I heard him say, that for his part he believed there was no God: but said he, I can profess one, and be religious too, if the company I am in, and the circumstances of other things, shall put me upon it.

Clerk. You are sure you have heard him say thus?

Know-all. Upon mine oath, I heard him say thus.

Mr Tell-true called. Then said the clerk, Mr Tell-true, what say you to the king's judges touching the prisoner at the bar?

Tell-true. My lord, I formerly was a great companion of his (for which I now repent me) and I have often heard him say, and that with very great stomach fulness, that he believed there was neither God, angel, or spirit.

Clerk. Where did you hear him say so?

Tell-true. In Black-mouth-lane, and in Blasphemers-row, and in many other places besides.

Clerk. Have you much knowledge of him?

Tell-true. I know him to be a Diabolonian, the son of a Diabolonian, and a horrible man to deny a Deity; his father's name was Never-be-good, and he had more children than this Atheism. I have no more to say.

Clerk. Mr Hate-lies, look upon the prisoner at the bar; do you know him?

Hate-lies. My lord, this Atheism is one of the vilest wretches that ever I came near, or had to do with in my life: I have heard him say that there is no God; I have heard him say that there is no world to come, no sin, nor punishment hereafter; and moreover, I have heard him say, that it was as good to go to a whorehouse as to hear a sermon.

The evidence of Mr Hate-lies.

Clerk. Where did you hear him say these things?

Hate-lies. In Drunkard's-row, just at Rascal's-lane-end, at the house in which Mr Impiety lived.

Lustings set to the bar. *Clerk.* Set him by, gaoler,* and set Mr Lustings to the bar.

His indictment. Mr Lustings, thou art here indicted by the name of Lustings (an intruder upon the town of Mansoul) for that thou hast devilishly and traitorously taught by practice and filthy words, that it is lawful

---

* Atheism is fairly tried and justly condemned. Alas! how much practical atheism is there among professed Christians! For if men live without prayer, and in opposition to his will, they live " without God in the world," and what is this but atheism?

and profitable to man to give way to his carnal desires; and that thou, for thy part, hast not, nor ever wilt, deny thyself of any sinful delight as long as thy name is Lustings. How sayest thou? art thou guilty of this indictment or not?

Lustings. Then said Mr Lustings, My lord, I am a man of high birth, and have been used to pleasures, and pastimes, and greatness. I have not been wont to be snubbed for my doings, but have been left to follow my will as if it were law. And it seems strange to me that I should this day be called into question for what not only I, but almost all men, do either secretly or openly countenance, love, and approve of.

His plea.

Clerk. Sir, we concern not ourselves with your greatness, (though the higher, the better you should have been) but we are concerned, and so are you, about an indictment preferred against you. How say you? are you guilty of it, or not?

Lustings. Not guilty.

Clerk. Crier, call upon the witnesses to stand forth and give their evidence.

Witnesses called against Lustings.

Crier. Gentlemen, you the witnesses for the king, come and give in your evidence for our lord the king against the prisoner at the bar.

Clerk. Come, Mr Know-all, look upon the prisoner at the bar. Do you know him?

Know-all. Yes, my lord, I know him.

Clerk. What is his name?

Know-all. His name is Lustings: he is the son of one Beastly; his mother bare him in Flesh-street: she was one Evil-concupiscence's daughter. I knew all the generation of them.

Clerk. Well said. You have heard his indictment: what say you to it? is he guilty of the things charged him or not?

Know-all. My lord, he has, as he saith, been a great man indeed; and greater in wickedness than by pedigree, more than a thousand fold.

Clerk. But what do you know of his particular actions, and especially with reference to his indictment?

Know-all. I know him to be a swearer, a liar, a sabbath-breaker; I know him to be a fornicator, and an unclean person; I know him to be guilty of abundance of evils. He has been, to my knowledge, a very filthy man.

His guilt proved.

Clerk. But where did he use to commit his wickedness? in some private corner, or more openly and shamelessly?

Know-all. All the town over, my lord.

Clerk. Come, Mr Tell-true, what have you to say for our lord the king against the prisoner at the bar?

Tell-true. My lord, all that the first witness has said I know to be true, and a great deal more besides.

Clerk. Mr Lustings, do you hear what these gentlemen say?

Lustings. I was ever of opinion, that the happiest life that a man could live on earth, was, to keep himself from nothing that he desired in the world; nor have I been false at any time to this opinion of mine, but have lived in the love of my notions all my days: nor was I ever so churlish, having found such sweetness in them myself, as to keep the commendation of them from others.

Lustings sets up his defence.

Court. Then said the court, There hath proceeded enough from his own mouth to lay him open to condemnation; wherefore set him by,* gaoler, and set Mr Incredulity to the bar.

Incredulity set to the bar.

Clerk. Mr Incredulity, thou art here indicted by the name of Incredulity (an intruder upon the town of Mansoul,) for that thou hast feloniously and wickedly, and that when thou wert an officer in the town of Mansoul, made head against the captains of the great Shaddai, when they came and demanded possession of Mansoul; yea, thou didst bid defiance to the name, forces, and cause of the king; and didst also, as did Diabolus thy captain, stir up and encourage the town of Mansoul to make head against and resist the said force of the king. What sayest thou to this indictment? art thou guilty, or not?

His indictment.

Then said Incredulity, I know not Shaddai: I loved my old prince; I thought it my duty to be true to my trust, and to do what I could to possess the minds of the men of Mansoul to do their utmost to resist strangers and foreigners, and with might to fight against them. Nor have I, nor shall I, change my opinion for fear of trouble, though you at present are possessed of place and power.

His plea.

Court. Then said the court; The man, as you see, is incorrigible; he is for maintaining his villanies by stoutness of words, and his rebellion with impudent confidence. And therefore set him by, gaoler;† and set Mr Forget-good to the bar.

Forget-good set to the bar.

---

* Lustings, or the sinful lusts of the flesh, is well described; he is the son of one Beastly, his mother a daughter of Evil-concupiscence, a swearer, a liar, a fornicator, &c. &c. He is a true Diabolonian; and as all God's people are to walk, not according to the flesh, but according to the spirit, he must die.

† Unbelief is the great instigator of rebellion against God; out of his own mouth he is condemned as absolutely incorrigible.

Clerk. Mr Forget-good, thou art here indicted by the name of Forget-good (an intruder upon the town of Mansoul,) for that thou, when the whole affairs of the town of Mansoul were in thy hand, didst utterly forget to serve them in what was good, and didst fall in with the tyrant Diabolus against Shaddai the king, against his captains, and all his host, to the dishonour of Shaddai, the breach of his law, and the endangering of the destruction of the famous town of Mansoul. What sayest thou to this indictment? art thou guilty, or not guilty?

His indictment.

Then said Forget-good, Gentlemen, and at this time my judges, as to the indictment by which I stand accused of several crimes before you, pray attribute my forgetfulness to my age, and not to my wilfulness; to the craziness of my brain, and not the carelessness of my mind; and then I hope I may by your charity be excused from great punishment, though I be guilty.

His plea.

Then said the court, Forget-good, Forget-good, thy forgetfulness of good was not simply of frailty, but of purpose and for that thou didst loath to keep virtuous things in thy mind. What was bad, thou couldst retain; but what was good thou couldst not abide to think of: thy age, therefore, and thy pretended craziness, thou makest use of to blind the court withal, and as a cloak to cover thy knavery. But let us hear what the witnesses have to say for the king, against the prisoner at the bar. Is he guilty of this indictment, or not?

Witnesses called.

Hate-lies. My lord, I have heard this Forget-good say, that he could never abide to think of goodness, no not for a quarter of an hour.

Clerk. Where didst thou hear him say so?

Hate-lies. In All-base-lane, at a house next door to the sign of the Conscience-seared-with-a-hot-iron.

Clerk. Mr Know-all, what can you say for our lord the king, against the prisoner at the bar?

General character of Forget-good.

Know-all. My lord, I know the man well; he is a Diabolonian, the son of a Diabolonian, his father's name was Love-naught; and for him I have often heard him say, that he counted the very thoughts of goodness the most burthensome thing in the world.

Clerk. Where have you heard him say these words?

Know-all. In Flesh-lane, right opposite to the church.

Then said the clerk, Come, Mr Tell-true, give in your evidence concerning the prisoner at the bar, about that for which he stands here, as you see, indicted before this honourable court.

Tell-true. My Lord, I have heard him often say, he had rather think of the vilest thing, than of what is contained in the holy scriptures.

Clerk. Where did you hear him say such grievous words?

Tell-true. Where? in a great many places; particularly in Nauseous-street, in the house of one Shameless; and in Filth-lane, at the sign of the Reprobate, next door to the Descent-into-the-pit.

Court. Gentlemen, you have heard the indictment, his plea, and the testimony of the witnesses.*

Gaoler, set Mr Hard-heart to the bar.

He is set to the bar.

Clerk. Mr Hard-heart, thou art here indicted by the name of Hard-heart (an intruder upon the town of Mansoul,) for that thou didst most desperately and wickedly possess the town of Mansoul with impenitency and obdurateness; and didst keep them from remorse and sorrow for their evils all the time of their apostacy from, and rebellion against, the blessed king Shaddai. What sayest thou to this indictment? art thou guilty, or not guilty?

Hard-heart set to the bar.

His indictment.

Hard-Heart. My lord, I never knew what remorse or sorrow meant, in all my life: I am impenetrable, I care for no man; nor can I be pierced with men's grief, their groans will not enter into my heart; whomsoever I mischief, whomsoever I wrong, to me it is music when to others mourning.

Court. You see the man is a right Diabolonian, and has convicted himself.† Set him by, Gaoler, and set Mr False-peace to the bar.

Mr False-peace, thou art here indicted by the name of False-peace (an intruder upon the town of Mansoul), for that thou didst most wickedly and satanically bring, hold, and keep the town of Mansoul, both in her apostacy and in her hellish rebellion, in a false, groundless, and dangerous peace, and damnable security, to the dishonour of the king, the transgression of his law, and the great damage of the town of Mansoul. What sayest thou? art thou guilty of this indictment, or not?

False-peace set to the bar.

His indictment.

Then said Mr False-peace, Gentlemen, and you now appointed to be my judges, I acknowledge that my name is Mr Peace;

---

* Forgetfulness of good, pleads a weak head, but the witnesses prove an avowed hatred of every thing scriptural and religious; it is therefore the fault of the heart rather than of the head, for, who is he that cannot remember what he loves?

† Hardness of heart is quite in character; he is impenetrable, and knows not how to relent; he is also self-condemned.

He denies his name. but that my name is False-peace, I utterly deny. If your honours should please to send for any that intimately know me, or for the mid-wife that laid my mother of me, or for the gossips that were at my christening, they will any or all of them prove, that my name is not False-peace, but Peace. Wherefore I cannot plead to this indictment, for as much as my name is not inserted therein; and as is my *true* name, so also are my conditions. I was always a man that loved to live at quiet; and what I loved myself, that I though others might love also. Wherefore when I saw that any of my neighbours laboured under a disquieted mind, I endeavoured to help them what I could; and I could give many instances of this good temper of mine: As,

1. When at the beginning our town of Mansoul declined the ways of Shaddai, some of them afterwards began to have diquieting reflections on themselves for what they had done: but I, as one troubled to see them disquieted, presently sought out means to get them quiet again.

False-peace justifies his conduct.

2. When the ways of the old world, and of Sodom, were in fashion; if any thing happened to molest those that were for the customs of the present times, I laboured to make them quiet again, and to cause them to act without molestation.

3. To come nearer home: when the wars broke out between Shaddai and Diabolus, if at any time I saw any of the town of Mansoul afraid of destruction, I often used, by some way, device, invention, or other, to labour to bring them to peace again. Wherefore, since I have been always the man of so virtuous a temper, as some say a peace-maker is, and if a peace-maker be so deserving a man, as some have been bold to attest he is; then let me, gentlemen, be accounted by you, who have a great name for justice and equity in Mansoul, for a man that deserveth not this inhuman way of treatment, but liberty, and also a licence to seek damage of those that have been my accusers.

Then said the clerk, Crier, make proclamation.

Crier. "O yes! Forasmuch as the prisoner at the bar hath denied his name to be that which is mentioned in the indictment; the court requireth, that if there be any in this place, who can give information to the court, of the original and right name of the prisoner, they would come forth and give in their evidence: for the prisoner stands upon his own innocence."

Proclamation for the witnesses to come forth.

Then came two into the court, and desired that they might have leave to speak what they knew concerning the prisoner at the bar; the name of the one was Search-truth, and the name of the other Vouch-truth: so the court demanded of these men if they knew the prisoner, and what they could say concerning him for he stands, said they, upon his own vindication.

Then said Mr Search-truth, My lord—

Court. Hold; give him his oath. Then they swore him: so he proceeded.

Search-truth. My lord, I know, and have known this man from a child, and can attest that his name is False-peace. I knew his father, his name was Mr Flatterer, and his mother, before she was married, was called by the name of Mrs Sooth-up: and these two, when they came together, lived not long without this son; and when he was born, they called his name False-peace. I was his playfellow, only I was somewhat older than he; and when his mother used to call him home from his play, she would say to him False-peace, False-peace, come home quick, or I will fetch you. Yea, I knew him when he sucked; and though I was then but little, yet I can remember, that when his mother used to sit at the door with him, or played with him in her arms, she would call him twenty times together, My little False-peace, my pretty False-peace! and O my sweet rogue, False-peace! and again, O my little bird, False-peace! and How do I love my child! The gossips also know it is thus, though he has had the face to deny it in open court.

The evidence given by Mr Search-truth.

Then Mr Vouch-truth was called upon, to speak what he knew of him. So they sware him.

Then said Mr Vouch-truth, My lord, all that the former witness hath said is true: his name is False-peace, the son of Mr Flatterer, and Mrs Sooth-up his mother. And I have in former times seen him angry with those that called him any thing else but False-peace, for he would say that all such mocked and nick-named him; but this was at the time when Mr False-peace was a great man, and when the Diabolonians were the brave men in Mansoul.

Mr Vouch-truth's evidence against False-peace.

Court. Gentlemen, you have heard what these two men have sworn against the prisoner at the bar. And now, Mr False-peace, to you: You have denied your name to be False-Peace; yet you see that these honest men have sworn that this is your name. As to your plea, in that you are quit; besides the matter of your indictment, you are not by it charged for evil doing, because you are a man of peace, or a peace-maker among your neighbours, but that you did wickedly and satanically bring, keep, and hold the town of Mansoul both under its apos-

The true character of False-peace discovered.

tacy from, and in its rebellion against its king, in a false, lying and damnable peace, contrary to the law of Shaddai, and to the hazard of the destruction of the then miserable town of Mansoul. All that you have pleaded for youself, is, that you have denied your name, &c. but here you see, we have witnesses to prove that you are the man.

For the peace that you so much boast of making among your neighbours, know, that the peace that is not a companion of truth and holiness, but is without this foundation, is grounded upon a lie, and is both deceitful and damnable, as also the great Shaddai hath said: thy plea therefore, hath not delivered thee from what by thy indictment thou art charged with, but rather it doth fasten all upon thee.

But thou shalt have very fair play: let us call the witnesses that are to testify as to matters of fact, and see what they have to say for our lord the king, against the prisoner at the bar.

Clerk. Mr Know-all, what say you for our lord the king, against the prisoner at the bar?

Know-all. My lord, this man hath for a long time made it, to my knowledge, his business to keep the town of Mansoul in a sinful quietness, in the midst of all her lewdness, filthiness, and turmoils, and hath said, and that in my hearing, Come, come, let us fly from all trouble, on what ground soever it comes, and let us be for a quiet and peaceable life though it wanteth a good foundation.

Mr Know-all's evidence.

Clerk. Come, Mr Hate-lies, what have you to say?

Hate-lies. My lord, I have heard him say, that peace, though in a way of unrighteousness, is better than trouble with truth.

Clerk. Where did you hear him say this?

Hate-lies. I heard him say it in Folly-yard, at the house of one Mr Simple, next door to the sign of the Self-deceiver. Yea, he hath said this, to my knowledge, twenty times in that place.*

Court. We may spare further witness; this evidence is plain and full. Set him by, Gaoler, and set Mr No-truth to the bar.——Mr No-truth thou art here indicted by the name of No-truth (an intruder upon the town of Mansoul) for that thou hast always, to the dishonour of Shaddai, and to the endangering of the utter ruin of the famous town of Mansoul, set thyself to de-

No truth set to the bar.
His indictment.

---

* False-peace denies his name, justifies his conduct, and pleads his mild pacific disposition; but the witnesses, Search-truth, Vouch-truth, and others, prove he is rightly called False-peace, and that he had laboured to keep the town in a state of sinful quiet, in the midst of all its abominations, and when it ought to have been alarmed; for " there is no peace, saith my God, to the wicked." Every gracious soul will unite in its condemnation.

face and utterly to spoil all the remainders of the law and image of Shaddai, that have been found in Mansoul, after her deep apostacy from her king, to Diabolus, that envious tyrant. What sayest thou? art thou guilty of this indictment, or not?

No-truth. Not guilty, my lord.

Then the witnesses were called; and Mr Know-all first gave in his evidence against him.

Know-all. My lord, this man was at the pulling down of the image of Shaddai; yea this is he that did it with his own hands. I myself stood by and saw him do it, and he did it at the command of Diabolus. Yea, this Mr No-truth did more than this, he did also set up the horned images of the beast Diabolus, in the same place. This is also he that, at the bidding of Diabolus, rent and tore, and caused to be consumed, all that he could of the remainders of the law of the king, even whatever he could lay his hands on in Mansoul.

His guilt clearly proved.

Clerk. Who saw him do this, besides yourself?

Hate-lies. I did, my lord, and so did many others beside; for this was not done by stealth, or in a corner, but in the open view of all; yea, he chose himself to do it publicly, for he delighted in doing it.

Clerk. Mr No-truth, how could you have the face to plead Not guilty, when you were so manifestly the doer of all this wickedness?

No-truth. Sir, I thought I must say something; and as my name is, so I speak: I have been advantaged thereby, before now, and did not know but, by speaking no truth, I might have reaped the same benefit now.*

His defence.

Clerk. Set him by, Gaoler, and set Mr Pitiless to the bar —Mr Pitiless thou art here indicted by the name of Pitiless (an intruder upon the town of Mansoul,) for that thou didst most treacherously and wickedly shut up all bowels of compassion, and wouldst not suffer poor Mansoul to console her own misery, when she apostatized from her rightful king; but didst evade, and at all times turn her mind away from those thoughts that had in them a tendency to lead her to repentance. What sayest thou to this indictment? guilty, or not guilty?

Pitiless set to the bar.

His indictment.

Pitiless. Not guilty of pitilessness: all I did, was to cheer up,

---

* No-truth, or Falsehood, is a desperate Diabolonian; it was he who defaced the image of God, hated his law, and endeavoured utterly to destroy all goodness in the town; but he that knows all, and who requireth truth in the inward parts, will detect and destroy him.

Pitiless denies his name. according to my name; for my name is not Pitiless, but Cheer-up; and I could not abide to see Mansoul inclined to melancholy.

Clerk. How! do you deny your name, and say it is not Pitiless, but Cheer-up? Call for witness: what say you the witnesses to this plea?

Know-all. My lord, his name is Pitiless; so he hath wrote himself in all papers of concern wherein he has had to do. But these Diabolonians love to counterfeit their names. Mr Covetousness covers himself with the name of Good-husbandry, or the like: Mr Pride can, when need is, call himself Mr Neat, Mr Handsome, or the like, and so of all the rest of them.

Clerk. Mr Tell-true, what say you?

Tell-true. His name is Pitiless, my lord: I have known him from a child; and he hath done all that wickedness wherewith he stands charged in the indictment; but there is a company of them that are not acquainted with the danger of damning, therefore they call all those melancholy, who have serious thoughts how that state should be shunned by them.*

Clerk. Set Mr Haughty to the bar, Gaoler.——Mr Haughty, *Haughty set to the bar.* thou art here indicted by the name of Haughty (an intruder upon the town of Mansoul,) for that thou didst most traitorously and devilishly teach the town of Mansoul to carry it loftily and stoutly against the *His indictment.* summonses that were given them by the captains of the king Shaddai. Thou didst also teach the town of Mansoul to speak contemptuously and villifying of their great king Shaddai; and didst moreover encourage, both by words and example, Mansoul to take up arms both against the king, and his son Immanuel. How sayest thou? art thou guilty of this indictment or not?

Haughty. Gentlemen, I have always been a man of courage and valour, and have not used, when under the greatest clouds, to sneak or hang down the head like a bulrush; nor did it at all at any time please me to see men veil their bonnets to those that have opposed them. Yea, though their adversaries seemed to *Mr Haughty justifies himself.* have ten times the advantage of them. I did not use to consider who was my foe, nor what the cause was in which I was engaged;

---

* Pitiless is charged with wickedly evading all those thoughts which should have led to repentance; but endeavours to exculpate himself under the name of Cheer-up; so many sins shelter themselves under pleasing names:

"With names of virtue she deceives
  The aged and the young;
And while the heedless wretch believes,
  She makes his fetters strong."

it was enough for me if I carried it bravely, fought like a man, and came off a victor.

Court. Mr Haughty, you are not here indicted for that you have been a valiant man, nor for your courage and stoutness in times of distress; but for that you have made use of this your pretended valour to draw the town of Mansoul into acts of rebellion both against the great king and Immanuel his son. This is the crime, and the thing wherewith thou art charged in and by the indictment. But he made no answer to that.*

Now when the court had thus far proceeded against the prisoners at the bar, then they put them over to the verdict of their jury, to whom they addressed themselves after this manner:

Court. Gentlemen of the jury, you have been here, and have seen these men: you have heard their indictments, their pleas, and what the witnesses have testified against them: now what remains, is, that you forthwith withdraw yourselves to some place, where without confusion you may consider of what verdict, in a way of truth and righteousness, you ought to bring in for the king against them, and bring it in accordingly.

The Court's address to the jury.

Then the jury, to wit, Mr Belief, Mr True-heart, Mr Upright, Mr Hate-bad, Mr Love-good, Mr See-truth, Mr Heavenly-mind, Mr Moderate, Mr Thankful, Mr Humble, Mr Goodwork, and Mr Zeal-for-God, withdrew themselves, in order to their work. Now when they were shut up by themselves, they fell to discourse among themselves, in order to the drawing up of their verdict.

And thus Mr Belief (for he was the foreman) began "Gentlemen," quoth he, "for the men, the prisoners at the bar; for my part, I believe that they all deserve death." "Very right," said Mr True-heart, "I am wholly of your opinion.' "And so am I," said Mr Upright. "O what a mercy is it," said Mr Hate-bad, "that such villains as these are apprehended!" "Ay, ay," said Mr Love-good, "this is one of the joyfullest days that ever I saw in my life." Then said Mr See-truth, "I know that if we judge them to death, our verdict shall stand before Shaddai himself." "Nor do I at all question it," said Mr Heavenly-mind; he said moreover, "when all such beasts as these are cast out of Mansoul, what a goodly town will it be then!" Then said Mr Moderate, "It is not my manner to pass my judgment with rashness; but for these, their crimes

The jury deliver in their verdict distinctly.

---

* The haughtiness of man must be brought low, for God abaseth the proud, but giveth grace to the humble.

are so notorious, and the witness so palpable, that that man must be wilfully blind who says the prisoners ought not to die." "Blessed be God," said Mr Thankful, "that the traitors are in safe custody." "And I join with you in this, upon my bare-knees," said Mr Humble. "I am glad also," said Mr Good-work. Then said the warm man, and true-hearted Mr Zeal-for-God, "Cut them off; they have been the plague, and sought the destruction of Mansoul."*

Thus therefore being all agreed in their verdict, they came instantly into the court.

Clerk. Gentlemen of the jury, answer all to your names. Mr Belief, One: Mr True-heart, Two: Mr Upright, Three: Mr Hate-bad, Four: Mr Love-good, Five: Mr See-truth, Six: Mr Heavenly-mind, Seven: Mr Moderate, Eight: Mr Thankful, Nine: Mr Humble, Ten: Mr Good-work, Eleven: Mr Zeal-for-God, twelve: Good men and true, stand together in your verdict: are you all agreed?

Jury. Yes, my lord.

Clerk. Who shall speak for you?

Jury. Our foreman.

Clerk. You, the Gentlemen of the jury, being empannelled for our lord the king, to serve here in a matter of life and death, have heard the trials of each of these men the prisoners at the bar: what say you? are they guilty of that, and those crimes of which they stand here indicted, or are they not guilty?

All pronounced guilty.

Foreman. Guilty, my lord.

Clerk. Look to your prisoners, gaoler.

This was done in the morning, and in the afternoon they received sentence of death according to the law.

The gaoler, therefore, having received such a charge, put them all in the inward prison, to preserve them there till the day of execution, which was to be the next morning.

But now to see how it happened, one of the prisoners, Incredulity by name, in the interim betwixt the sentence and time of execution, broke prison, and made his escape, and got him away quite out of the town of Mansoul, and lay lurking in such places and holes as he might, until he should again have opportunity to do

Incredulity breaks prison.

---

* There is, in the renewed soul, a sincere detestation of all sin. As this jury are unanimous in their verdict, so all real Christians will most cordially unite in the dooming his lusts to death.

"Yes, my Redeemer, they shall die,
My heart hath so decreed;
Nor will I spare the guilty things
That made my Saviour bleed."

the town of Mansoul a mischief for their thus handling of him as they did.

Now when Mr Trueman the gaoler perceived that he had lost his prisoner, he was in a heavy taking, because *he* (that prisoner we speak of) was the very worst of all the gang: wherefore first he goes and acquaints my Lord-mayor, Mr Recorder, and my Lord Will-be-will, with the matter, and to get of them an order to make search for him throughout the town of Mansoul. So an order he got, and search was made, but no such man could now be found in all the town of Mansoul.

All that could be gathered, was, that he had lurked awhile about the outside of the town, and that here and there one or other had a glimpse of him as he made his escape out of Mansoul; one or two also affirmed, that they saw him without the town, going apace quite over the plain.* Now when he was quite gone, it was affirmed by one Mr Did-see, that he ranged all over dry places, till he met with Diabolus his friend, but where should they meet one another but upon Hell-gate-hill. But oh! what a lamentable story did the old gentleman tell to Diabolus, concerning what sad alteration Immanuel had made in Mansoul.

Incredulity goes to Diabolus.

As, first, how Mansoul had after some delays, received a general pardon at the hands of Immanuel; and that they had invited him into the town, and had given him the castle for his possession. He said, moreover, that they had called his soldiers into the town, coveted who should quarter the most of them; they also entertained him with the timbrel, song, and dance. But that, said Incredulity, that is the sorest vexation to me, that he hath pulled down, O father, thy image, and set up his own; pulled down thy officers and set his own. Yea, and Will-be-will, that rebel, who, one would have thought, should never have turned from us, is now in as great favour with Immanuel as ever he was with thee. But, besides all this, this Will-be-will has received a special commission from his Master, to search for, to apprehend, and put to death, all, and all manner of Diabolonians that he shall find in Mansoul: yea, and this Will-be-will has taken and committed to prison already eight of my lord's most trusty friends in Mansoul; nay

And tells him what Immanuel is now doing in Mansoul.

---

* Unbelief was apprehended and condemned—but, alas! he escapes. This incident is introduced by the author with great skill; he eludes justice, and flies to hell, to meditate new mischiefs. Ah! where is the believer who is at all times wholly free from the assaults of this arch-rebel? where is the christian who has not occasion to say, and that with tears, "Lord! I believe, help thou mine unbelief?"

further, my lord, (with grief I speak it,) they have been all arraigned, condemned, and I doubt, before this, executed in Mansoul. I told my lord of eight; and myself was the ninth, who should assuredly have drunk of the same cup, but that through craft I have made mine escape from them.

When Diabolus had heard this lamentable story, he yelled,

Diabolus yells at the news.

and snuffed up the wind like a dragon, and made the sky look dark with his roaring: he also sware that he would try to be revenged of Mansoul for this. So they concluded to enter into great consultation, how they might get the town of Mansoul again.*

Now before this time, the day was come, in which the prisoners in Mansoul were to be executed, Rom. viii. 13. vi. 12, 13, 14. So they were brought to the cross, and that by Mansoul, in most solemn manner: for the prince said, that this should be done by the hand of the town of Mansoul; that I may see, said he, the forwardness of my now redeemed Mansoul to keep my word, and to do my commandments; and that I may bless Mansoul in doing this deed, Gal. v. 24. Proof of sincerity pleases me well, let Mansoul therefore first lay their hands upon these Diabolonians to destroy them.

So the town of Mansoul slew them, according to the word of

The prisoners executed.

their prince; but when the prisoners were brought to the cross to die, you can hardly believe what troublesome work Mansoul had of it to put the Diabolonians to death; for the men knowing that they must die, and all of them having implacable enmity in their heart to Mansoul, what did they do but take courage at the cross, and there resist the men of the town of Mansoul! Wherefore the men of Mansoul were forced to cry out for help to the captains and men of war. Now the great Shaddai had a secretary in the town, and he was a great lover of the men of Mansoul, and he was at the place of execution also; so he hearing the men of Mansoul cry out against the strugglings and unruliness of the prisoners, rose up from his place, and came and put his hands upon the hands of the men of Mansoul. So they crucified the Diabolonians that had been a plague, a grief, and an offence to the town of Mansoul, Rom. viii. 13.†

---

*As the conversion of sinners occasions joy in heaven, so, probably, it produces vexation and grief in hell.

† The greatest proof of our sincere attachment to Christ is the destruction of our sins; not suffering them to reign in our mortal bodies, but crucifying the flesh with its affections and lusts: But indeed our sins struggle much, and die hard, and our own native strength is insufficient for their mortification; the Spirit therefore is introduced as helping in this work;—for, "if we, through the Spirit, do mortify the deeds of the body, we shall live," Rom. viii. 13.

CHAPTER XI.

Mr Experience is made an officer. The Charter of the Town graciously renewed, and enlarged with special privileges. The ministry of the Gospel regularly established under the direction of the secretary. Mr Conscience ordained a preacher. Directions how to behave to the ministers. The inhabitants are clad in white. God's peace appointed to rule. The unexampled felicity of the town.

NOW when this good work was done, the prince came down to see, to visit, to speak comfortably to the men of Mansoul, and to strengthen their hands in such work. And he said to them, that by this act of their's he had proved them, and found them to be lovers of his person, observers of his laws, and such as had also respect to his honour. He said moreover (to show them that they by this should not be losers, nor the town of Mansoul weakened by the loss of them,) that he would make them another captain, and that of one of themselves; and that this captain should be the ruler of a thousand, for the good and benefit of the now flourishing town of Mansoul.

The prince comes down to congratulate them.

He promises to make them a new captain.

So he called one to him whose name was Waiting, and said to him, Go quickly up to the castle-gate, and inquire there for one Mr. Experience, that waiteth upon the noble captain the captain Credence, and bid him come hither to me. So the messenger that waited upon the good Prince Immanuel went and said as he was commanded. Now the young gentleman was waiting to see the captain train and muster his men in the castle-yard. Then said Mr Waiting to him, Sir, the prince would that you should come down to his highness forthwith. So he brought him down to Immanuel, and he came and made obeisance before him.

Experience must be the new captain.

Now the men of the town knew Mr Experience well, for he was born and bred in Mansoul; they also knew him to be a man of conduct, of valour, and a person prudent in matters; he was also a comely person, well spoken, and very successful in his undertakings.

The qualifications of their new captain.

Wherefore the hearts of the townsmen were transported with joy when they saw that the prince himself was so taken with Mr Experience that he would needs make him a captain.

So with one consent they bowed the knee before Immanuel, and with a shout said, Let Immanuel live for ever! Then said the prince to the young gentleman whose name was Mr Experience, I have thought good to confer upon thee a place of trust and honour in this my town of Mansoul (then the young man bowed his head and worshipped:) it is, said Immanuel, that thou shouldst be a captain, a captain over a thousand men in my beloved town of Mansoul. Then said the captain, Let the king live! So the prince gave out orders forthwith to the king's secretary, that he should draw up for Mr Experience a commission to make him a captain over a thousand men; and let it be brought to me, said he, that I may set to it my seal. So it was done as commanded. The commission was drawn up, brought to Immanuel, and he set his seal thereto. Then by the hand of Mr Waiting, he sent it away to the captain.

His commission sent him.

Now so soon as the captain had received his commission, he sounded his trumpet for volunteers, and young men came to him apace; yea, the greatest and chief men in the town sent their sons to be inlisted under his command. Thus Captain Experience came under command to Immanuel, for the good of the town of Mansoul. He had for his lieutenant one Mr Skilful, and for his cornet one Mr Memory. His under-officers I need not name; 1 Sam. xvii. 36 37. His colours were the white colours for the town of Mansoul; and the escutcheon was the dead lion and the dead bear.* So the prince returned to his royal palace again.

His under-officers.

Now when he was returned thither, the elders of the town of Mansoul, to wit, My Lord-mayor, the Recorder and the Lord Will-be-will, went to congratulate him, and in special way to thank him for his love, care, and the tender compassion which he showed to his ever-obliged town of Mansoul. So after a while, and some sweet communion between them, the townsmen, having solemnly ended their ceremony, returned to their place again.

Immanuel also appointed them a day wherein he would renew their charter, yea wherein he would renew and enlarge it, mending several faults therein, that Mansoul's yoke might be yet more easy, Heb. viii.

He renews their charter.

3. Matt. xi. And this he did without any desire of their's, even of his own frankness and noble mind. So when he had

---

* Experience in divine things is often of great use to the Christian, especially in seasons of darkness and danger; a recollection of what God has done for us encourages us still to hope in him. The author refers to 1 Sam. xvii. 35, 37, where the stripling David boldly undertakes to encounter Goliath the Philistine giant: " Thy servant, (said he to Saul) slew both the lion and the bear; the Lord who delivered me from the paw of the lion and the bear, will deliver me out of the hand of this Philistine."

sent for and seen their old one, he laid it by, and said, " Now that which decayeth and waxeth old, is ready to vanish away." He said moreover, the town of Mansoul shall have another, and a better.* An epitome whereof take as follows:

"I, Immanuel, Prince of peace, and a great lover of the town of Mansoul, do, in the name of my Father, and of my own clemency, give, grant, and bequeath to my beloved town of Mansoul:

The charter of the town of Mansoul. "First, Free and full forgiveness of all wrongs, injuries, and offences, done by them against my father, me, their neighbours, or themselves, Heb. viii. John xvii. 8. 14.

"Secondly, I do give them the holy law, and my testament, with all therein contained, for their everlasting comfort and consolation, 2 Pet. i. 4. 2 Cor. vi. 1. 1. John, i. 16.

"Thirdly, I do also give them a portion of the self-same grace and goodness that dwells in my father's heart and mine.

"Fourthly, I do give, grant, and bestow upon them freely the world, and what is therein, for their good, 1 Cor. iii. 21, 22. And they shall have that power over it, as shall stand with the honour of my father, my glory, and their comfort; yea, I grant them the benefits of life and death, and of things present and things to come. This privilege, no other city, town, or corporation shall have, but my Mansoul only.

"Fifthly, I do give and grant them leave, and free access to me in my palace at all seasons, there to make known their wants to me; and I give them moreover a promise, that I will hear and redress all their grievances, Heb. x. 19, 20. Matt. vii. 7.

"Sixthly, I do give, grant to, and invest the town of Mansoul with full power and authority to seek out, take, enslave and destroy, all, and all manner of Diabolonians, that at any time, from whencesoever, shall be found straggling in or about the town of Mansoul.

"Seventhly, I do further grant to my beloved town of Mansoul, that they shall have authority not to suffer any foreigner or stranger, or their seed, to be free in and of the blessed town of Mansoul, nor to share in the excellent privileges thereof: but that all the grants, privileges, and immunities, that I bestow upon the famous town of Mansoul, shall be for those the old natives, and true inhabitants thereof; to them, I say, and to their right seed after them, Eph. iv. 22. Col. iii. 5—9. But all Dia-

* The new charter is the covenant of grace, which is established on better promises than the old dispensation. It contains many great and precious privileges here judiciously enumerated.

bolonians, of what sort, birth, country or kingdom soever, shall be debarred a share therein."

So when the town of Mansoul had received their gracious charter (which in itself is infinitely more large,) they carried it to audience, that is, to the market-place, and there Mr Recorder read it in the presence of all the people, 2 Cor. iii. 5. Jer. xxxi. 33. Heb viii. 10. This being done, it was had back to the castle-gates, and there fairly engraven upon the doors thereof, and laid in letters of gold, to the end that the town of Mansoul, with all the people thereof, might always have it in their view, or might go where they might see what a blessed freedom their prince had bestowed upon them, that their joy might be increased in themselves, and their love renewed to their great and good Immanuel.

Their charter set upon the castle-gates.

But what joy, what comfort, what consolation, think you, did now possess the hearts of the men of Mansoul! The bells rung, the minstrels played, the people danced, the captains shouted, the colours waved in the wind, the silver trumpets sounded, and all the Diabolonians now were glad to hide their heads.*

When this was over, the prince sent for the elders of Mansoul, and communed with them about a ministry he intended to establish among them; such a ministry, that might open unto them, and instruct them in the things that concerned their present and future state; for, said he, you, of yourselves, unless you have teachers and guides, will not be able to know, and, if not to know, to be sure not to do, the will of my father, Jer. x. 23. 1 Cor. ii. 14.

At this news, when the elders of Mansoul brought it to the people, the whole town came running together (for it pleased them well, as whatever the prince now did, pleased the people,) and all with one consent implored his majesty, that he would forthwith establish such a ministry among them, as might teach them both law and judgment, statute and commandment; that they might be documented in all good and wholesome things. So he told them he would grant their requests; and would establish two among them, one that was of his father's court, and one that was a native of Mansoul.

The common good thoughts.

---

* Well may the Christian exult in the blessings of the new and everlasting covenant, which is "ordered in all things and sure." The world, life, death, things present, and things to come, all is our's if we are Christ's." This charter was set upon the castle-gates; may it be inscribed, in indelible characters, on our hearts; while every power of the soul is filled with joy, and sin, abashed, hides its head.

He that s from the court, said he, is a person of no less
quality and dignity than my father and I, 2
Pet. i. 21. 1 Cor. ii. 10. John i. 1. v. 7.
And he is the lord chief secretary of my father's house; for he
is, and always has been, the chief dictator of all my father's laws;
a person well skilled in all mysteries, and knowledge of mysteries, as is my father, or as myself is. Indeed he is one with
us in nature, and also as to loving of, and being faithful to, and in
the eternal concerns of, the town of Mansoul.

The Holy Spirit.

And this is he, said the prince, that must be your chief teacher; for 'tis he, and he only, that can teach you clearly in all
high and supernatural things: he, and he only, it is, that knows
the ways and methods of my father's court; nor can any, like
him, show how the heart of my father is at all times, in all things,
upon all occasions, towards Mansoul; for, " as no man knows
the things of a man, but the spirit of a man which is in him,"
John xiv. 26. xiv. 13. 1 John ii. 27; so the things of my father
knows no man, but this his high and mighty secretary; nor can
any (as he) tell Mansoul how and what they shall do, to keep
themselves in the love of my father. He also it is that can bring
lost things to your remembrance, and that can tell you things to
come. This teacher, therefore, must have the pre-eminence
(both in your affections and judgment) before your other teacher;
his personal dignity, the excellency of his teaching, also the
great dexterity that he hath to assist you to make and draw up
petitions to my father for your help, and to his pleasing, must
lay obligations upon you to love him, fear him, and to take heed
that you grieve him not, 1 Thess. i. 5, 6.

This person can put life and vigour into all he says; yea, and
can also put it into your hearts, Acts xxi. 10,
11. This person can make seers of you, and
can make you tell what shall be hereafter,
Jude 20. Eph. vi. 18. Rom. viii. 16. Rev. ii. 7, 11, 17, 29.
Eph. iv. 30. Isaiah lxiii. 10. By this person you must frame
all your petitions to my father and me; and without his advice
and counsel first obtained, let nothing enter into the town or
castle of Mansoul, for that may disgust and grieve this noble
person.

The office of the Holy Spirit.

Take heed, I say, that you do not grieve this minister; for if
you do he may fight against you; and should he once be moved
by you to set himself against you in battle array, that will distress
you more than if twelve legions should be sent from my father's
court to make war upon you.

But (as I said) if you shall hearken unto him, and shall love him; if you shall devote yourselves to his teaching, and shall seek to have converse, and to maintain communion with him; you shall find him ten times better than is the whole world to any, 1 Cor. xiii. 14. Rom. v. 5. Yea, he will shed abroad the love of my father in your hearts, and Mansoul will be the wisest and most blessed of all people.*

Conscience made a minister.
Then did the prince call unto him the old gentlemen, who afore had been the recorder of Mansoul, Mr Conscience by name, and told him, that forasmuch as he was well skilled in the law and government of the town of Mansoul, and was also well-spoken, and could pertinently deliver to them his master's will in all terrene and domestic matters, therefore he would also make him a minister for, in, and to the goodly town of Mansoul, in all the laws, statutes, and judgments of the famous town of Mansoul. And thou must, said the prince, confine thyself to the teaching of moral virtues, to the civil and natural duties; but thou must not attempt or presume to be a revealer of those high and supernatural mysteries that are kept close in the bosom of Shaddai my father, for those things knoweth no man, nor can any reveal them but my father's secretary only. Thou art a native of the town of Mansoul, but the lord secretary is a native with my father; wherefore, as thou hast knowledge of the laws and customs of the corporation, so he of the things and will of my father.

Wherefore, oh Mr Conscience, although I have made thee minister and a preacher to the town of Mansoul, yet as to the things which the lord secretary knoweth, and shall teach to this people, there thou must be his scholar, and a learner, even as the rest of Mansoul are. Thou must, therefore, in all high and supernatural things, go to him for information; for though there be a spirit in man, this person's inspiration must give him understanding, Job xxviii. 2. Wherefore, O thou Mr Recorder, be humble, and remember, that the Diabolonians, that kept not their first charge, but left their own standing, are now made prisoners in the pit. Be therefore content with thy station.

His power in Mansoul.
I have made thee my father's vicegerent on earth, in such things of which I have made mention before. And take thou power to teach them to Mansoul, yea, and to impose them with whips and chastisements, if

---

* The ministry of the gospel is established in Mansoul, under the direction of the Holy Spirit. He is the chief teacher in all divine things: from him all spiritual wisdom proceeds; by him the ordinary pastors of the church are instructed, and by his power alone their ministrations become useful. His gracious offices and influences are here charmingly stated.

they shall not willingly hearken to do thy commandments. And Mr Recorder, because thou art old and feeble, therefore I give thee leave and license to go when thou wilt to my fountain, my conduit, and there to drink freely of the blood of my grape, for my conduit doth always run wine, Heb. ix. 14. Thus doing, thou shalt drive from thy heart and stomach all foul, gross, and hurtful humours. It will also lighten thine eyes and strengthen thy memory for the reception and keeping of all that the king's most noble secretary teacheth.

When the prince had thus put Mr Recorder (that once so was) into the place and office of a minister of Mansoul, and the man had thankfully accepted thereof, then did Immanuel address himself to the townsmen themselves.

"Behold (said the prince to Mansoul) my love and care towards you; I have added to all that is past this mercy, to appoint you preachers, the most noble secretary, to teach you in all sublime mysteries; and this gentleman (pointing to Mr Conscience) is to teach you in all things human and domestic, for therein lieth his work. He is not, by what I have said, debarred of telling to Mansoul any thing that he hath heard from the lord high secretary; only he shall not attempt or presume to pretend, to be a revealer of those high mysteries himself; for the breaking of them up, and the discovery of them to Mansoul, lieth only in the power, authority, and skill of the lord high secretary himself. Talk of them he may, and so may the rest of the town of Mansoul, as they have opportunity, press them upon each other for the benefit of the whole. These things I would have you observe and do: for it is for your life, and the lengthening of your days.

The prince's speech to Mansoul.

A license to Mansoul.

"And one thing more to my beloved town of Mansoul: You must not dwell in, nor stay upon, any thing of that which he hath in commission to teach you as to your trust and expectation of the next world: of the next world, I say, for I propose to give another to Mansoul when this with them is worn out, but for that you must wholly and solely have recourse to, and make stay upon his doctrine, that is your teacher after the first order. Yea, Mr Recorder himself must not look for life from that which he himself revealeth; his dependance for that must be founded in the doctrine of the other preacher. Let Mr Recorder also take heed that he receive not any doctrine, or point of doctrine, that is not communicated to him by his superior teacher, nor yet within the precincts of his own formal knowledge."*

---

* Admirably judicious is this charge to the Rev. Mr Conscience, ordained a preacher in Mansoul. The office of Conscience is to compare the heart and

Now after the prince had thus settled things in the famous town of Mansoul, he proceeded to give the elders of the corporation a necessary caution; to wit how they should carry it to the noble captains that he had sent or brought with him from his father's court, to the famous town of Mansoul. "These captains," said he, "love the town of Mansoul, and they are men picked out of abundance, as men that best suit, and that will most faithfully serve in the wars of Shaddai against the Diabolonians, for the preservation of the town of Mansoul. I charge you, therefore, said he, O ye inhabitants of the now flourishing town of Mansoul, that you carry it not untowardly to my captains and their men; since they are picked and choice men, men chosen out of many for the good of the town of Mansoul. I say, I charge you, that you carry it not untowardly to them; for though they have the hearts and faces of lions, when at any time they shall be called forth to engage and fight with the king's foes, and the enemies of the town of Mansoul, yet a little discountenance cast upon them from the town of Mansoul, will deject and cast down their faces, will weaken and take away their courage. Do not, therefore, carry it unkindly to my valiant captains, and courageous men of war, but love them, nourish them, succour them, and lay them to your bosoms, and they will not only fight for you, but cause to fly from you all those Diabolonians that seek, and will, if possible, prove your utter destruction.

He gives them caution about the captains.

The citizens of Mansoul must behave kindly to the captains.

"If, therefore, any of them should at any time be sick, or weak, and so not able to perform that office of love which with all their hearts they are willing to do (and will do also when well and in health,) Heb. xii. 12. Isa. xxxv. 3, slight them not, nor despise them, but rather strengthen and encourage them, though weak and ready to die; for they are your fence and your guard, your walls, gates, locks, and bars, Rev. iii. 2. 1 Thess. v. 14. And although, when they are weak they can do but little, but rather need to be helped by you, than that you should then expect great things from them; yet when well, you know what exploits and warlike achievements they can do, and will perform for you.

walk of the christian with the word of God, and so to judge whether it be good or bad; but Conscience is not to decide on the secret decrees of God, nor pretend to reveal new doctrines; Conscience is not the legislator, but the minister of the law, and must ever look up to the Holy Spirit for his teaching. Yet Conscience is here armed with great authority, and permitted to chastise the soul when it offends. But conscience itself needs purifying by the blood of Christ, and refreshment also from the same source. Heb. ix. 14.

"Besides, if they be weak, the town of Mansoul cannot be strong; if they be strong, then Mansoul cannot be weak: your safety therefore doth lie in their health, and in your countenancing them. Remember also, that if they be sick, they catch that disease of the town of Mansoul itself.*

"These things I have said unto you, because I love your welfare, and your honour: observe, therefore, oh my Mansoul, to be punctual in all things that I have given in charge unto you, and that not only as a town corporate, and so to your officers and guard and guides in chief, but to you as you are a people whose well-being, as single persons, depends on the observation of the orders and commandments of their Lord. Next, oh my Mansoul! I warn you of that, of which, notwithstanding the reformation that is at present wrought among you, you have need to be warned about; wherefore hearken diligently unto me. I am now sure, and you will know hereafter, that there are yet some Diabolonians remaining in the town of Mansoul; Diabolonians that are sturdy and implacable, and that do already, while I am yet with you, and that will yet more when I am from you, study, plot, contrive, invent, and jointly attempt to bring you to desolation, and so to a state far worse than that of Egyptian bondage; they are the avowed friends of Diabolus, therefore look about you, Matt. vii. 21, 22. They used, therefore, to lodge with their prince in the castle, when Incredulity was lord-mayor of this town; but since my coming hither they lie more in the outsides and walls, and have made themselves dens, and caves, and holes, and strong holds therein, Rom. vii. 18. Wherefore, oh Mansoul! thy work as to this will be so much the more difficult and hard; that is, to take, mortify, and put them to death, according to the will of my father. Nor can you utterly rid yourselves of them, unless you should pull down the walls of your town, the which I am by no means willing you should. Do you ask me, what shall we then do? Why, be you diligent, and quit you like men; observe their holds, find out their haunts, assault them, and make no peace with them; wherever they haunt, lurk, or abide, and what terms of peace soever they offer you, abhor; and all shall be well betwixt you and me. And that you may the better know them from the natives of Mansoul, I will give you this brief schedule of the

A caution about the Diabolonians that yet remain in Mansoul.

---

* The instructions given to Mansoul respecting their behaviour to the ministers of the gospel is perfectly scriptural. They are to be "esteemed very highly in love for their works sake;" they are to be encouraged and strengthened; for this is profitable to the people, as well as a debt of love due to God and them.

names of the chief of them; and they are these that follow: The Lord Fornication, the Lord Adultery, the Lord Murder, the Lord Anger, the Lord Lasciviousness, the Lord Deceit, the Lord Evil-eye, Mr Drunkenness, Mr Revelling, Mr Idolatry, Mr Witchcraft, Mr Variance, Mr Emulation, Mr Wrath, Mr Strife, Mr Sedition, and Mr Heresy. These are some of the chief, O Mansoul! of those that will seek to overthrow thee for ever: these, I say, are the skulkers in Mansoul; but look well into the law of the king, and thou shalt find their physiognomy and such other characteristical notes of them whereby they may be known.*

The names of some of the Diabolonians in Mansoul.

"These, O my Mansoul! (and I would gladly that you should certainly know it) if they be suffered to run and range about the town as they wish, would quickly, like vipers, eat out your bowels, yea, poison your captains, cut the sinews of your soldiers, break the bars and bolts of your gates, and turn your now most flourishing Mansoul into a barren, desolate wilderness and ruinous heap. Wherefore, that you may take courage to yourselves to apprehend those villians wherever you find them, I give to you, my Lord-mayor, my Lord Will-be-will, and Mr Recorder, with all the inhabitants of the town of Mansoul, full power and commission to seek out, to take, and cause to be put to death by the cross, all manner of Diabolonians, wherever you shall find them lurk within or without the walls of the town of Mansoul. I told you before that I had placed a standing ministry among you; not that you have but these with you, for my four first captains, who came against the master and lord of the Diabolonians that was in Mansoul, they can, and (if need be) if they be required, will not only privately inform, but publicly preach to the corporation, good and wholesome doctrine. yea, they will set up a weekly, and, if need be, a daily lecture in thee, O Mansoul! and will instruct thee in such profitable lessons, that, if attended to, will do thee good at the end. And take good heed that you spare not the men whom you have a commission to take and crucify.

A commission to destroy the Diabolonians.

"Now, as I have set before your eyes the vagrants and runagates by name, so I will tell you, that among yourselves some of them shall creep in to beguile you,

A caution.

---

* It is absolutely necessary for Christians to watch and pray against their remaining corruptions, the sin that dwelleth in them; for though their lusts do not possess the castle of the heart, yet they have their private lurking places. They are therefore to be diligently sought after, and may be known by their physiognomy (the distinguishing cast of the face.) They are truly wise who study this scriptural physiognomy, and so detect the true character of sin.

even such as would seem, and that in appearance are, very rife and hot for religion: and they, if you watch not, will do you a mischief, such an one as you do not think of. These will show themselves to you in another hue than those under the description before; wherefore watch and be sober, and suffer thyself not to be betrayed."*

When the prince had thus far new-modelled the town of Mansoul, and had instructed them in such matters as were profitable for them to know; then he appointed another day, on *Another privilege in Mansoul.* which he intended, when the townsfolk came together, to bestow a further badge of honour upon the town of Mansoul: a badge that should distinguish them from all people, kindreds and tongues that dwell in the kingdom of Universe. Now it was not long before the day appointed came, and the prince and the people met in the king's palace, where first Immanuel made a short speech unto them, and then did for them as he had said, and unto them as he had promised.

His speech to Mansoul. "My Mansoul," said he "that which I now am about to do, is, to make you known to the world to be mine, and to distinguish you also in your own eyes, from all false traitors that may creep in among you."

Then he commanded that those that waited upon him should go and bring forth out of his treasury those white glittering robes that I, said he, have provided and laid up in store for my Mansoul. So the white garments were fetched, and laid forth to the eyes of the people, Rev. xix. 8. Moreover, it was granted to them, that they should take them and put them on. So the people were put into white, into fine linen, white and clean.

Then said the prince unto them, "This, O Mansoul! is my livery, and the badge by which mine are known from the servants of others. Yea, it is that which I grant to all that are mine, and without which no man is permitted to see my face. Wear them, therefore, for my sake, who gave them unto you; and also if you would be known by the world to be mine."

But now, can you think how Mansoul shone! It was fair as the sun, clear as the moon, and terrible as an army with banners.

The prince added further, and said, "No prince, potentate, or mighty one of Universe, giveth this livery but myself: behold, therefore, as I said before, you shall be known by it to be mine.

---

* There are spiritual wickedness, lusts of the mind, as well as of the flesh, which are more apt to deceive, as they assume the mask of religion; such as spiritual pride, self-righteousness, self-seeking and superstition.

"And now," said he, "I have given you my livery, let me give you also in commandment concerning them: and be sure that you take good heed to my words.

"First, Wear them daily, day by day, least you should at some times appear to others as if you were none of mine," Eccl ix. 8.

"Secondly, Keep them always white: for if they be soiled, it is dishonour to me," Rev. iii. 2.

"Thirdly, Wherefore gird them up from the ground, and let them not be soiled with dust or dirt.

"Fourthly, Take heed that you lose them not, least you walk naked and they see your shame.

"Fifthly, But if you should sully them, if you should defile them (the which I am unwilling you should, and the prince Diabolus would be glad if you would,) Rev. vii. 14—17, then speed to do that which is written in my law, that yet you may stand, and not fall before me, and before my throne, Luke xxi. 36. Also, this is the way to cause that I may not leave you nor forsake you while here, but dwell in this town of Mansoul for ever.*

And now was Mansoul, and the inhabitants of it, as the signet upon Immanuel's right hand: where was there now a town, a city, a corporation, that could compare with Mansoul! A town redeemed from the hand and power of Diabolus! A town that the king Shaddai loved, and that he sent Immanuel to regain from the prince of the infernal cave; yea, a town that Immanuel loved to dwell in, and that he chose for his royal habitation; a town that he fortified for himself, and made strong by the force of his arm. What shall I say! Mansoul has now a most excellent prince, golden captains and men of war, weapons proved, and garments as white as snow. Nor are these benefits to be counted little, but great; can Mansoul esteem them so, and improve them to that end and purpose for which they are bestowed upon them.

The glorious state of Mansoul.

When the prince had thus completed the modelling of the town, to show that he had great delight in the works of his hands, and took pleasure in the good that he had wrought for

---

* This idea of the white raiment is borrowed from Rev. xix. 3, "And to her (that is to the church, the spouse of the Lamb) was granted that she should be arrayed in fine linen, clean and white, for the fine linen is the righteousness of the saints." This is a lively emblem of honour and favour, of purity and holiness; "for the fine linen (says Dr Guise) signifies the righteousness both of justification by faith in the righteousness of Christ, to entitle her to heavenly bliss, and of sanctification by his spirit, to make her meet for enjoying it.

The prince's standard set up. the famous and flourishing town of Mansoul, he commanded, and they set his standard upon the battlements of the castle. And then,

First, he gave them frequent visits: not a day now but the elders of Mansoul must come to him (or he to them) into his palace, 2 Cor. vi. 16. Now they must walk together, and talk of all the great things that he had done, and yet further promised to do for the famous town of Mansoul. Thus would he often do with the Lord-mayor, my Lord Will-be-will, and the honest subordinate preacher Mr Conscience, and Mr Recorder. But oh how graciously, how lovingly, how courteously and tenderly, did this blessed prince carry it towards the town of Mansoul! In all the streets, gardens, orchards, and other places where he came, to be sure the poor should have his blessing and benediction; yea, he would kiss them, and, if they were ill, he would lay hands on them, and make them well. The captains also he would daily, yea sometimes hourly, encourage with his presence and goodly words: for you must know, that a smile from him upon them would put more vigour, life, and stoutness into them, than any thing else under heaven.

The prince would now also feast them, and be with them continually; hardly a week would pass, but a banquet must be had betwixt him and them, 1 Cor. v. 8. You may remember, that some pages before we made mention of one feast that they had together, but now to feast them was a thing more common, every day with Mansoul was a feast-day now. Nor did he, when they returned to their places, send them empty away;

Marks of the prince's favour. either they must have a ring, a gold chain, a bracelet, a white stone, or something; so dear was Mansoul to him now, so lovely was Mansoul in his eyes.*

Secondly, When the elders and townsmen did not come to him, he would send in much plenty of provision upon them; meat that came from court, wine and bread that were prepared for his father's table; yea, such delicates would be send unto them, and therewith would so cover their table, that whoever saw it, confessed that the like could not be seen in any kingdom.

Thirdly, If Mansoul did not frequently visit him as he desired they should, he would walk out to them, knock at their doors, and desire entrance, that amity might be maintained betwixt them and him; if they heard and opened to him, as com-

---

* This describes the blessedness of a close walk with God, and the enjoyment of communion with him; in this happy state and frame every day is a feast day.

monly they would if they were at home, then would he renew his former love, and confirm it too, with some new tokens, and signs of continued favour, Rev. iii. 20. Cant. v. 2.

And it was now amazing to behold, that in that very place where sometimes Diabolus had his abode, and enter- tained the Diabolonians, to the almost utter destruc- tion of Mansoul, the prince of princes should sit eating and drinking with them, while all his mighty captains, men of war, trumpeters, with the singing-men and singing-women of his father, stood round about to wait upon them! Now did Man- soul's cup run over, now did her conduits run sweet wine, now did she eat the finest of the wheat, and drink milk and honey out of the rock! Now she said, How great is his goodness! for since I found favour in his eyes, how honourable have I been!

Mansoul's glory.

The blessed prince also ordained a new officer in the town, Col. iii. 15, and a goodly person he was, his name was Mr God's-peace; this man was set over my Lord Will-be-will, my Lord-mayor, Mr Recorder, the subordinate preacher, Mr Mind, and over all the natives of the town of Mansoul. Himself was not a native of it; but came with the prince Immanuel from the court. He was a great acquaintance of Captain Credence and Captain Good-hope; some say they were akin, and I am of that opinion too, Rom. xv. 13. This man, as I said, was made governor of the town in general, especially over the castle, and Captain Credence was to help him there. And I made great observations of it, that so long as all things went in Mansoul as this sweet-natured gentleman would, the town was in most happy condition. Now there were no jars, no chidings, no inter- ferings, no unfaithful doings, in all the town of Mansoul; every man in Mansoul kept close to his own employment. The gentry, the officers, the soldiers, and all in place, observed their order. And as for the women and children of the town, they followed their business joyfully, they would work and sing from morning till night; so that quite through the town of Mansoul now nothing was to be found but harmony, quietness, joy, and health; and this lasted all that summer. But there was a man in the town of Mansoul, and his name was Mr Carnal-security; this man, after all the mercy bestowed upon this corporation, brought the town of Mansoul into great and grievous slavery and bondage. A brief account of him, and of his doings, take as followeth.*

Holy concep- tions and good thoughts.

---

* "The peace of God, which passeth all understanding, is appointed to keep the heart and mind through Christ Jesus." Phil. iv. 7. Yea, it is authorised

MR. GOD'S-PEACE.   P. 158.

CHAPTER XII.

Carnal security prevailing in the town, a coolness takes place between Immanuel and the inhabitants. He is offended, and privately withdraws. Godly-fear publicly detects the cause, and excites the people to destroy Carnal-security. Measures taken to procure the return of Immanuel.

WHEN Diabolus at first took possession of the town of Mansoul, he brought thither with himself a great number of Diabolonians, men of his own conditions. Now among these there was one whose name was Mr Self-Conceit; and a notable brisk man he was, as any that in those days possessed the town of Mansoul. Diabolus, then, perceiving this man to be active and bold, sent him upon many desperate designs; the which he managed better, and more to the pleasing of his lord, than most that came with him from the dens could do. Wherefore finding him so fit for his purpose, he preferred him, and made him next to the great Lord Will-be-will, of whom we have spoken so much before. Now the Lord Will-be-will, being in those days very well pleased with him and with his atchievements, gave him his daughter, the Lady Fear-nothing, to wife. Now of my Lady Fear-nothing did this Mr Self-conceit beget this gentleman, Mr Carnal-security. Wherefore there being then in Mansoul those strange kind of mixtures, it was hard for them, in some cases, to find out who were natives, who not; for Mr Carnal-security sprang from my Lord Will-be-will by his mother's side, though he had for his father a Diabolonian by nature.

The story of Mr Carnal-Security.

Mr Self-conceit.

Carnal security's original.

Well, this Carnal-security took much after his father and mother: he was self-conceited, he feared nothing, he was also a very busy man: nothing of news, nothing of doctrine, nothing of alteration or talk of alteration, could at any time be on foot in Mansoul, but Mr Carnal-security would be at the head or tail of it. But to be sure he would decline those that he deemed the weakest, and stood always with them (in his way of standing) that he supposed was the strongest side.

His qualities.

Now when Shaddai the mighty and Immanuel his son made

"to rule in the heart always, by all means." This is enjoyed only in the exercise of faith. Happy is the heart where God's peace takes the lead. It is the Christian's first and daily business to maintain this peace within, and then all goes well.

war upon Mansoul to take it, this Mr Carnal-security was then in the town, and was a great doer among the people, encouraging them in their rebellion, and putting them upon hardening themselves in their resisting the king's forces: but when he saw that the town of Mansoul was taken and converted to the use of the glorious prince Immanuel; and when he also saw what was become of Diabolus, and how he was unroosted, and made to quite the castle in the greatest contempt and scorn; and that the town of Mansoul was well lined with captains, engines of war, and men, and also provisions; what doth he but wheel about also, and as he had served Diabolus against the good prince, so he feigned that he would serve the prince against his foes; and, having got some little smattering of Immanuel's things by the end (being bold) he ventures himself into the company of the townsmen, and attempts also to chat among them. Now he knew that the power and strength of the town of Mansoul was great, and that it could not but be pleasing to the people, if he cried up their might and their glory; wherefore he beginneth his tale with the power and strength of Mansoul, and affirmeth, that it was impregnable; now magnifying the captains, and their slings and their rams; then crying up their fortifications and strong holds; and lastly, the assurance that they had from their prince, that Mansoul should be happy forever. But when he saw that some of the men of the town were tickled and taken with this discourse, he makes it his business, and, walking from street to street, house to house, and man to man, he brought also Mansoul to dance after his pipe, and to grow almost as carnally secure as himself; so from talking they went to feasting, and from feasting to sporting, and so to some other matters (now Immanuel was yet in the town of Mansoul, and he wisely observed their doings:) my Lord-mayor, my Lord Will-be-will, and Mr Recorder, were also taken with the words of this tattling Diabolonian gentleman; forgetting that their prince had given them warning before, to take heed that they were not beguiled with any Diabolonian sleight; he had further told them, that the security of the now flourishing town of Mansoul did not so much lie in her present fortifications and force, as in her so using of what she had, as might oblige her Immanuel to abide within her castle. For the right doctrine of Immanuel was that the town of Mansoul should take heed that they forget not his father's love and his; also that they should so demean themselves as to continue to keep themselves therein. Now

How Mr Carnal-security begins the misery of Mansoul.

The heads of Mansoul seduced.

this was not the way to do it, namely, to fall in love with one of the Diabolonians, and with such an one too as Mr Carnal-security was, and to be led up and down by the nose by him: they should have heard their prince, feared their prince, loved their prince, and have stoned this naughty pack to death, and taken care to have walked in the ways of their prince's prescribing; for then should their peace have been as a river; when their righteousness had been like the waves of the sea.*

Now when Immanuel perceived that through the policy of Mr Carnal-security the hearts of the men of Mansoul were chilled and abated in their practical love to him;

Immanuel bemoans Mansoul.

First, he bemoans them, and bewails their state with the secretary, saying, "O that my people had hearkened unto me, and that Mansoul had walked in my ways! I would have fed them with the finest of the wheat; and with honey out of the rock would I have sustained them." This done, he said in his heart, I will return to the court, and go to my place, till Mansoul shall consider and acknowledge their offence. And he did so, and the cause and manner of his going away from them was thus, for that Mansoul declined him, as is manifest in these particulars:

1. They left off their former way of visiting him, they came not to his royal palace as afore.

2. They did not regard, nor yet take notice, that he came, or came not to visit them.

3. The love feasts that had wont to be between their prince and them, though he made them still, and called them to them, yet they neglected to come to them, or to be delighted with them.

4. They waited not for his counsel, but began to be headstrong and confident in themselves, concluding that now they were strong and invincible, and that Mansoul was secure, and beyond all reach of the foe, and that her state must needs be unalterable for ever.

Now, as was said, Immanuel, perceiving that, by the craft of

* Carnal-security is well described, as it is the offspring of Self-conceit and Fear-nothing. This is one of those evils into which the professors of religion may be unwarily drawn; and it proceeds from an abuse of the doctrines of grace. The true doctrine of God, as the author observes, is, that believers should not forget the love of the father and of the son, but so demean themselves as to continue therein; but carnal-security makes men trust to their fortifications, their privileges, rather than to the Lord; and while they boast of perseverance take no care to persevere, but grow careless about prayer, communion with God, and coming to his table; while pride, sloth, and conformity to the world prevail. The spirit has been much encouraged lately by some preachers, and many have been " tickled and taken with their discourse "

Mr Carnal-security, the town of Mansoul was taken off from their dependance upon him, and upon his father by him, and set upon what by them was bestowed upon it; he first, as I said, bemoaned their state; then he used means to make them understand that the way they went on in was dangerous: for he sent my lord high secretary to them, to forbid them such ways; but twice when he came to them, he found them at dinner in Mr Carnal-security's parlour; and perceiving also that they were not willing to reason about matters concerning their good, he took grief and went his way. The which when he had told to the prince Immanuel, he was grieved also, and returned to his father's court.

He endeavours to reclaim them.

They grieve the Holy Ghost and Christ.

Christ withdraws not all at once.

Now the methods of his withdrawing, as I was saying before, were thus:

1. Even while he was yet with them in Mansoul, he kept himself close, and more retired than formerly.

2. His speech was not now, if he came into their company, so pleasant and familiar as formerly.

3. Nor did he, as in times past, send to Mansoul from his table those dainty bits which he was wont to do.

4. Nor, when they came to visit him, as now and then they would, would he be so easily spoken with, as they found him in times past. They might now knock once, yea twice, but he would seem not at all to regard them; whereas formerly he would run and meet them half way, and take them too and lay them in his bosom.*

The working of their affections.

Thus Immanuel carried it now; and by this his carriage he thought to make them bethink themselves, and return to him. But alas! they did not consider, they did not know his ways, they regarded not, they were not touched with these, nor with the true remembrance of former favours, Ezek. xi. 21. Hosea, v. 15. Lev. xxvi. 21—24. Wherefore what does he but in private manner withdraw himself, first from his palace, then to the gate of the town, and so away from Mansoul he goes, till they should acknowledge their offence, and more earnestly seek his face. Mr God's-peace also laid down his commission, and would for the present act no longer. Thus they walked contrary to him, and he again, by way of retaliation, walked contrary to them, Jer. ii. 32. But alas! by this time they were so hard-

---

* Carnal-security, however pleasing to the flesh, grieves the Holy Spirit, destroys spiritual comfort, and causes the Lord to withdraw from the soul. Miserable is this condition, and yet it is often little observed or lamented, such as the hardness of the heart.

ened in their way, and had so drunk in the doctrine of Mr Carnal-security, that the departing of their prince touched them not, nor was he remembered by them when gone; and so of consequence his absence was not bewailed by them.

Now there was a day wherein this old gentleman, Mr Carnal-security, again made a feast for the town of Mansoul, and there was at that time in the town one Mr Godly-fear; one now but little set by, though formerly one of great request. This man, old Carnal-security had a mind if possible, to gull and abuse as he did the rest, and therefore he now bids him to the feast with his neighbours. So the day being come, they prepared, and he goes and appears with the rest of the guests; and being all set at the table, they ate and drank, and were merry, even all but this one man (for Mr Godly-fear set like a stranger, and neither ate nor was merry); which when Mr Carnal-security perceived, he addressed himself in a speech thus to him:

A trick put upon Mr Godly-fear.

He goes to the feast, and sits there like a stranger.

Talk between Mr Carnal-security and Mr Godly-fear.

"Mr Godly-fear are you not well? you seem to be of ill body or mind, or both. I have a cordial of Mr Forget-good's making, which, Sir, if you will take, I hope it may make you bonny and blithe, and so make you more fit for us feasting companions."

Unto whom the good old gentleman discreetly replied: "Sir, I thank you for all things courteous and civil; but for your cordial, I have no list thereto. But a word to the natives of Mansoul: You the elders and chief of Mansoul, to me it is strange to see you so jocund and merry, when the town of Mansoul is in such woful case."

Then said Mr Carnal-security, "You want sleep, good Sir, I doubt. If you please, lie down and take a nap, and we the mean while will be merry."

Then said Mr Godly-fear as follows: "Sir, if you were not destitute of an honest heart, you could not do as you have done, and do."

Then said Mr Carnal-security, "Why?"

Godly-fear. "Nay, pray interrupt me not. It is true, the town of Mansoul was strong and (with a proviso) impregnable; but you have weakened it, and it now lies obnoxious to its foes; nor is it a time to be silent; it is you, Mr Carnal-security, that have stripped Mansoul, and driven her glory from her; you have pulled down her towers; you have broken down her gates, you have spoiled her locks and bars.

"And now to explain myself: From that time that my lord of Mansoul, and you, Sir, grew so great, from that time the strength of Mansoul has been offended; and now he is risen and is gone. If any shall question the truth of my words, I will answer him by this and such like questions: Where is the Prince Immanuel? When did a man or woman in Mansoul see him? When did you hear from him, or taste any of his dainty bits? You are now a feasting with this Diabolonian monster, but he is not your prince; I say, therefore, though enemies from without, had you taken heed, could not have made a prey of you, yet since you have sinned against your prince, your enemies within have been too hard for you."

Mr Godly-fear explains himself.

Then said Mr Carnal-security, "Fie! fie! Mr Godly-fear, fie! Will you never shake off your timorousness? Are you afraid of being sparrow-blasted? Who hath hurt you? Behold, I am on your side; only you are for doubting, and I am for being confident. Besides, is this a time to be sad in? A feast is made for mirth, why then do you now, to your shame and our trouble, break out into such passionate, melancholy language, when you should eat and drink, and be merry?

Then said Mr Godly-fear again, "I may well be sad, for Immanuel is gone from Mansoul: I say again, he is gone, and you, sir, are the man that has driven him away; yea, he is gone without so much as acquainting the nobles of Mansoul with his going; and if that is not a sign of his anger, I am not acquainted with the methods of godliness.

"And now, my lords and gentlemen, my speech is still to you. You gradually declining from him, provoked him to depart from you; the which he did gradually, if perhaps you would have been made sensible thereby, and have been renewed by humbling yourselves: but when he saw that none would regard, or lay these fearful beginnings of his anger and judgment to heart, he went away from this place; and this I saw with mine own eyes. Wherefore now, while you boast, your strength is gone; you are like the man that lost his locks which before waved about his shoulders. You may, with this lord of your feast, shake yourselves and think to do as at other times; but since without him you can do nothing, and he is departed from you, turn your feast into a sigh, and your mirth into lamentation."*

His speech to the elders of Mansoul.

---

* The fear of God in the heart is placed there to prevent utter apostacy, and to detect that carnal security which proves so mischievous. Godly-fear cannot enjoy that carnal mirth which security provides, nor stupify himself

Then the subordinate preacher, old Mr Conscience by name, he that of old was recorder of Mansoul, being startled at what was said, began to second it thus:

Conscience startled.

Conscience. "Indeed, my brethren, quoth he, I fear that Mr Godly-fear tells us true: I, for my part, have not seen my prince a long season. I cannot remember the day, for my part: nor can I answer Mr Godly-fear's question. I am afraid that all is nought with Mansoul."

Godly-fear. "Nay, I know that you will not find him in Mansoul, for he is departed and gone; yea, and gone for the faults of the elders, and for that they rewarded his grace with unsufferable unkindness."

Then did the subordinate preacher look as if he would fall down dead at the table; also, all there present, except the man of the house, began to look pale and wan. But having a little recovered themselves, and jointly agreeing to believe Mr Godly-fear and his sayings, they began to consult what was best to be done [now Mr Carnal-security was gone into his withdrawing room, for he liked not such dumpish doings] both to the man of the house, for drawing them into evil, and also to recover Immanuel's love.

They are all aghast.

Then the saying of their prince came very hot into their minds, concerning the false prophets that should arise to delude the town of Mansoul. So they took Mr Carnal-security (concluding that he was the person) and burnt his house upon him with fire, for he also was a Diabolonian by nature.*

They consult and burn their feast-maker.

When this was past and over, they bespeed themselves to look for Immanuel their prince, Cant. v. 6, and "they sought him, but they found him not;" then were they more confirmed in the truth of Mr Godly-fear's sayings, and began also severely to reflect upon themselves for their vile and ungodly doings; for they concluded now, that their prince had left them.

They apply themselves to the Holy Ghost; but he is grieved, &c.

with Forget-good's cordial; but boldly remonstrates against that gradual decline in religion which occasioned the Lord to withdraw his gracious presence:

"So Samson, when his hair was lost,
Met the Philistines to his cost;
Shook his vain limbs with sad surprise,
Made feeble fight and lost his eyes. *Watts.*

* Carnal-security is such an enemy to the soul, that he should be utterly destroyed. When conscience is roused to oppose this deceitful foe, the business will be done; and measures will be taken to procure, if possible, the return of forfeited blessings.

Then they agreed and went to my lord Secretary, whom before they refused to hear, and had grieved with their doings, to know of him (for he was a seer, and could tell where Immanuel was) how they might direct a petition to him. But the lord Secretary would not admit them to a conference about this matter, nor would admit them to his royal palace, nor come out to them, Isa. lxiii. 10. Eph. iv. 30. 1 Thess. v. 19.

Now was it a day gloomy and dark, a day of clouds and of thick darkness with Mansoul. Now they saw that they had been foolish, and began to perceive what the company and prattle of Mr Carnal-security had done, and what desperate damage his swaggering words had brought poor Mansoul into: but what further it was likely to cost them, that they were ignorant of. Now Mr Godly-fear began to be in great repute with the men of the town; yea, they were ready to look upon him as a prophet.

Well, when the sabbath-day was come, they went to hear their subordinate preacher; but oh, how did it thunder and lighten this day! His text was that in the prophet Jonah, "They that observe lying vanities, forsake their own mercies," ch. ii. 8. But there was then such power and authority in that sermon, and such a dejection seen in the countenances of the people that day, that the like hath seldom been heard or seen. The people, when sermon was done, were scarce able to go to their homes, or to betake themselves to their employs the week after; they were so sermon-smitten, and also so sermon sick, that they knew not what to do,

A thundering sermon.

Hos. vi. 13. He not only showed Mansoul their sin, but trembled before them under the sense of his own, still crying out of himself, as he preached to them, "Unhappy man that I am! that I should do a wicked thing! that I, a preacher! whom the prince did set up to teach Mansoul his law, should myself live senseless and sottishly here, and be one of the first found in transgression! This transgression also fell within my precincts: I should have cried out against the wickedness; but I let Mansoul lie wallowing in it, until it had driven Immanuel from its borders." With these things he also charged all the lords and gentry of Mansoul, to the almost distracting of them, Psalm lxxxviii.

The subordinate preacher acknowledges his fault, and bewails his compliance with Mr Carnal-security.

About this time also there was a great sickness in the town of Mansoul, and most of the inhabitants were greatly afflicted: yea, the captains also and men of war were brought thereby to a languishing condition, and that for a long time together; so that in

A great sickness in Mansoul.

on, nothing could to purpose now have been
he townsmen or field officers, Heb. xii. 12, 13.
ii. 24. Oh, how many pale faces, weak hands,
l staggering men, were now seen to walk the
ul! Here were groans, there pants, and yonder
re ready to faint.
too, which Immanuel had given them, were but
some were rent, some were torn, and all in a
some also hung so loosely upon them, that the
ame at was ready to pluck them off.
ne spent in this sad and desolate condition, the
cher called for a day of fasting, and to humble
being so wicked against the great Shaddai and
s Son: and he desired that Captain Boanerges
ould preach; which he consented to do: and the
y being come, his text was this: "Cut it down;
y cumbereth it the ground?" and a very smart
upon the text. First, he showed what was
the words, to wit, "because the fig-tree was
he showed what was contained in the sentence,
e or utter desolation. He next showed by whose
ntence was pronounced, and that was by Shad-
nd lastly, he showed the reasons of the point:
led his sermon. But he was very pertinent in
insomuch that he made poor Mansoul tremble:
is well as the former, wrought much upon the
en of Mansoul; yea, it greatly helped to keep
were roused by the preaching that went before;
ighout the whole town there was little or noth-
or seen but sorrow, and mourning, and wo.*

mon they got together, and consulted what was
est to be done. But, said the subordinate preach-
, I will do nothing of my own head, without ad-
sing with my neighbour Mr Godly-fear. So
ient for Mr Godly-fear, and he forthwith appear-
desired that he would further show his opinion
had best to do: wherefore the old gentlemen
i; "It is my opinion that this town of Mansoul
ay of her distress, draw up and send an humble
offended prince Immanuel, that he, in favour

was one of the first messengers to the town, had with-
preachers were introduced, as more suited to the state of
they need to be roused from their sloth, and Boanerges
i times of spiritual declension awakening sermons are very

and grace, will turn again unto them, and not keep his anger forever."

When the townsmen had heard this speech, they unanimously agreed to his advice; so they presently drew up their request; and the next question was, But who shall carry it? At last they all agreed to send it by my Lord-mayor, who accepted the service, and addressed himself to his journey; after which, he came to the court of Shaddai, whither Immanuel the prince of Mansoul was gone, Lam. iii. 8, 44; but the gate was shut, and a strict watch kept thereat; so that the petitioner was forced to stand without for a great while together. Then he desired that som would go in to the prince, and tell him who stood at the gate, and also what his business was. Accordingly one went and told Shaddai and Immanuel his son, that the Lord-mayor of the town of Mansoul stood without at the gate of the king's court, desiring to be admitted into the presence of the prince, the king's son. He also told the Lord-mayor's errand both to the king and his son Immanuel. But the prince would not come down, nor admit that the gate should be opened, but sent an answer to this effect, Jer. ii. 27, 28. "They have turned their back unto me, and not their face; but now, in the time of their trouble, they say unto me, Arise and save us. But can they not now go to Mr Carnal-security, to whom they went when they turned from me, and make him their leader, their lord, and their protector? And now in their trouble they visit me, from whom in their prosperity they went astray."

They send the Lord-mayor to court.

This answer made my Lord-mayor look black in the face; it troubled, it perplexed, it rent him sore, Lam. iv. 7, 8. And now he began to see what it was to be familiar with Diabolonians, such as Mr Carnal-security was. When he saw that at court (as yet) there was little help to be expected, either for himself or friends in Mansoul; he smote upon his breast and returned weeping, and all the way bewailing the lamentable state of Mansoul.

The lord mayor returns and how.

When he was come within sight of the town, the elders and chief of the people of Mansoul went out at the gate to meet him, and to salute him, and to know how he sped at court. But he told them his tale in so doleful a manner, that they all cried out and mourned and wept. Wherefore they threw ashes and dust upon their heads, and put sackcloth upon their loins, and went crying out through the town of Mansoul; which when the rest of the townsfolk saw, they all mourned and wept. This therefore was a day of re-

The state of Mansoul now.

uke, trouble and anguish to the town of Mansoul, and also of great distress.

After some time, when they had somewhat recovered themselves, they came together to consult again what was yet to be done; and they asked advice, as they did before, of the Rev. Mr Godly-fear; who told them, that there was no way better to do than to do as they had done, nor would he that they should be discouraged at all with what they had met with at court; yea, though several of their petitions should be answered with naught but silence or rebuke; for, said he, it is the way of the wise Shaddai to make men wait, and to exercise patience; and it should be the way of them in want to be willing to stay his leisure.

They again consult Godly-fear.

Then they took courage, and sent again and again, and again and again; for there was not a day nor an hour, that went over Mansoul's head, wherein a man might not have met upon the road one or other riding post from Mansoul to the court of king Shaddai, and all with letters petitionary in behalf of, and for the prince's return, to Mansoul. The road, I say, was now full of messengers, going and returning, and meeting one another; some from the court, and some from Mansoul; and this was the work of the miserable town of Mansoul all that long, that sharp, that cold and tedious winter.*

See now what is the work of a backsliding saint awakened.

Groaning desires.

Now you may remember that I told you before that after Immanuel had taken Mansoul, yea, and after he had new modelled the town, there remained, in several lurking places of the corporation, many of the old Diabolonians, that either came with the tyrant when he invaded and took the town, or that had there (by reason of unlawful mixtures in their birth, breeding, and bringing up) their holes, dens, and lurking places in, under, or about the walls of the town; some of their names are, the Lord Fornication, the Lord Adultery, the Lord Murder, the Lord Anger, the Lord Lasciviousness, the Lord Deceit, the Lord Evil-eye, the Lord Blasphemy, and that horrible villain the old and dangerous Lord Covetousness; these, with many more, had yet their abode in the town of Mansoul, even after Immanuel had driven Diabolus out of the castle.

A memento.

Against these the good prince granted a commission to the

---

* Prayer, at all times necessary, becomes peculiarly seasonable when a state of backsliding is discovered. Prayer may not immediately receive an answer, nor forfeited comfort return; but as Godly-fear said, there is no better way than to pray and pray again, and wait the Lord's pleasure.

Lord Will-be-will and others, yea, to the whole town of Mansoul, to seek, take, secure, and destroy, any or all that they could lay hands of; for that they were Diabolonians by nature, enemies to the prince, and those who sought to ruin the blessed town of Mansoul. But Mansoul did not pursue this warrant, but neglected to apprehend, secure, and destroy those Diabolonians; wherefore what do these villains, but by degrees take courage to show themselves to the inhabitants of the town; yea, and as I was told, some of the men of Mansoul grew too familiar with several of them, to the sorrow of the corporation, as you will hear more in time and place.*

Mansoul heeded not the prince's caution, nor put his commission in execution.

CHAPTER XIII.

The Diabolonians take courage from the departure of Immanuel, and plots are formed, in concert with Hell, for a counter-revolution in Mansoul. Covetousness, Lasciviousness, and Anger, by changing their names, are introduced into respectable families, where they corrupt their masters and do incredible mischief. An army of twenty thousand Doubters is raised to surprise the town.

WHEN the Diabolonian lords perceived that Mansoul had, through sinning, offended Immanuel their prince, and that he had withdrawn himself and was gone, what do they but plot the ruin of Mansoul? Accordingly they met together at the hold of one Mr Mischief, who was a Diabolonian, and here consulted how they might deliver up Mansoul into the hands of Diabolus again. Now some advised one way, and some another, every man according to his own liking. At last my Lord Lasciviousness proposed, that some of the Diabolonians in Mansoul should offer themselves for servants to some of the natives of the town; for, said he, if they do so, and Mansoul shall accept of them, they may for us, and for Diabolus our lord, make the taking of the town of Mansoul more easy than otherwise it would be. But then stood up the lord Murder, and said, This may not be done at this time,

The Diabolonians' plot.

---

* When Mansoul first received Immanuel, a strict charge was given to discover and destroy the Diabolonians; but this was too much neglected: the consequence was, that they became to Mansoul what the Canaanites were to Israel, according to the prediction, Numb. xxxiii. 55. "If ye will not drive out the inhabitants of the land from before you, then shall it come to pass, that those which ye let remain of them shall be pricks in your eyes, and thorns in your sides, and shall vex you in the land wherein ye dwell."

CONSPIRATORS   P. 278

for Mansoul is now in a kind of rage, because, by our friend Mr Carnal-security she hath been once ensnared already, and made to offend against her prince; and how shall she reconcile herself unto her lord again, but by the heads of these men? Besides, we know that they have in commission to take and slay us wherever they shall find us; let us therefore be wise as foxes: when we are dead, we can do them no hurt; but while we live, we may.

They send to hell for advice Thus when they had tossed the matter to and fro, they jointly agreed that a letter should forthwith be sent away to Diabolus in their name, by which the state of the town of Mansoul should be showed him, and how much it is under the frowns of their prince; we may also, said some, let him know our intentions, and ask his advice in the case. So a letter was presently framed, the contents of which were these:

"*To our great lord, the Prince Diabolus, dwelling below in the Infernal cave.*

"O great father, and mighty prince Diabolus, we the true Diabolonians, yet remaining in the rebellious town of Mansoul, having received our beings from thee, and our nourishment at thy hands, cannot with content and quiet endure to behold, as we do this day, how thou art dispraised, disgraced and reproached among the inhabitants of this town; nor is thy long absence at all delightful to us, because greatly to our detriment.

"The reason of this our writing to our Lord is, that we are not altogether without hope that this town may become thy habitation again: for it is greatly declined from its prince Immanuel, and he is departed from them; yea, and though they send and send after him, to return to them, yet can they not prevail, nor get good words from him.

"There has been also of late, and is yet remaining, a very great sickness and faintings among them; and that not only upon the poorer sort of the town, but upon the lords, captains, and chief gentry of the place; [we only, who are Diabolonians by nature, remain well, lively and strong]; so that through their great transgression on one hand, and their dangerous sickness on the other, we judge they lie open to thy hand and power. If

They propose a second attempt against Mansoul. therefore it shall stand with thy horrible cunning, and with the cunning of the rest of the princes with thee, to come and make an attempt to take Mansoul again, send us word, and we shall to our utmost power be ready to deliver it into thy hand. Or if what we have said shall not be thought best and most meet to be done, send us thy mind in a few words, and we are all ready to follow thy counsel, to the hazard of our lives, and what else we have.

"Given under our hands this day and date above written, after a close consultation at the house of Mr Mischief, who is yet alive, and hath his place in our desirable town of Mansoul.

Mr Profane is carrier: he brings the letter to Hellgate-hill, and presents it to Cerberus the porter.

When Mr Profane (for he was the carrier was come with his letter to Hellgate-hill, he knocked at the gate for entrance. Then did Cerberus the porter (for he was the keeper of that gate) open to Mr Profane; to whom he delivered his letter which he had brought from the Diabolonians in Mansoul. So he carried it in, and presented it to Diabolus his lord, and said, Tidings, my lord, from Mansoul; and from our trusty friends in Mansoul.

Then came together Beelzebub, Lucifer, Apollyon, with the rest of the rabble there, to hear what news from Mansoul. So the letter was read and Cerberus stood by. When the letter was openly read, and the contents thereof spread into all the corners of the den, command was given, that without lett,

Deadmen's bell, and how it went.

or stop, Deadman's bell should be rung for joy. So the bell was rung, and the princes rejoiced that Mansoul was like to come to ruin. Now the clapper of the bell went, "The town of Mansoul is coming to dwell with us; make room for Mansoul." This bell, therefore, they rang, because they hoped that they should have Mansoul again.*

Now when they had performed this their horrible ceremony, they got together again, to consult what answer to send to their friends in Mansoul; and some advised one thing, and some another; but at length, because the business required haste, they left the whole business to Diabolus, judging him the most proper lord of the place. So he drew up a letter in answer to what Mr Profane had brought, and sent it to the Diabolonians in Mansoul, by the same hand that brought their's to him; and these were the contents thereof:

---

* Wilful departure from God gives courage to our spiritual foes, who rejoice in the hope of making backsliders apostates. Satan will renew his temptations with double force; while lasciviousness, murder, and mischief will unite with him in cunning devices to ruin the soul.

A letter from Diabolus to the Diabolonians his servants in Mansoul.

"*To our Offspring, the high and mighty Diabolonians that yet dwell in the town of Mansoul; Diabolus, the great Prince of Mansoul, wisheth a prosperous issue and conclusion of those many brave enterprises, conspiracies, and designs, that you, of your love and respect to our honour, have in your hearts to attempt to do against Mansoul.*

"Beloved children and disciples, my Lord Fornication, Adultery, and the rest; we have here, in our desolate den, received, to our highest joy and content, your welcome letter, by the hand of our trusty Mr Profane; and to show how acceptable your tidings were, we rang out our bell for gladness; for we rejoiced as much as we could, when we perceived that yet we had friends in Mansoul, and such as sought our honour and revenge in the ruin of the town of Mansoul. We also rejoiced to hear that they are in a degenerate condition, have offended their prince, and that he is gone. Their sickness also pleaseth us, as does also your health, might, and strength. Glad also would we be, right horribly beloved, could we get this town into our clutches again. Nor will we be sparing of our wit, cunning, craft, and hellish inventions, to bring to a wished conclusion this your brave beginning.

"And take this for your comfort, our birth and offspring, that if we again surprise and take it, we will attempt to put all your foes to the sword, and make you the great lords and captains of the place. Nor need you fear (if ever we get it again) that we after that shall be cast out any more; for we will come with more strength, and so take faster hold than we did at first. Besides, it is the law of that prince, which now they own, that if we get them a second time, they shall be our's for ever. Matt. xii. 43—45.

"Do you therefore, our trusty Diabolonians, yet more pry into and endeavour to spy out, the weakness of the town of Mansoul. We would also that you yourselves do attempt to weaken them more and more. Send us word also by what means we had best to attempt the regaining thereof, to wit, whether by persuasion to a vain and loose life; by tempting them to doubt and despair; or by blowing up the town by the gunpowder of pride and self-conceit.* Do you also, O ye brave Diabolonians, and true sons of the pit, be always in a readiness to make a most hor-

---

* These means of destruction are proposed in hell: 1. A Vicious life. 2. Despair of mercy. 3. Prevailing pride; either of these would prove our ruin. But grace prevents.

rid assault within, when we shall be ready to storm it without. Now speed you in your project, and we in our desires, the utmost power of our gates, which is the wish of your great Diabolus, Mansoul's enemy, and him that trembles when he thinks of judgment to come. All the blessing of the pit be upon you! and so we close up our letter.

" Given at the Pit's Mouth, by the joint consent of all the princes of darkness, to be sent (to the force and power that we have yet remaining in Mansoul) by the hand of Mr Profane. "By me, DIABOLUS."

Profane comes home again.

This letter was sent to the Diabolonians that yet remained in Mansoul, and that yet inhabited the wall, from the dark dungeon of Diabolus, by the hand of Mr Profane, by whom they also in Mansoul sent their's to the pit. Now when this Mr Profane returned to Mansoul, he came, as he was wont, to the house of Mr Mischief, for that was the place where the contrivers were met. Now when they saw that their messenger was returned safe and sound, they rejoiced at it. Then he presented them his letter; which when they had read and considered, much augmented their gladness. They asked him after the welfare of their frends; as how their Lord Diabolus, Lucifer, and Beelzebub did, with the rest of those in the den. To which this Profane made answer, Well, well, my Lords, they are well, even as well as can be in their place. They also, said he, rang for joy at reading your letter, as you will perceive by this, when you read it.

Now, as was said, when they had read their letter, and perceived that it encouraged them in their work, they fell to their way of contriving again, how they might complete their design upon Mansoul; and the first thing they agreed upon, was, to keep all things from Mansoul as close as they could.* Let it not be known, let not Mansoul be acquainted with what we design against it. The next thing was, how or by what means they should try to bring to pass the ruin and overthrow of Mansoul; and one said after this manner, and another said after that. Then stood up Mr Deceit, and said, My right Diabolonian friends, our lords, and the high ones of the dungeon, propound unto us these three ways:

The Diabolonians plot the overthrow of Mansoul.

1. Whether we had best to seek its ruin, by making Mansoul loose and vain:

---

* Were the stratagems of Satan obvious, they would not succeed. Let us not be ignorant of his devices.

2. Or, by driving them to doubt and despair:

3. Or, by endeavouring to blow them up with the gun-powder of pride and self-conceit.

Now I think, if we shall tempt them to pride, that may do something; and if we tempt them to wantonness, that may help. But in my mind, if we could drive them into desperation, that would knock the nail on the head; for then we should have them, in the first place, question the truth of the love of the heart of their prince towards them, and that will disgust him much. This, if it works well, will quickly make them leave off their way of sending petitions to him; then farewell earnest solicitations for help and supply; for then this conclusion lies naturally before them, " As good do nothing, as to do to no purpose." So they unanimously approved of Mr Deceit's advice.

Then the next question was, But how shall we do to bring our project to pass? And it was answered by the same gentleman, that this might be the best way to do it: Even let, quoth he, so many of our friends, as are willing to venture themselves for the promoting of their prince's cause, disguise themselves with apparel, change their names, and go into the market like far-countrymen, proffer themselves for servants to the famous town of Mansoul, and let them pretend to do for their masters as beneficially as may be: for by so doing they may, if Mansoul shall hire them, in little time so corrupt and defile the corporation, that her now prince shall be not only further offended with them, but in conclusion spue them out of his mouth. And when this is done, our prince Diabolus shall prey upon them with ease: yea, of themselves, they shall fall into the mouth of the eater.

The advice given by Mr Deceit.

This project was no sooner propounded, but was as readily accepted, and forward were all Diabolonians now to engage in the enterprise: but it was not thought fit that all should do thus; wherefore they pitched on two or three, namely, the Lord Covetousness, the Lord Lasciviousness, and the Lord Anger: the Lord Covetousness called himself by the name of Prudent-thrifty; the Lord Lasciviousness called himself by the name of Harmless-mirth; and the Lord Anger called himself by the name of Good-zeal.*

So upon a market-day they came into the market-place; three lusty fellows they were to look on, and they were clothed in

---

* How deceitful is sin! how seldom does it own its true name; it deceives the soul by plausible appearances, and is too often entertained to our unspeakable injury. Had these villains owned their true names, who would have received them?

sheep's russet, which was now in a manner as white as the robes of the men of Mansoul. Now the men could speak the language of Mansoul well: so when they came into the market-place and offered themselves to the townsmen, they were presently entertained; for they asked but little wages, and promised to do their masters great service.

Mr Mind hired Prudent-thrifty, and Mr Godly-fear hired Good-zeal. True, this fellow Harmless-mirth hung a little in hand, and could not so soon get a master as the others did, because the town of Mansoul was now in Lent; but after a while, because Lent was almost out, Lord Will-be-will hired Harmless-mirth, to be both his waiting-man and his lacquey; and thus they got them masters.

These villains, being now got into the houses of the men of *Covetousness Lasciviousness and Anger work mischief in the town of Mansoul.* Mansoul, quickly began to do great mischief therein; for, being filthy, arch, and sly, they quickly corrupted the families where they were, yea, they tainted their masters much, especially this Prudent-thrifty, and him they called Harmless-mirth. True, he that went under the visor of Good-zeal was not so well liked by his master, who quickly found that he was but a counterfeit rascal; which when the fellow perceived, he with speed made his escape from the house, or I doubt not but his master would have hanged him.*

When these vagabonds had thus far carried on their design, and corrupted the town as much as they could, in the next place they considered with themselves, at what time their prince Diabolus without, and themselves within the town, should make an attempt to seize upon Mansoul; and they all agreed upon this, that a market-day would be the best for that work; because then the townsfolk will be busy in their ways: and always take this for a rule, " when people are most busy in the world, they least fear a surprise."† We also then, said they, shall be able with less suspicion to gather ourselves together for the work of our friends and lords; yea, on such a day should we attempt our work, and miss it, we may, when they give us the rout, the better hide ourselves in the crowd, and escape.

---

* When covetousness prevails in the mind, and lasciviousness corrupts the will, how great is the mischief that must ensue; the former prevails unperceived under the idea of prudent thrift, and the latter acquires dominion under the notion of harmless mirth; let heads of families be on their guard against the one, and young people especially against the other. Covetousness is spiritual idolatry, and infinitely hateful to God. Lasciviousness is a sin that, in a peculiar manner, defiles the soul, and grieves the Holy Spirit.

† Let busy tradesmen, and all who are deeply engaged in worldy concerns mark this well. Take care of your hearts on market-days. Be diligent in business, but fervent in spirit, watching unto prayer

The Diabolonians send another letter to Diabolus.

Having thus far agreed upon these things, they wrote another letter to Diabolus, and sent it by the hand of Mr Profane; **the contents of which were these:**

"*The Lords of Looseness send to the great and high Diabolus from our dens, caves, holds, and strong-holds, in and about the wall of the town of Mansoul, greeting.*

"Our great lord, and the nourisher of our lives, Diabolus; how glad we were when we heard of your fatherhood's readiness to comply with us, and to forward our design, in **attempting to ruin** Mansoul; none can tell but those, who, as we do, set themselves against all appearance of good, when and wheresoever we find it, Rom. vii. 21. Gal. v. 17.

"Touching **the encouragement that your greatness is pleased** to give us, to continue to **devise, contrive, and study the utter** desolation of Mansoul, that we are **not solicitous about;** for we know right well, that it **cannot** but be pleasing **and profitable to** us, to see our enemies, and them that seek our lives, die at our feet, or fly before us. We therefore are **still contriving, to the** best of our cunning, to make this work more facile and **easy to** your lordship, and to us.

"First, we considered of that most **hellishly cunning, compacted,** threefold project, that by you was propounded **to us in** your last; and have concluded, that though **to blow them up** with the gunpowder of pride would do well, and to do it by tempting them to be loose and vain will help on, yet to contrive to bring them into the gulf of desperation, we think will do best of all. Now we who are at your beck, have **thought of two** ways to do this: first, we, for our parts, will **make them as vile** as we can, and then you with us, at a time appointed, shall be ready to fall upon them with the utmost force. And of all the

An army of Doubters proposed to be sent against Mansoul.

nations that **are at your whistle, we** think that an army of Doubters **may be the most likely to attack** and overcome the town of Mansoul.* Thus shall we overcome these enemies, else the pit shall open her mouth upon them, and desperation shall thrust them down into it. We have also, **to ef-** fect this our so much wished design, sent already three of our trusty Diabolonians among them; they are disguised in garb,

---

* This scheme is contrived with consummate skill: first, let the christian be drawn into a light, vain, worldly walk, "make him as vile as you can," and then assault him with doubts and fears about his salvation. This plan too often succeeds.

have changed their names, and are now accepted of them, to wit Covetousness, Lasciviousness and Anger. The name of Covetousness is changed into Prudent-thrifty, and him Mr Mind has hired, and is almost become as bad as our friend. Lasciviousness has changed his name to Harmless-mirth, and he is got to be the Lord Will-be-will's lacquey; but he has made his master very wanton. Anger changed his name into Good-zeal, and was entertained by Mr Godly-fear, but the peevish old gentleman took pepper in the nose, and turned our companion out of his house: nay, he has informed us since, that he ran away from him, or else his old master had hanged him for his labour.* Now these have much helped forward our work and design upon Mansoul; for notwithstanding the spite and quarrelsome temper of the old gentleman last mentioned, the other two ply their business well, and are likely to ripen the work apace.

"Our next project is, that it be concluded that you come upon the town upon a market-day, and that when they are upon the heat of their business; for then to be sure they will be more secure, and least think that an assault will be made upon them. They will also at such a time be less able to defend themselves, and to offend you in the prosecution of our design. And we your trusty (and we are sure your beloved) ones shall, when you make your furious assault without, be ready to second the business within. So shall we in all likelihood be able to put Mansoul to utter confusion, and swallow them up before they can come to themselves. If your serpentine heads, most subtle dragons, and our highly esteemed lords, can find out a better way than this, let us quickly know your minds.

"To the Monsters of the Infernal Cave, from the House of Mr Mischief, in Mansoul, by the hand of Mr Profane."

Now all the while that the raging runagades, and hellish Diabolonians were thus contriving the ruin of the town of Mansoul, *The sad state of Mansoul.* they, to wit, the poor town itself, was in a sad and woful case, partly because they had so grievously offended Shaddai and his son, and partly because that the enemies thereby got strength within them afresh, and also because, though they had by many petitions made suit to the prince Immanuel, and to his father Shaddai, by him, for their pardon and favour, yet hitherto obtained they not one smile; but contrariwise, through the craft and subtlety of the domestic Diabolonians, their sky was made to grow blacker and blacker, and their Immanuel to stand at further distance. The sickness also still greatly raged in Mansoul, but among the cap-

---

* Godly-fear cannot long entertain sinful anger.

tains, and the inhabitants of the town, their enemies, and their enemies only, were now lively and strong; and like to become the head, whilst Mansoul was made the tail.*

By this time the letter last mentioned, that was written by the Diabolonians that yet lurked in the town of Mansoul, was conveyed to Diabolus, in the black den, by the hand of Mr Profane. He carried the letter by Hellgate-hill as afore, and conveyed it by Cerberus to his lord.

But when Cerberus and Mr Profane met, they were presently great as beggars, and thus they fell into discourse about Mansoul, and about the project against her.

Talk between him and Cerberus. Ah! old friend, quote Cerberus, art thou come to Hellgate-hill again? By St. Mary, I am glad to see thee.

Profane. Yes, my lord, I am come again about the concerns of the town of Mansoul.

Cerberus. Prithee tell me, what condition is that town of Mansoul in at present?

Profane. In a brave condition, my lord, for us, and for my lords, the lords of this place, I trow; for they are greatly decayed as to godliness, and that is as well as our heart can wish; their lord is greatly out with them, and that doth also please us well. We have already also a foot in their dish, for our Diabolonian friends are laid in their bosoms, and what do we lack but to be masters of the place? Besides, our trusty friends in Mansoul are daily plotting to betray it to the lords of this town; also the sickness rages bitterly among them, and that which makes up all, we hope at last to prevail.

Then said Cerberus, No time like this to assault them. I wish that the enterprise be followed close, and that the success desired may be soon effected: yes, I wish it for the poor Diabolonians' sakes, that live in the continual fear of their lives in that traitorous town of Mansoul.

Profane. The contrivance is almost finished, the lords in Mansoul that are Diabolonians are at it day and night; and the other are like silly doves, that want heart to be concerned with their state, and to consider that ruin is at hand.† Besides, you may, yea, must think, when you put all things together, that there are many reasons that prevail with Diabolus to make what haste he can.

* Backsliding from God naturally produces clouds that grow blacker and blacker; corruptions grow stronger and stronger; while grace in the soul becomes sick and weakly.

† This is the misery of the case; backsliding souls want heart to consider their own state. This shows the great importance of vigilance and self-examination.

Cerberus. Thou hast said as it is, I am glad things are at this pass. Go in, my brave Profane, to my lords, they will give thee for thy welcome as good a coranto as this kingdom will afford. I have sent thy letter in already.

Then Mr Profane went into the den, and his Lord Diabolus met him, and saluted him with, Welcome, my trusty servant, I have been made glad with thy letter. The rest of the lords of the pit gave him also their salutations. Then Profane, after obeisance made to them all, said; Let Mansoul be given to my lord Diabolus, and let him be her king for ever. And with that the yawning gorge of hell gave so loud and hideous a groan (for that is the music of that place) that it made the mountains about it totter, as if they would fall in pieces.

Profane's entertainment.

Now after they had read and considered the letter, they consulted what answer to return, and the first that spake to it was Lucifer.

Lucifer. Then said he, The first project of the Diabolonians in Mansoul is like to be lucky, and to take; to wit, that they will, by all the means they can, make Mansoul yet more vile; no way to destroy a soul like this; our old friend Balaam went this way, and prospered many years ago, Numb. xxxi. 16. Rev. ii. 14. Let this therefore stand with us for a maxim, and be to Diabolonians for a general rule in all ages; for nothing can make this to fail but grace, in which I would hope that this town has no share. But whether to fall upon them on a market-day, because of their cumber in business, that I would should be under debate. And there is more reason why this head should be debated, than why some other should; because upon this will turn the whole of what we shall attempt. If we time not our business well, our whole project may fail. Our friends the Diabolonians say, that a market-day is best, for then will Mansoul be most busy, and have fewest thoughts of a surprise. But what if they shall double their guards on those days (and methinks nature and reason should teach them to do it?) and what if they should keep such a watch on those days, as the necessity of their present case requires? Yea, what if their men should be always in arms in those days? Then you may, my lords, be disappointed at your attempts, and may bring our friends in the town to utter danger of unavoidable ruin.*

They consult what answer to give to the letter.

Lucifer's speech.

Beelzebub. Then said the great Beelzebub, There is some-

---

* "Learn wisdom from the devil. Nature and reason should teach men to be doubly on their guard when much engaged in the world—on market-days;

Beelzebub's speech. thing in what my lord hath said, but his conjecture may or may not fall out. Nor hath my lord laid it down as that which must not be receded from: for I know that he said it only to provoke a warm debate thereabout. Therefore we must understand, if we can, whether the town of Mansoul has such sense and knowledge of her decayed state, and of the designs that we have on foot against her, as to set watch and ward at her gates, and to double them on market-days. But if after inquiry made, it shall be found that they are asleep, then any day will do, but a market-day is best; and this is my judgment.

Diabolus. Then quoth Diabolus, How shall we know this? And it was answered, Inquire about it at the mouth of Mr Profane. So Profane was called in, and asked the question, and he made his answer as follows:

Profane. My lords so far as I can gather, this is at present the condition of the town of Mansoul: they are decayed in their faith and love; Immanuel, their prince, has given them the back; they send often by petition to fetch him again, but he makes no haste to answer their request; nor is there much reformation among them.

Profane's description of the present state of Mansoul.

Diabolus. I am glad that they are backward to a reformation, but yet I am afraid of their petitioning. However, their looseness of life is a sign that there is not much heart in what they do, and without the heart things are little worth.* But, go on my masters, I will divert you, my lords, no longer.

Beelzebub. If the case be so with Mansoul, as Mr Profane has described it to be, it will be no great matter what day we assault it; not their prayers nor their power will do them much service.

When Beelzebub had ended his oration, then Apollyon began, My opinion, said he, concerning this matter is, that we go on fair and softly, not doing things in a hurry. Let our friends in Mansoul go on still to pollute and defile it, by seeking to draw it yet more into sin (for there is nothing like sin to devour Mansoul.) If this be done, and takes effect, Mansoul itself will leave off to watch, petition, or any thing else, that should tend to her secu-

Dreadful advice against Mansoul.

"Men should be always in arms on those days." Would to God this hint were duly regarded in the country on market-days, and in London always, where every day in the week is market-day!

* Good reasoning. Looseness of life is a proof that, whatever of religion men may profess, there is not much heart in it, and if not, it is of little worth, and will do them little service.

city and safety; for she will forget her Immanuel, she will not desire his company; and can she be gotten thus to live, her prince will not come to her in haste. Our trusty friend, Mr Carnal-security, with one of his tricks, drove him out of the town; and why may not my Lord Covetousness, and my Lord Lasciviousness, by what they **may** do, keep him out of the town?* And this I will tell you (not because you know it not, but) that two or three Diabolonians, if entertained and countenanced by the town of Mansoul, will do more to the keeping Immanuel from them, and towards making the town our own, than an army or a legion that should be sent out from us to withstand him.

Let, therefore, this first project that our friends in Mansoul have set on foot, be strongly and diligently carried on with all cunning and craft imaginable; and let them send continually under one guise or other, more and other of their men to play with the people of Mansoul; and then perhaps we shall not need to be at the charge of making a war upon them; or if that must of necessity be done, yet the more sinful they are, the less able they will be **to resist us, and** then the more easily **we** shall overcome them. And besides, suppose (and that is the worst that can be supposed) that Immanuel should come to them again, why may not the same means (or the like) drive him from them once more? Yea, why may he not, by their lapse into that sin again be driven from them for ever, for the sake of which he was at the first driven from them for a season? And if this should happen, **then away** will go with him his rams, his slings, his captains, his soldiers, and he leaveth Mansoul naked and bare. Yea, will not this town, when she sees herself utterly forsaken of her prince, of her own accord open her gates again unto you? But this must be done by time, a few days will not effect so great a work as this.†

Apollyon gives his advice that they should carry on the war with craft and guile.

When Apollyon had made **an end** of speaking, Diabolus began to blow out his own malice, and plead his own cause, and he said, **My lords and** powers of the cave, my true and trusty friends, I have with much impatience, as becomes me, given ear to your long **and tedious orations.** But my furious gorge and empty paunch so lusteth after a repossession of my famous town of Mansoul, that whatever comes on it, I can **wait** no longer to see the

Diabolus can brook no delay, but is determined to retake the town immediately.

---

* Very true, though said by the father of lies. Sin will do more to hurt the soul than a legion of devils.

† Apostacy is often a gradual affair, a sure poison, but slow

events of lingering projects. I must, and that without further delay, seek by all means I can, to fill my unsatiable gulf with the soul and body of the town of Mansoul. Therefore lend me your heads, your hearts, and your helps, **now I** am going to recover my town of Mansoul.

When the lords and princes of the pit saw the flaming **desire** that was in Diabolus to devour the miserable town of Mansoul, they left off to raise any more objections, **but consented to lend** him what strength they could: though, had Apollyon's advice been taken, they had far more fearfully distressed the town of Mansoul. But I say, they were willing to lend him what strength they could, not knowing what need they might have of him, when they should engage for themselves, as he. Wherefore they **fell** to devising about the next thing propounded; to wit, what soldiers they were, and also how many, with whom Diabolus should go against the town of Mansoul, to take it; and, after **some** debate, it was concluded, according as in the letter the Diabolonians had suggested, that none was more fit for that expedition, **than an** army of terrible doubters. They therefore concluded **to send** against Mansoul an army of sturdy Doubters. **The number** thought fit to be employed in that service was between twenty and thirty thousand.* So then the result of that **great council** of those high and mighty lords was, That Diabolus should even now out of hand beat up his drum for men in the land of Doubting, which land lieth upon the confines of the place called Hellgate-hill, for men that might be employed by him against the miserable town of Mansoul. It was also concluded, that these lords themselves should help him in the war, and that they would, to that end, head and manage his men. So they drew up a letter, and sent it back to the Diabolonians that lurked in **Mansoul, and** that waited for the coming back of Mr Profane, to signify to them into what method they had put their design. The contents whereof follow:

An army of Doubters raised to go against the town of Mansoul.

The princes of the pit go with nem.

"*From the dark and horrible dungeon of Hell, Diabolus, with all the society of the princes of darkness, sends to our trusty ones, in and about the walls of the town of Mansoul, now impatiently waiting for our most devilish answer to their venomous and most poisonous design against the town of Mansoul.*

* When the enemy has so far prevailed by temptation, that sin has been entertained in the soul, as lasciviousness and covetousness, then is the time to pour into the soul a crowd of distressing doubts respecting our own salvation, and this is the natural and usual counsequence of sin indulged.

"Our native ones, in whom from day to day we boast, and in whose actions all the year long we greatly delight ourselves, we received your welcome, because highly esteemed letter, at the hand of our trusty and greatly beloved, the old gentleman, Mr Profane; and do give you to understand, that when we had broken it up, and had read the contents thereof (to your amazing memory be it spoken) our yawning hollow-bellied place where we are, made so hideous and yelling a noise for joy, that the mountains that stand round about Hellgate-hill had like to have been shaken to pieces at the sound thereof.

"We could also do no less than admire your faithfulness to us, with the greatness of that subtlety that now hath showed itself to be in your heads to serve us against the town of Mansoul. For you have invented for us so excellent a method for our proceeding against that rebellious people, that a more effectual cannot be thought of by all the wits of hell. The proposals therefore which now at last you have sent us, since we saw them, we have done little else but highly approved and admired them.

"Nay, we shall, to encourage you in the profundity of your craft, let you know, that at a full assembly and conclave of our princes and principalities of this place, your project was discoursed and tossed from one side of our cave to the other by their mightinesses; but a better, and, as was by themselves judged, a more fit and proper way, by all their wits could not be invented, to suprise, take, and make our own, the rebellious town of Mansoul.

"Wherefore, in fine, all that was said that varied from what you had in your letter propounded, fell of itself to the ground, and yours only was stuck to by Diabolus the prince; yea, his gaping gorge and yawning paunch was on fire to put your invention into execution.

An army of more than twenty thousand Doubters to go against Mansoul.

"We therefore give you to understand, that our stout, furious, and unmerciful Diabolus, is raising for your relief, and the ruin of the rebellious town of Mansoul, more than twenty thousand Doubters to come against that people. They are all stout and sturdy men, and men that of old have been accustomed to war. I say, he is doing this work of his, with all the speed he can, for with his heart and spirit he is engaged in it. We desire, therefore, that as you have hitherto stuck to us, and given us both advice and encouragement, you still will prosecute our design, nor shall you lose, but be gainers thereby; yea, we intend to make you the lords of Mansoul.

"One thing may not by any means be omitted, that is, those with us desire, that every one of you that are in Mansoul would still use all your power, cunning, and skill, with delusive persuasions, yet to draw the town of Mansoul into more sin and wickedness, even that sin may be finished, and bring forth death.

"For thus it is concluded with us, that the more vile, sinful and debauched the town of Mansoul is, the more backward will their Immanuel be to come to their help, either by presence, or other relief: yea, the more sinful, the more weak, and so the more unable will they be to make resistance, when we shall make our assault upon them to swallow them up. Yea, they may cause that their mighty Shaddai himself may cast them out of his protection; yea, and send for his captains and soldiers home, with his slings and rams, and leave them naked and bare, and then the town of Mansoul will of itself open to us, and fall as a fig into the mouth of the eater. Yea, to be sure that we then with a great deal of ease shall come upon her, and overcome her.

"As to the time of our coming upon Mansoul, we as yet have not fully resolved upon that, though at pre-

Mansoul is to be assaulted both without and within.

sent some of us think, as you, that a market-day, or a market-day at night, will certainly be the best.* However, do you be ready, and when you shall hear our roaring drum without, do you be as busy to make the most horrible confusion within 1 Pet. v. 8; so shall Mansoul certainly be distressed before and behind, and shall not know which way to betake herself for help. My Lord Lucifer, my Lord Beelzebub, my Lord Apollyon, my Lord Legion, with the rest, salute you, as does also my Lord Diabolus; and we wish both you, with all that you do or shall possess, the very self-same fruit and success for your doing, as we ourselves at present enjoy for ours.

"From our dreadful confines in the most fearful pit, we salute you, and so do those many legions here with us, wishing you may be as hellishly prosperous as we desire to be ourselves. By the letter-carrier, Mr Profane."

Then Mr Profane addressed himself for his return to Mansoul, with his errand from the horrible pit to the Diabolonians that dwelt in that town. So he came up the stairs from the deep to the mouth of the cave where Cerberus was. Now when Cer-

---

* A market-day at night. At that season how many tradesmen are full of the world; and too many, who visit markets from the country, "overcharged with surfeiting, drunkenness, and the cares of this life!" "Be sober, be vigilant." 1 Pet. v. 8.

berus saw him, he asked how matters went below, about and against the town of Mansoul.

Profane. Things go as well as we can expect. The letter that I carried thither was highly approved, and well liked by all my lords, and I am returning to tell our Diabolonians so. I have an answer to it here in my bosom, that I am sure will make our masters that sent me, glad; for the contents thereof are to encourage them to pursue their design to the utmost, and to be ready also to fall on within, when they shall see my Lord Diabolus beleaguering of the town of Mansoul.

Conversation between the keeper of hell-gate, and the bearer of the letter

Cerberus. But does he intend to go against them himself?

Profane. Does he? Ay, and he will take along with him more than twenty thousand, all sturdy Doubters and men of war, picked men from the land of Doubting, to serve him in the expedition.

Cerberus. Then was **Cerberus** glad, and said, And are there such brave preparations a making to go against the miserable town of Mansoul? And would I might be put at the head of a thousand of them, that I might also show my valour against the famous town of Mansoul.

Profane. Your wish may come to pass, you look like one that has mettle enough, and my lord will have with him those that are valiant and stout. But my business requires haste.

Cerberus. Ay, so it does. Speed thee to the town of Mansoul, with all the deepest mischiefs that this place can afford thee. And when thou shalt come to the house of Mr Mischief, the place where the Diabolonians meet to plot, tell them that Cerberus doth wish them his service, and that if he may, he will with the army come up against the famous town of Mansoul.

Profane. That I will. And I know that my lords that are there will be glad to hear it, and to see you also.

So after a few more such kind of compliments, Mr Profane took leave of his friend Cerberus; and Cerberus again, with a thousand of their pit wishes, bid him haste with all speed to his masters. The which when he had heard he made obeisance, and began to gather up his heels to run.

The messenger, Mr Profane, proceeds on his errand.

Thus therefore he returned, and came to Mansoul, and going as afore to the house of Mr Mischief, there he found the Diabolonians, assembled, and waiting for his return. Now when he was come, and had presented himself, he delivered his letter and adjoined his compliment to them therewith: My lords, from the confines of the pit, the high and mighty principalities and powers of the den salute you here, the true Diabolonians of the town of Mansoul: wishing you always the most proper of their benediction, for the great service, high attempts, and brave achievements, that you have put yourselves upon, for the restoring to our prince Diabolus the famous town of Mansoul.

This was therefore the present state of the miserable town of Mansoul. She had offended her prince, and he was gone; she had encouraged the powers of hell, by her foolishness, to come against her to seek her utter destruction.

State of the town of Mansoul at this critical juncture.

True, the town of Mansoul was somewhat made sensible of her sin, but the Diabolonians were gotten into her bowels; she cried, but Immanuel was gone and her cries did not fetch him as yet again. Besides, she knew not whether ever or never he would return, and come to his Mansoul again; nor did they know the power and industry of the enemy nor how forward they were to put in execution that plot of hell that they had devised against her.

They did indeed still send petition after petition to the prince but he answered all with silence. They did neglect reformation, and that was as Diabolus would have it; for he knew, if they regarded iniquity in their heart, their king would not regard their prayer; they therefore still grew weaker and weaker, and were as a rolling thing before the whirlwind. They cried to their king for help, and laid Diabolonians in their bosoms. what therefore should a king do to them? Yea, there seemed now to be a mixture in Mansoul, the Diabolonians and Mansoulians would walk the streets together. Yea, they began to seek their peace, for they thought, that since the sickness had been so mortal in Mansoul, it was in vain to go to handy-gripes with them. Besides, the weakness of Mansoul was the strength of their enemies; and the sins of Mansoul the advantage of the Diabolonians. The foes of Mansoul also now began to promise themselves the town for a possession; there was no great difference now betwixt the Mansoulians and Diabolonians; both seemed to be masters of Mansoul. Yea, the Diabolonians increased and grew, but the town of Mansoul diminished greatly. There were more than eleven thousand men, women, and children, that died by the sickness of Mansoul.*

* When there is grace in the soul, there can scarce be a total insensibility. They had petitioned again and again; but they regarded iniquity in the heart, therefore their prayers were not heard. O what a change had taken place. Time was, when Immanuel first came to dwell in Mansoul, that all was joy, and peace, and love; but sin was indulged, and Jesus departed.

CHAPTER XIV.

The Plot discovered by Mr Prywell. Preparations made for defence. More Diabolonians executed. The army of Doubters described; they approach the town, and make an assault upon Ear-gate, but are repelled. The Drummer beats a parley, but is disregarded. Diabolus attempts to deceive by his flatteries, but in vain. Jolly and Griggish, two young Diabolonians, executed. Gripe and Rake-all hanged. Any-thing and Loose-foot imprisoned.

BUT now, as Shaddai would have it, there was one whose name was Mr Prywell, a great lover of the people of Mansoul. And he, as his manner was, went listening up and down in Mansoul, to see and hear if at any time he might, whether there was any design against it, or no. For he was always a jealous man, and feared some mischief some time would befal it, either from the Diabolonians within or from some power without. Now upon a time it so happened, as Mr Prywell went listening here and there, that he lighted upon a place called Vile-hill in Mansoul, where Diabolonians used to meet; so hearing a muttering, (you must know that it was in the night,) he softly drew near to hear; nor had he stood long under the house-end (for there stood a house there,) but he heard one confidently affirm, that it was not, or would not be long, before Diabolus should possess himself again of Mansoul, and that then the Diabolonians did intend to put all Mansoulians to the sword, and would kill and destroy the king's captains, and drive all his soldiers out of the town.*

The story of Mr Prywell.

The Diabolonians' lot discovered and by whom.

He said, moreover, That he knew there were above twenty thousand fighting men prepared by Diabolus for the accomplishing of his design, and that it would not be many months before they all should see it. When Mr Prywell had heard this story

Religion was now at so low an ebb, that they mixed freely with the world, and "there was no great difference between the Mansoulians and the Diabolonians—between professors and profane." This is an awful case; a case, alas! too common.

Reader, pause and examine thyself. Is this thy state? If it be not, bless the Lord who hath kept thee from falling. If it be, O cry to him for pardon and grace, for dreadful danger is at hand.

Sin is, indeed, the sickness of the soul. Many thousands are said to have died by it. This is not intended as if any of the Lord's truly gracious and elect people had finally perished; (which would be contrary to the truth;) but that very great and dreadful loss had been sustained by this awful backsliding from him, the deadful consequences of which appear in the next chapter.

* Holy jealousy and careful examination will detect the plans and devices of Satan. We cannot watch and pry too narrowly when we consider the deceitfulness of sin and of the heart.

Understanding and Conscience. he quickly believed it was true; wherefore he went forthwith to my Lord-mayor's house, and acquainted him therewith, who sending for the subordinate preacher, brake the business to him, and he as soon gave the alarm to the town; for he was now the chief preacher in Mansoul, because as yet my lord Secretary was ill at ease.* And this was the way that the subordinate preacher took to alarm the town therewith. The same hour he caused the lecture-bell to be rung, and the people came together; he then gave them a short exhortation to watchfulness, and made Mr Prywell's news the argument thereof.

The alarm-bell rung.

For, said he, a horrible plot is contrived against Mansoul, even to massacre us all in a day; nor is this story to be slighted, for Mr Prywell is the author thereof. Mr Prywell was always a lover of Mansoul, a sober and judicious man, a man that is no tattler, nor raiser of false reports, but one that loves to look into the very bottom of matters, and talks nothing of news but by very solid argument.

I will call him, and you shall hear him your own selves; so he called him, and he came and told his tale so punctually, and affirmed its truth with such ample grounds, that Mansoul fell presently under a conviction of the truth of what he said. The preacher also backed him, saying, Sirs, it is not irrational for us to believe it, for we have provoked Shaddai to anger, and have sinned Immanuel out of the town; we have had too much correspondence with Diabolonians, and have forgotten our tender mercies; no marvel, then, if the enemy both within and without should design and plot our ruin; and what time like this to do it? The sickness is now in the town, and we have been made weak thereby. Many a good-meaning man is dead, and the Diabolonians of late grown stronger and stronger.

Besides, quoth the subordinate preacher, what I have received from this good truth-teller is one inkling further, that he understood by those that he overheard, that several letters have lately passed between the furies of the pit and the Diabolonians, in order to our destruction.

They take the alarm.

When Mansoul heard all this, and not being able to gainsay it, they lift up their voice and wept. Mr Prywell also, in the presence of the townsmen, confirmed all that their subordinate preacher had said. Wherefore they now set afresh to bewail their folly, and to a doubling of petitions to Shaddai, and his son. They also brake the business to the captains, high

---

* The Holy Spirit was grieved, and suspended his usual influences. Gospel ministers are watchmen, and must sound the alarm in the time danger

They tell these things to the captains. commanders, and men of war in the town of Mansoul, intreating of them to use the means to be strong, and to take good courage, and that they would look after their harness, and make themselves ready to give Diabolus battle by night or by day, should he come, as they are informed he will, to beleaguer the town of Mansoul.

When the captains heard this, they being always true lovers of the town of Mansoul, what do they, but like so many Samsons, they shake themselves, and come together to consult and contrive how to defeat those bold and hellish contrivances that were upon the wheel, by the means of Diabolus and his friends, against the now sickly, weakly, and much impoverished town of Mansoul; and they agreed upon these following particulars.

1. That the gates of Mansoul should be kept shut, and made *Their agreement.* fast with bars and locks, and that all persons that went out or came in should be very strictly examined by the captains of the guards, 1 Cor. xvi. 13, to the end, said they, that those that are managers of the plot amongst us may, either coming or going, be taken; and that we may also find out who are the great contrivers (amongst us) of our ruin, Lam. iii. 40.

2. The next thing was, that a strict search should be made for all kind of Diabolonians, throughout the whole town of Mansoul; and that every man's house from top to bottom, should be looked into, and that too house by house, that if possible a farther discovery might be made of all such among them as had a hand in these designs, Heb. xii. 15, 16.

3. It was further concluded upon, that wheresoever or with whomsoever any of the Diabolonians were found, that even those of the town of Mansoul, that had given them house and harbour, should, to their shame and the warning of others, do penance in the open place, Jer. ii. 34. chap. v. 26. Ezek. xvi. 52.

4. It was moreover resolved by the famous town of Mansoul, *A public fast and day of solemn humiliation.* that a public fast, and a day of humiliation, should be kept throughout the whole corporation, to the justifying of their prince, the abasing of themselves before him for their transgressions against him, and against Shaddai his father, Joel i. 14. chap. ii. 15, 16. It was further resolved, that all such in Mansoul as did not on that day endeavour to keep that fast, and to humble themselves for their faults, but should mind their worldly employments, or be found wandering up or down the streets, should be taken for Diabolonians, and suffer as Diabolonians for such wicked doings.

5. It was further concluded then, that with what speed, and with what warmth of mind they could, they would renew their humiliation for sin, and their petitions to Shaddai for help, they also resolved to send tidings, to the court of all that Mr Prywell had told them, Jer. xxxviii. 4.

6. It was also determined, that thanks should be given by the town of Mansoul to Mr Prywell, for his diligent seeking of the welfare of their town; and further, that forasmuch as he was so naturally inclined to seek their good, and also to undermine their foes, they gave him a commission of Scout-master-general, for the good of the town of Mansoul.*

When the corporation, with their captains, had thus concluded, they did as they had said, they shut their gates, they made for Diabolonians strict search, they made those with whom any were found, to do penance in the open place. They kept their fast, and renewed their petition to their prince, and Mr Prywell managed his charge, and the trust that Mansoul had put into his hands, with great conscience and good fidelity; for he gave himself wholly up to his employ, and that not only within the town, but he went out to pry, to see, and to hear.

Mr Prywell goes a scouting.
Not many days after, he provided for his journey, and went towards Hellgate-hill, into the country where Doubters were, where he heard of all that had been talked of in Mansoul, and he perceived also that Diabolus was almost ready for his march, &c. So he came back with speed, and calling the captains and elders of Mansoul together, he told them where he had been, what he had heard, and what he had seen. Particularly he told them, that Diabolus was almost ready for his march, and that he had made old Mr Incredulity, that once brake prison in Mansoul, the general of his army; that his army consisted of all Doubters, and that their number was above twenty thousand. He told, moreover, that Diabolus intended to bring with him the chief princes of the Infernal Pit, and that he would make them chief captains over his Doubters. He told them, moreover, that it was certainly true, that several of the black den would with Diabolus ride reformades, to reduce the town of Mansoul to the obedience of Diabolus their prince.

He returns with great news.

He said, moreover, that he understood by the Doubters, among whom he had been, that the reason why old Incredulity was made general of the whole army, was, because none truer than he to

---

* All these were wise regulations. They show that we should be earnest in supplication, very diligent in self-examination, deeply humbled for sin, and zealous in detecting our corruptions.

the tyrant; and because he had an implacable spite against the town of Mansoul. Besides, said he, he remembers the affront that Mansoul has given him, and he is resolved to be revenged of them.*

But the black princes shall be made high commanders; only Incredulity shall be over them all, because he can more easily and dexterously beleaguer the town of Mansoul, than any of the princes besides, Heb. xii. 1.

Now when the captains of Mansoul, with the elders of the town, had heard the tidings that Mr Prywell brought, they thought it expedient, without further delay, to put into execu-
The laws of Immanuel against the Diabolonians put into execution. tion the laws against the Diabolonians, which their prince had made, and given them in commandment to manage against them. Wherefore, forthwith a diligent and impartial search was made in all houses in Mansoul, for all and all manner of Diabolonians. Now in the house of Mr Mind, and in the house of the great Lord Will-be-will, were two Diabolonians found. In Mr Mind's house was one Lord Covetousness found; but he had changed his name to Prudent-thrifty. In my Lord Will-be-will's house, one Lasciviousness was found; but he had changed his name to Harmlessmirth. These two the captains and elders of the town of Mansoul took and committed to custody, under the hand of Mr Trueman, the gaoler; and this man handled them so severely, and loaded them so well with irons, that they both fell into a very deep consumption, and died in the prison; their masters also, according to the agreement of the captains and elders, were brought to do penance in the open place, to their shame, and a warning to the rest of the town of Mansoul.†

Now this was the manner of penance in those days. The persons offending, being made sensible of the evil of their doings, were enjoined open confession of their faults, and a strict amendment of their lives.‡

After this the captains and elders of Mansoul sought yet to find out more Diabolonians, wherever they lurked, whether in

---

* The design of Satan was to overwhelm the soul with doubts and fears, in consequence of sin indulged; incredulity, therefore, or unbelief, is, with great propriety, appointed general of the army, for the doubts and fears of serious persons usually arise from unbelief.

† In the time of danger we are more engaged in the mortification of our sinful lusts; and it is well when the deceitfulness of sin is detected, its false names and pretences discovered, and when covetousness and lasciv. usness consume away and die.

‡ This godly discipline is almost unknown in our day; yet is it consonant with the word of God, and if practised, would promote the holiness of the church, and its credit in the eyes of the world.

dens, caves, holes, vaults, or where else they could, in or about the wall or town of Mansoul. But though they could plainly see their footing, and so follow them by their track and smell to their holes, even to the mouths of their caves and dens, yet take and do justice upon them they could not, their ways were so crooked, their holes so strong, and they so quick to take sanctuary there.

The Diabolonians hide themselves in their dens. But Mansoul ruled now with so stiff a hand over the Diabolonians that were left, that they were glad to shrink into corners: time was, when they durst walk openly and in the day but now they were forced to embrace privacy and the night: time was, when a Mansoulian was their companion, but now they counted them deadly enemies. This change did Mr Prywell's intelligence make in the town of Mansoul.*

By this time Diabolus had finished his army which he intended to bring with him for the ruin of Mansoul; and had set over them captains, and other field officers, such as liked his furious stomach best: himself was lord paramount. Incredulity was general of his army. Their highest captains shall be named afterwards; but now for their officers, colours, and scutcheons.

1. Their first captain was Captain Rage, he was captain over the Election-Doubters, his were the red colours; his standard-bearer was Mr Destructive, and the great red dragon he had for his scutcheon, Rev. xii. 3, 4, 13, 15, 17.

2. The second captain was Captain Fury, he was captain over the Vocation-Doubters, his standard-bearer was Mr Darkness, his colours were those that were pale, and he had for his scutcheon the fiery flying serpent, Numb. xx. 6.

3. The third captain was Captain Damnation, he was captain over the Grace-Doubters, his were the red colours; Mr No-life bare them, and he had for his scutcheon the black den, Matt. iii. 22, 23. Rev. ix. 1.

4. The fourth captain was Captain Insatiable, he was captain over the Faith-Doubters,† his were the red colours; Mr Devourer bare them, and he had for his scutcheon the yawning-jaws, Prov. xxvii. 20.

5. The fifth captain was Captain Brimstone, he was captain

---

* When grace reigns in the heart, sin cannot show itself as it once did: but yet in-dwelling sin, the law in the members, is so subtle, that it will hide itself in secret places, difficult to be discovered, and far more difficult to be destroyed. There it is, and the believer is constrained to say—"O wretched man that I am, who shall deliver me," &c.

† The doubts of God's people are, frequently, concerning their election, their calling, their being partakers of saving grace, their final perseverance, their resurrection, salvation, and glory. To nourish and increase these doubts is the aim of hell, as represented in this formidable armament.

over the Perseverance-Doubters, his also were the red colours, Mr Burning bare them, and his scutcheon was the blue and stinking flame, Ps. xi. 6. Rev. xiv. 11.

6. The sixth captain was Captain Torment, he was captain over the Resurrection-Doubters, his colours were those that were pale, Mr Gnaw was his standard-bearer, and he had the black worm for his scutcheon, Mark. ix. 44, 46, 48.

7. The seventh captain was Captain No-ease, he was captain over the Salvation-Doubters, his were the red colours, Mr Restless bare them, and his scutcheon was the ghastly picture of death, Rev. iv. 11. chap. vi. 8.

8. The eighth captain was Captain Sepulchre, he was captain over the Glory-Doubters, his also were the pale colours, Mr Corruption was his standard-bearer, and he had for his scutcheon a scull, and dead men's bones, Jer. v. 16. ch. ii. 25.

9. The ninth captain was Captain Past-hope, he was captain of those that are called the Felicity-Doubters, his standard-bearer was Mr Despair; his also were the red colours, and his scutcheon was the hot iron and the hard heart, Tim ii. 4. Rom. ii. 5

These were his captains, and these were their forces, these were the standards, these were their colours, and these were their scutcheons. Now over these did the great Diabolus make superior captains, and they were in number seven: as namely, *The seven chief captains of Diabolus's army.* the Lord Beelzebub, the Lord Lucifer, the Lord Legion, the Lord Apollyon, the Lord Python, the Lord Cerberus, and the Lord Belial; these seven he set over the captains, and Incredulity was lord general, and Diabolus was king.

The reformades also, such as were like themselves, were made some of them captains of hundreds, and some of them captains of more. And thus was the army of Incredulity completed.

So they set out at Hellgate-hill (for there they had their rendezvous,) from whence they came with a straight course upon their march towards the town of Mansoul. Now, as was hinted before, the town had, as Shaddai would have it, received from the mouth of Mr Prywell the alarm of their coming before. Wherefore they set a strong watch at the gates, and had also doubled their guards; they also mounted their slings in good places, where they might conveniently cast out their great stones to the annoyance of the enemy.

Nor could those Diabolonians that were in the town do that hurt as was designed they should; for Mansoul was now awake. But alas, poor people, they were sorely affrighted at the first appearance of their foes, and at their sitting down before the town, especially when they heard the roaring of their drum,

Pet. v. 8. This, to speak truth, was amazingly hideous to hear, it frightened all men seven miles round.* The streaming of their colours, was also terrible and dejecting to behold.

When Diabolus was come up against the town, first he made his approach to Ear-gate; and gave it a furious assault, supposing, as it seems, that his friends in Mansoul had been ready to do the work within; but care was taken of that before, by the vigilance of the captains. Wherefore missing of the help that he expected from them, and finding his army warmly attacked with the stones from the slingers (for that I will say for the captains, that considering the weakness that yet was upon them by reason of the long sickness that had annoyed the town of Mansoul, they behaved themselves gallantly,) he was forced to make some retreat from Mansoul, and intrench himself and his men in the field, without the reach of the slings of the town, James iv. 7.

He makes an assault upon Ear-gate and is repelled.

He retreats and intrenches himself.

Now having intrenched himself, he cast up four mounts against the town; the first he called Mount Diabolus, putting his own name thereon, the more to affright the town of Mansoul; the other three he called thus, Mount Alecto, Mount Megara, and Mount Tisiphone, for these are the names of the dreadful furies of hell. Thus he began to play his game with Mansoul, and to serve it as the lion his prey, even to make it fall before his terror. But, as I said, the captains and soldiers, resisted so stoutly, and did so much execution, that they made him, though against stomach, to retreat; wherefore Mansoul began to take courage.

Now upon Mount Diabolus, which was raised on the north side of the town, there did the tyrant set up his standard, and a fearful thing it was to behold, for he had wrought in it by devilish art after the manner of his scutcheon, a flaming fire, fearful to behold, and the picture of Mansoul burning in it.

Diabolus's standard set up.

When Diabolus had thus done, he commanded that his drummer should every night approach the walls of the town of Mansoul, and beat a parley; the command was to do it at night, as in the day-time they annoyed him with their slings; for the tyrant said, that he had a mind to parley with the now trembling town of Mansoul, and he commanded that the drum should beat every night, that through weariness they might at last, if possible, (at the first they were unwilling, yet) be forced to do it.

So the drummer did as he was commanded; he arose, and

---

* 1 Pet. v. 8. "Be sober, be vigilant: because your adversary the devil, as a roaring lion, walketh about, seeking whom he may devour."

beat his drum. But when his drum did go, if one looked towards the town of Mansoul, behold darkness and sorrow, and the light was darkened in the heaven thereof, Isa. v. 30. No noise was ever heard upon earth more terrible, except the voice of Shaddai when he speaketh. But how did Mansoul tremble! it now looked for nothing but forthwith to be swallowed up.*

The drummer makes a speech by order of Diabolus.

When this drummer had beaten a parley, he made this speech to Mansoul: "My master has bid me tell you, that if you will willingly submit, you shall have the good of the earth; but if you shall be stubborn, he is resolved to take you by force."

But by that the fugitive had done beating his drum, the people of Mansoul had betaken themselves to the captains that were in the castle, so that there was none to regard nor to give this drummer an answer: so he proceeded no further that night, but returned again to his master to the camp.

When Diabolus saw that, by drumming, he could not work out Mansoul to his will, the next night he sendeth this drummer without his drum, still to let the townsmen know that he had a mind to parley with them. But when all came to all, his parley was turned into a summons to the town, to deliver up themselves: but they gave him neither heed nor hearing, for they remembered what at first it cost them to hear him a few words.†

The next night he sends again, and then who should be his messenger to Mansoul but the terrible Captain Sepulchre; so Captain Sepulchre came up to the walls of Mansoul, and made this oration to the town:

"O ye inhabitants of the rebellious town of Mansoul! I summon you in the name of the prince Diabolus, that without any more ado you set open the gates of your town, and admit your lord to come in. But if you shall still rebel, when we have taken the town by force, we will swallow you up as the grave; wherefore if you will hearken to my summons, say so; and if not, then let them know.

"The reason of this my summons;" quoth he, "is, for that my lord is your undoubted prince and lord, as you yourselves have formerly owned. Nor shall that assault that was given to my lord, when Immanuel dealt so dishonourably by him, prevail with him to lose his right, and to forbear to attempt to recover his own. Consider then, O Mansoul, with thyself, wilt thou show thyself peaceably, or not? If thou wilt quietly yield up thy-

---

* The miseries of the damned may sometimes greatly terrify a true Christian, who, being delivered by Jesus from the wrath to come, has no reason to fear them.

† We must not parley with the tempter, or hold any correspondence with him. A few words with him ruined us all in our first parents.

self, then our old friendship shall be renewed; but if thou wilt yet refuse and rebel, then expect nothing but fire and sword."*

When the languishing town of Mansoul heard this summoner, and his summons, they were yet more put to their dumps, but made the captain no answer at all; so away he went as he came.

The Mansoulians apply for advice to their lord secretary. After some consultation among themselves, as also with some of their captains, they applied themselves afresh to the lord secretary for counsel and advice from him; for this lord secretary was their chief preacher (as mentioned before) only now he was ill at ease; and of him they begged favour in these two or three things.

1. That he would look comfortably upon them, and not keep himself so much retired from them as formerly. Also, that he would be prevailed with to give them a hearing while they should make known their miserable condition to him. But to this he told them as before. That as yet he was but ill at ease, and therefore could not do as he had formerly done.

2. The second thing they desired, was, that he would be pleased to give them his advice about their now so important affairs, for that Diabolus was come and set before the town with no less than twenty thousand Doubters. They said, moreover, that both he and his captains were cruel men, and that they were afraid of them. But to this he said, You must look to the law of the prince, and there see what is laid upon you to do.†

3. Then they desired that his highness would help them to frame a petition to Shaddai, and unto Immanuel his son, and that he would set his own hand thereto, as a token that he was one with them in it: for said they, my Lord, many a one have we sent, but can get no answer of peace, but now surely one with thy hand unto it, may obtain good for Mansoul.

But all the answer he gave to this, was, That they had offended Immanuel, and had also grieved himself, and that therefore they must as yet partake of their own devices.

This answer of the lord secretary fell like a mill-stone upon them; yea, it crushed them so, that they could not tell what to do, yet they durst not comply with the demands of Diabolus,

---

* The fear of death sometimes seizes the mind of a child of God: but Jesus came to deliver us from that cruel bondage. This Captain Sepulchre often pays a visit to the doubting soul. But Christians should remember, that Jesus has disarmed death of his sting, and that death itself shall be rendered gain.

† It was wisely done to seek the assistance of the Holy Spirit. He refers them to the written word, for there is sufficient direction in every case. While we earnestly desire the help of the good spirit we must not neglect the directions of the word.

The sad straits of Mansoul. nor with the demands of his captain," Lam. i. 5. So then here were the straits that the town of Mansoul was in when the enemy came upon her: her foes were ready to swallow her up, and her friends forbore to help her.

Then stood up my lord-mayor, whose name was my Lord Understanding, and he began to pick and pick, until he had picked comfort out of that seemingly bitter saying of the ord secretary; for thus he descanted upon it: First, said he, This unavoidably follows upon the saying of my lord, That we must yet suffer for our sins. 2. But, quoth he, the word "yet" sounds as if at last we should be saved from our enemies, and that, after a few more sorrows, Immanuel will come and be our help. Now the lord-mayor was the more critical in his dealing with the secretary's words, because my lord was more than a prophet, and because none of his words were such, but that at all times they were most exactly significant, and the townsmen were allowed to pry into them, and to expound them to their best advantage.*

So they took their leaves of my lord, and returned to the captains, to whom they told what my lord secretary had said, who, when they had heard it, were all of the same opinion as was my lord-mayor himself; the captains therefore began to take courage, and prepared to make some brave attempt upon the camp of the enemy, and to destroy all that were Diabolonians, with the roving Doubters that the tyrant had brought with him to ruin the poor town of Mansoul.

The town of Mansoul in order. So all betook themselves forthwith to their places, the captains to theirs, the lord-mayor to his, the subordinate preacher to his, and my Lord Will-be-will to his. The captains longed to be at some work for their prince, for they delighted in warlike achievements. The next day, therefore, they came together and consulted; and after consultation had, they resolved to give an answer to the captain of Diabolus with slings; and so they did at the rising of the sun on the morrow; for Diabolus had adventured to come nearer again, but the sling-stones were to him and his like hornets. For as there is nothing to the town of Mansoul so terrible as the roaring of Diabolus's drum, so there is nothing to Diabolus so terrible as the well playing of Immanuel's slings. Wherefore Diabolus was forced to make another retreat, yet further off from the famous town of Mansoul. Then did the lord-mayor of Mansoul cause the bells to be rung, and that

---

* To search the scripture carefully is our duty, and it is a great privilege to possess an enlightened understanding for that purpose.

thanks should be sent to the lord high secretary by the mouth of the subordinate preacher; for that by his words the captains and elders of Mansoul had been strengthened against Diabolus.*

When Diabolus saw that his captains and soldiers, high lords, and renowned, were frightened and beaten down by the stones that came from the golden slings of the prince of the town of Mansoul, he bethought himself, and said, I will try to catch them by fawning, I will try to flatter them into my net.

Diabolus changes his way. Wherefore, after a while he came down again to the wall, not now with his drum, nor with Captain Sepulchre, but having all so besugarded his lips; he seemed to be a very sweet-mouthed, peaceable prince, designing nothing for honour sake, nor to be revenged on Mansoul for injuries by them done to him; but the welfare, and good, and advantage of the town and people therein, was now, as he said, his only design. Wherefore, after he had called for audience, and desired that the townsfolk would give it to him, he proceeded in his oration and said,†

"Oh! the desire of my heart, the famous town of Mansoul, how many nights have I watched, and how many weary steps have I taken, if perhaps I might do thee good! 1 Pet. v. 8. Rev. xii. 10. Far be it, far be it from me to desire to make war upon you; if ye will but willingly and quickly deliver up yourselves unto me. You know that you were mine of old, Matt. iv. 8. Luke iv. 6, 7. Remember also, that so long as you enjoyed me for your lord, and that I enjoyed you for my subjects, you wanted for nothing of all the delights of the earth, that I, your lord and prince could get for you; or that I could invent to make you bonny and blithe withal. Consider, you never had so many hard, dark, troublesome and heart-afflicting hours, while you were mine, as you have had since you revolted from me, nor shall you ever have peace again until you and I become one as before. Be but prevailed with to embrace me *Diabolus exerts himself to bring the townsfolk over to him.* again, and I will grant, yea, enlarge your old charter with abundance of privileges, so that your license and liberty shall be to take, hold, enjoy and make your own, all that is pleasant from east to west. Nor shall any of those incivilities, wherewith you have offended me, be ever charged

---

* Resist the devil and he will flee from you. A little encouragement from the Holy Spirit excites fresh courage in the soul to oppose Satan; and, no doubt, the holy resistance of the Christian is as formidable to him as his assaults are to the tempted.

† Satan has various modes of attack. If he succeed not as the roaring lion, he will assume the crafty serpent; if he prevail not by fear he will resort to flattery; in the latter way he obtained his purpose with our first mother.

upon you by me, so long as the sun and moon endure. Nor shall any of those dear friends of mine, that now, for the fear of you, lie lurking in dens and holes and caves in Mansoul, be hurtful to you any more; yea, they shall be your servants, and shall minister unto you of their substance, and of whatever shall come to hand. I need speak no more, you know them, and have some time since been much delighted in their company; why then should we abide at such odds? Let us renew our old acquaintance and friendship again.

"Bear with your friend, I take the liberty at this time to speak thus freely unto you. The love that I have to you presses me to do it, as also does the zeal of my heart for my friends with you; put me not therefore to further trouble, nor yourselves to further frights. Have you I will, in a way of peace or war, nor do you flatter yourselves with the power and force of your captains, or that your Immanuel will shortly come in to your help; for such strength will do you no pleasure.

"I am come against you with a stout and valiant army, and all the chief princes of the den are even at the head. Besides, my captains are swifter than eagles, stronger than lions, and more greedy of prey than are the evening wolves. What is Og or Bashan! what is Goliath of Gath? and what are a hundred more of them to one of the least of my captains! how then shall Mansoul think to escape my hand and force?"*

Diabolus having thus ended his flattering, fawning, deceitful, and lying speech to the famous town of Mansoul; the Lord-mayor replied unto him as follows:

"O Diabolus, prince of darkness, and master of all deceit;

The lord-mayor's answer. thy lying flatteries we have had, and made sufficient probation of, and have tasted too deeply of that destructive cup already; should we therefore again hearken unto thee, and so break the commandment of our great Shaddai, to join affinity with thee, would not our prince reject us, and cast us off for ever, and, being cast off by him, can the place that he has prepared for thee be a place of rest for us! Besides, O thou that art empty and void of all truth, we are rather ready to die by thy hand than to fall in with thy flattering and lying deceits."†

When the tyrant saw that there was little to be got in parleying with my lord mayor, he fell into a hellish rage, and resolved

---

* This infernal liar promises great things—wonderful liberty—all sensual gratifications, with perfect freedom from all religious fears and restraints; but he does not say, that after all this—"ye shall lie down in sorrow."

† An excellent answer! Past experience has proved that sin is bitterness in the end. Let us treat Satan as a liar, and maintain our allegiance to our prince.

that again with his army of Doubters he would another time assault the town of Mansoul.

So he called for his drummer, who beat up for his men (and while he did beat, Mansoul shook) to be in readiness to give battle to the corporation; then Diabolus drew near with his army and thus disposed of his men. Captain Cruel, and Captain Torment, these he drew up, and placed against Feel-gate, and commanded them to set down there for the war.*

Diabolus draws up his army against the town.

And he also appointed, that if need were, Captain No-ease should come into their relief. At Nose-gate he placed Captain Brimstone and Captain Sepulchre, and bid them look well to their ward on that side of the town of Mansoul. But at Eye-gate he placed that grim-faced one, the Captain Past-hope, and there also now did he set up his terrible standard.

Now Captain Insatiable was to look to the carriages of Diabolus, and was also appointed to take into custody that, or those persons and things that should at any time as prey be taken from the enemy. The inhabitants of Mansoul kept mouth-gate for a sally-port, wherefore that they kept strong, for that was it by and out of which the townsfolk sent their petitions to Immanuel their prince; that also was the gate, from the top of which the captains played their slings at the enemies, for that gate stood somewhat ascending, so that the placing of them here, and the letting of them fly from that place, did much execution against the tyrant's army; wherefore for these causes, with others, Diabolus sought, if possible, to stop up Mouth-gate with dirt.†

Now as Diabolus was busy and industrious in preparing to make his assault upon the town of Mansoul without, so the captains and soldiers in the corporation were as busy in preparing within; they mounted their slings, set up their banners, sounded their trumpets, and put themselves in such order as was judged most for the annoyance of the enemy, and for the advantage of Mansoul; and gave their soldiers orders to be ready at the sound of the trumpet for war. The Lord Will-be-will also, he took the charge of watching against the rebels within, and to do what he could to take them while without, or to stifle them within their caves, dens, and holes in the town-wall of Mansoul. And, to speak the truth of him, ever since he did

The Lord-Will-be-will plays the man.

---

* Satan's intention being to fill the soul with doubts, and, if possible, with despair, places his forces at Feel-gate; that is, he would lead the soul to doubt by trusting to his religious frames and feelings, instead of looking only to Jesus.

† The christian's chief weapon is prayer; no wonder, then, that the enemy wishes to obstruct it.

penance for his fault, he has showed as much honesty and bravery of spirit as may be in Mansoul, for he took one Jolly, and his brother Griggish, the two sons of his servant Harmless-mirth; (for to that day, though the father was committed to ward, the sons had a dwelling in the house of my lord) I say, he took them, and with his own hands put them to the cross. And this was the reason why he hanged them up; after their father was put into the hands of Mr Trueman the gaoler, his sons began to play their pranks, and to be tricking and toying with the daughters of their lord; nay, it was jealoused that they were too familiar with them, which was brought to his lordship's ear. Now his lordship being unwilling unadvisedly to put any man to death, did not suddenly fall upon them; but set watch and spies to see if the thing was true; of the which he was soon informed, for his two servants, whose names were Find-out and Tell-all, catched them together in an uncivil manner more than once or twice, and went and told their lord. So when my Lord Will-be-will had sufficient ground to believe the thing was true, he takes the two young Diabolonians, for such they were, (for their father was a Diabolonian born) and has them to Eye-gate, where he raised a very high cross just in the face of Diabolus, and of his army, and there he hanged the young villains, in defiance of Captain Past-hope, and the horrible standard of the tyrant.

Jolly and Griggish taken and executed.

Now this christian act of the brave Lord Will-be-will greatly abashed Captain Past-hope, discouraged the army of Diabolus, put fear into the Diabolonian runnagades in Mansoul, and put strength and courage into the captains that belonged to Immanuel the prince; for they without gathered, and that by this very act of my lord, that Mansoul was resolved to fight, and that the Diabolonians within the town could not do such things as Diabolus had hopes they would. Nor was this the only proof of the brave Lord Will-be-will's honesty to the town, nor of his loyalty to his prince, as will afterwards appear.*

Mortification of sin is a sign of hope of life.

Now when the children of Prudent-thrifty, who dwelt with Mr Mind, (for Thrift left children with Mr Mind, when he was also committed to prison, and their names were Gripe and Rake-all, these he begat of Mr Mind's bastard daughter, whose name

---

* The world pleads hard for gaity and freedom of behaviour between the sexes; dancing and other amusements are calculated to promote them. But experience, painful experience, and careful observation, prove their danger. Avoid the appearance of evil, and every approach towards it. The gracious will determines on the destruction of carnal jollity and frolic. In this way alone young persons will find their safety; and this act of mortification will please Christ, and dismay the enemy.

Mr Mind plays the man. was Mrs Hold-fast-bad,) I say, when his children perceived how the Lord Will-be-will had served them that dwelt with him, what do they but (lest they should drink of the same cup) endeavour to make their escape. But Mr Mind being wary of it, took them, and put them in hold in his house till the morning, (for this was done over-night,) and remembering that by the law of Mansoul all Diabolonians were to die (and to be sure they were at least by father's side such, and some say by mother's side too;) what does he, but takes them, and puts them in chains, and carries them to the self same place where my lord hanged his two before, there he hanged them. The townsmen also took great encouragement at this act of Mr Mind, and did what they could to have taken some more of these Diabolonian troublers of Mansoul; but at that time the rest lay so close, that they could not be apprehended; so they set against them a diligent watch and went every man to his place.*

I told you a little before, that Diabolus and his army were somewhat abashed and discouraged at the sight of what my Lord Will-be-will did, when he hanged up those two young Diabolonians; but his discouragement quickly turned itself into furious madness and rage against the town of Mansoul, and fight it he would. Also the townsmen and captains within had their hopes and expectations heightened, believing at last the day would be theirs, so they feared them the less. Their subordinate preacher too made a sermon about it, and took that theme for his text, "Gad, a troop shall overcome him, but he shall overcome at the last." Whence he showed, that though Mansoul should be sorely put to it at the first, yet the victory should most certanily be Mansoul's at the last, Gen. xlix. 19.†

So Diabolus commanded that his drummer should beat a charge against the town, and the captains also that were in the town sounded a charge against them, but they had no drum, they were trumpets of silver with which they sounded against them. Then they which were of the camp of Diabolus came down to the town to take it, and the captains *The battle begins between Mansoul and the army of Diabolus.* in the castle, with the slingers at Mouthgate, played upon them amain. And now there was nothing heard in the camp of Diabolus but horrible rage and blasphemy; but in the town good words, prayer, and singing of psalms.

---

* Covetousness, under whatever name it assumes, must be mortified, for it is of the devil.

† This was arguing wisely, and thus should the christian encourage himself in the Lord his God, when assaulted by an army of Doubters.

The enemy replied with horrible objections, and the terribleness of their drum; but the town made answer with the slapping of their slings, and the melodious noise of their trumpets. And thus the fight lasted for several days together, only now and then they had some small intermission, in which the townsmen refreshed themselves, and the captains made ready for another assault.

The captains of Immanuel were clad in silver armour, and the soldiers in that which was of proof; the soldiers of Diabolus were clad in iron, which was made to give place to Immanuel's engine shot. In the town some were hurt, and some were greatly wounded. Now the worst of it was, a surgeon was scarce in Mansoul, for that Immanuel at this time was absent, Rev. xxii. 2. Ps. xxxviii. 5. Howbeit, with the leaves of a tree the wounded were kept from dying, yet their wounds greatly putrified, and some did grievously stink. Of the townsmen these were wounded, to wit, my Lord Reason, he was wounded in the head. Another that was wounded, was the brave Lord-mayor; he was wounded in the eye. Another that was wounded, was Mr Mind; he received his wound about the stomach. The honest subordinate preacher also received a shot not far off the heart, but none of these were mortal. Many also of the inferior sort were not only wounded, but slain out-right. Now in the camp of Diabolus were wounded and slain a considerable number: for instance, Captain Rage was wounded, and so was Captain Cruel. Captain Damnation was made to retreat, and intrench himself further off of Mansoul; the standard also of Diabolus was beaten down, and his standard-bearer, Captain Much-hurt, had his brains beat out with a sling-stone, to the no little grief and shame of his prince Diabolus.

Who of Mansoul were wounded.

Hopeful thoughts.

Who in the camp of Diabolus were wounded and slain.

Many also of the Doubters were slain out-right, though enough of them were left alive to make Mansoul shake and totter. Now the victory that day being turned to Mansoul, put great valour into the townsmen and captains, and covered Diabolus's camp with a cloud, but withal it made them far more furious. So the next day Mansoul rested, and commanded that the bells should be rung, the trumpets also joyfully sounded, and the captains shouted round the town.*

The victory turned that day to Mansoul, &c.

My Lord Will-be-will also was not idle, but did notable service within against the domestics, or the Diabolonians, that were in

---

* By this battle we may understand the conflict that often takes place between faith and unbelief. The believer may be wounded, but shall not be slain.

the town, not only by keeping of them in awe; for he lighted on one at last whose name was Mr Any-thing, a fellow of whom mention was made before, for it was he, if you remember, that brought the three fellows to Diabolus, whom the Diabolonians took out of Captain Boanerges's companies, and that persuaded them to list themselves under the tyrant, to fight against the army of Shaddai; my Lord Will-be-will also took a notable Diabolonian, whose name was Loose-foot; this Loose-foot was a scout to the vagabonds in Mansoul, and used to carry tidings out of Mansoul to the camp, and out of the camp to those of the enemies in Mansoul; both these my lord sent away safe to Mr Trueman the goaler, with a commandment to keep them in irons; for he intended then to have them out to be crucified, when it would be for the best to the corporation, and most for the discouragement of the camp of the enemies.*

My Lord Will-be-will taketh one Any-thing, and one Loose-foot, and committeth them to ward.

My Lord-mayor also, though he could not stir about so much as formerly; because of the wound that he had lately received, yet gave he out orders to all that were the natives of Mansoul, to look to their watch and stand upon their guard, and, as occasion shall offer, to prove themselves men. Mr Conscience the preacher also did his utmost to keep all his good documents alive u_ in the hearts of the people of Mansoul.

CHAPTER XV.

The inhabitants of Mansoul made a rash sortie on the enemy by night, but are repulsed with loss. Diabolus makes a desperate attack upon Feel-gate, which being weak, he forces, and his army of Doubters possess the town, committing much violence. The inhabitants agree to petition Immanuel, and obtain the assistance of the secretary. Captain Credence presents the petition, is favourably received, and made Lord lieutenant of all the forces.

WELL, a while after the captains and stout ones of the town of Mansoul agreed, and resolved upon a time to make a sally out upon the camp of Diabolus, and this must be done in the night, and there was the folly of Mansoul (for the night is always the best for the enemy, but the worst for Mansoul to fight in), but yet they would do it, their courage was so high; their last victory also still stuck in their memories.

The captains consult to fall upon the enemy.

The night appointed being come, the prince's brave captains

---

* Any-thing means indifference about religion—a conformity, or opposition to it, as convenience requires. Loose-foot, may signify a careless walk and conversation.

cast lots who should lead the van in this new and desperate expedition against Diabolus, and against his Diabolonian army; and the lot fell to Captain Credence and Captain Experience; Captain Goodhope led the forlorn-hope (this Captain Experience the prince created such when himself resided in the town of Mansoul;) so as I said, they made their sally out upon the army that lay in the siege against them; and their hap was to fall in with the the main body of their enemies. Now Diabolus and his men, being expertly accustomed to night-work, took the alarm presently, and were as ready to give them battle, as if they had sent them word of their coming. Wherefore to it they went amain, and blows were hard on every side; the hell-drum also was beat most furiously, while the trumpets of the prince most sweetly sounded. And thus the battle was joined, and Captain Insatiable looked to the enemies' carriages, and waited when he should receive some prey.

They fight in the night.
Who lead the van.
How they fall on.

The prince's captain's fought it stoutly, beyond what indeed could be expected they should; they wounded many, they made the whole army of Diabolus to make a retreat. But I cannot tell how, but as the brave Captain Credence, Captain Good-hope, and Captain Experience, were upon the pursuit, cutting down and following hard after the enemy in the rear, Captain Credence stumbled and fell, by which fall he caught so great a hurt, that he could not arise, till Captain Experience helped him up, at which their men were put in disorder; the captain also was so full of pain, that he could not forbear but aloud to cry out; at this the other two captains fainted, supposing that Captain Credence had received his mortal wound; their men also were more disordered, and had no mind to fight. Now Diabolus being very observing, though at this time as yet he was put to the worst, perceiving that a halt was made among the pursuers, what does he, but taking it for granted that the captains were either wounded or dead, he therefore at first makes a stand, then faces about, and so comes up upon the prince's army with as much of his fury as hell could help him to, and his hap was to fall in just among the three captains, Captain Credence, Captain Good-hope, and Captain Experience, and did cut, wound, and pierce them so dreadfully, that what through discouragement, what through disorder, and what through the wounds that now they had received, and also the loss of much blood, they scarce were able (though they had for their power the

They fight bravely.
Captain Credence hurt.
The rest of the captains faint.
Diabolus takes place.
The prince's forces beaten.

three best hands in Mansoul) to get safe into the town again. Now when the body of the prince's army saw how these three Captains were put to the worst, they thought it their wisdom to make as safe and good a retreat as they could, and so returned by the sally port again, and so there was an end of the present action.*

Diabolus flushed. Diabolus was so flushed with this night's work, that he promised himself in a few days an easy and complete conquest over the town of Mansoul: wherefore on the day following he comes up to the sides thereof with great boldness, and demands entrance, and that forthwith they deliver themselves up to his government *He demands the town.* (the Diabolonians too that were within began to be somewhat brisk, as we shall show afterwards,) but the valiant lord-mayor replied, that what he got he must get by force; for as long as Immanuel their prince was *The mayor's answer.* alive, (though he at present was not so with them as they wished,) they could never consent to yield Mansoul up to another.

The Lord Will-be-will then stood up, and said, "Diabolus, thou master of the den, and enemy to all that *Brave Will-be-will's speech.* is good, we poor inhabitants of the town of Mansoul are too well acquainted with thy rule and government, and with the end of those things that for certain will follow submitting to thee, to do it. Wherefore, though a while we were without knowledge, we suffered thee to take us (as the bird that saw not the snare fell into the hands of the fowler,) yet since we have been turned from darkness to light, we have also been turned from the power of Satan to God. And though through thy subtlety, and the subtlety of the Diabolonians within, we have sustained much loss, and also plunged ourselves into much perplexity, yet give up ourselves, lay down our arms, and yield to so horrid a tyrant as thou, we will not; die upon the the place we chuse rather to do. Besides, we have hopes that in time deliverance will come from court unto us, and therefore we yet will maintain war against thee.†

This brave speech of the Lord Will-be-will, with that also of the lord-mayor, somewhat abated the boldness of Diabolus, though it kindled the fury of his rage. It *The captains encouraged.* also encouraged the townsmen and captains; yea, it was as a plaster to the brave Captain Credence's

* The night of darkness and desertion was not a proper season for this exertion. This sally seems intended to describe the prevalence of a self confident spirit, which cannot issue well; for faith, hope, and experience are wounded.

† Whatever temporary advantage Satan may gain over a gracious soul, yet "the root of the matter remaining," it will not give place to him, or patiently endure the thoughts of returning under his hellish tyranny.

wound; for you must know that a brave speech now, when the captains of the town, with their men of war, came home routed, and when the enemy took courage and boldness at the success that he had obtained, to draw up to the walls, and demand entrance, as he did, was in season, and also advantageous.

The Lord Will-be-will also played the man within, for while *Will-be-will's gallantry.* the captains and soldiers were in the field, he was in arms in the town, and wherever by him there was a Diabolonian found, they were forced to feel the weight of his heavy hand, and also the edge of his penetrating sword; many therefore of the Diabolonians he wounded, as the Lord Cavil, the Lord Brisk, the Lord Pragmatic, the Lord Murmur; several also of the meaner sort he sorely maimed: though there cannot at this time an account be given you of any that he slew outright. The cause, or rather the advantage that my Lord Will-be-will had at this time to do thus, was, for that the captains were gone out to fight the enemy in the field. For now, thought the Diabolonians within, is our time to stir and make an uproar in the town; what do they therefore but quickly get themselves into a body, and fall forthwith to hurricaning in Mansoul, as if now nothing but whirlwind and tempest should be there: wherefore, as I said, he takes this opportunity to fall in among them with his men, cutting and slashing with courage that was undaunted; at which the Diabolonians with all haste dispersed themselves to their holds, and my lord to his place as before.

This brave act of my lord somewhat revenged the wrong done by Diabolus to the captains, and also let them know, that *Nothing like faith to crush Diabolus.* Mansoul was not to be parted with, for the loss of a victory or two, wherefore the wing of the tyrant was clipt again, as to boasting, I mean, in comparison of what he would have done if the Diabolonians had put the town to the same plight to which he had put the captains.

Well, Diabolus yet resolves to have the other bout with Mansoul; for, thought he, since I beat them once, I may beat them twice: wherefore he commanded his men to be ready at such an hour of the night to make a fresh assault upon the town, and he gave it out in special, that they should bend all their force *He tries what he can do upon the sense and feelings of the christian.* against Feel-gate, and attempt to break into the town through that. The word that then he gave to his officers and soldiers was Hell-fire. And said he, if we break in upon them, as I wish we do, either with some, or with all our force, let them that break in look to it, that they forget not the word. And let nothing be heard in the town of Mansoul, but Hell-fire, hell-fire, hell-fire! The drummer was also to beat without ceasing, and the standard-bearers were to display their colours; the soldiers too were to put on what courage they could, and to see that they played manfully their parts against the town.*

So the night being come, and all things by the tyrant made ready for the work, he suddenly makes his assault upon Feel-gate, and after he had a while struggled there, he throws the gates wide open; for the truth is, those gates were but weak, and so most easily made to yield. When Diabolus had thus far made his attempt, he placed his captains, to wit, Torment and No-ease, there; so he attempted to press forward, but the prince's captains came down upon him, and made his entrance more difficult than he desired. And to speak truth, they made what resistance they could; but three of their best and most valiant captains being wounded, and by their wounds made much incapable of doing the town that service they would (and all the rest having more than their hands full of Doubters, and their captains that followed Diabolus,) they were overpowered with force, nor could they keep them out of the town. Wherefore the prince's men and the captains betook themselves to the castle, as to the strong-hold of the town: and this they did, partly, for their own security partly, for the security of the town, and partly, or rather chiefly, to preserve to Immanuel the prerogative royal of Mansoul, for so was the castle of Mansoul.

The army of Diabolus possess themselves of the town, while the captains of Immanuel fly to the castle.

The captains therefore being fled into the castle, the enemy, without much resistance, possessed themselves of the rest of the town, and spreading themselves as they went into every corner, they cried out as they marched, according to the command of the tyrant, Hell-fire, hell-fire, hell-fire! so that nothing for a while throughout the town of Mansoul could be heard but the direful noise of Hell-fire, together with the roaring of Diabolus's drum. And now did the clouds hang black over Mansoul, nor to reason, did any thing but ruin seem to attend it. Diabolus also quartered his soldiers in the houses of the inhabitants of the town of Mansoul. Yea, the subordinate preacher's house was as full of these outlandish Doubters as ever it could hold; and so

* It is now determined to bend all the force of Diabolus against *Feel-gate*, and the cry was incessantly to be *Hell-fire! Hell-fire!* The meaning is this: christians are to live by faith, not by sense, or feeling—they should derive their hope, not from their feelings and frames in religious duties, &c, but from Jesus alone, and his perfect righteousness. But if on the contrary, they depend on their feelings, Satan may possibly enter the soul with innumerable doubts, and the fear of hell-fire may be terrible.

was my Lord-mayor's and my Lord Will-be-will's also. Yea, where was there a corner, a cottage, a barn, or a hog-sty, that now was not full of these vermin? Yea, they turned the men of the town out of their houses, and would lie in their beds, and sit at their tables themselves. Ah, poor Mansoul! now thou feelest the fruits of sin, and what venom was in the flattering words of Mr Carnal-security! They made great havoc of whatever they

The Doubters make great havoc in the town.

laid their hands on; yea, they fired the town in several places; many young children also were by them dashed in pieces, yea, those that were yet unborn they destroyed in their mother's wombs; for you must needs think that it could not now be otherwise; for what conscience, what pity, what bowels of compassion can any expect at the hands of outlandish Doubters? Many in Mansoul that were women, both young and old, they forced, ravished, and beast-like abused, so that they swooned, miscarried, and many of them died, and so lay at the top of every street, and in all by-places of the town.

And now did Mansoul seem to be nothing but a den of dragons, an emblem of hell, and a place of total darkness. Now did Mansoul lie almost like the barren wilderness: nothing but nettles, briers, thorns, weeds, and stinking things seem now to cover the face of Mansoul. I told you before, how that these Diabolonian Doubters turned the men of Mansoul out of their beds; and now I will add, they wounded them, they mauled them, yea, and almost brained many of them. Many, did I say? yea, most, if not all of them. Mr Conscience they so wounded, yea, and his wounds so festered, that he could have no ease day nor night,

Sad work among the townsmen.

but lay as if continually upon a rack (but that Shaddai rules all, certainly they had slain him outright.) My Lord-mayor they so abused that they almost put out his eyes; my Lord Will-be-

Satan has a particular spite against a sanctified will.

will got into the castle; they intended to have chopped him all to pieces, for they looked upon him (as his heart now stood) to be one of the very worst that was in Mansoul against Diabolus and his crew. And indeed he showed himself a man, and more of his exploits you will hear of afterwards.

Now a man might have walked for many days together in Mansoul, and scarce have seen one in the town that looked like a religious man. Oh the fearful state of Mansoul now! now

The soul full of idle thoughts and blasphemies.

every corner swarmed with outlandish Doubters; red-coats and black-coats walked the town by clusters, and filled up all the houses with hideous noises, vain songs, lying stories and blasphemous language against Shaddai and his son. Now also those Diabolonians that lurked in the walls, and dens, and holes that were in the town of Mansoul, came forth and showed themselves; yea, walked with open face in company with the Doubters that were in Mansoul. Yea, they had more boldness now to walk the streets, to haunt houses, and to show themselves abroad than had any of the honest inhabitants of the now woful town of Mansoul. But Diabolus and his outlandish men were not at peace in Mansoul; for they were not there entertained as were the captains and forces of Immanuel; the townsmen browbeat them what they could: nor did they partake or make destruction of any of the necessaries of Mansoul, but that which they seized on against the townsmen's will; what they could they hid from them, and what they could not they had with an ill-will. They, poor hearts, had rather have had their room than their company, but they were at present their captives, and their captives for the present they were forced to be, Rom. vii. But I say, they discountenanced them as much as they were able, and showed them all the dislike that they could.*

The captains also from the castle held them in continual play with their slings, to the chafing and fretting of the minds of the enemies. True, Diabolus made a a great many attempts to have broken open the gates of the castle, but *Mr Godly-fear* Mr Godly-fear was made the keeper of that, *made keeper* and he was a man of courage, conduct, and *of the castle-* valour, so that it was in vain, as long as life last- *gates.* ed within him, to think to do that work, though mostly desired; wherefore all the attempts that Diabolus made against him were fruitless. (I have wished sometime that that man had had the whole rule of the town of Mansoul.)

Well, this was the condition of the town of Man- *The town of* soul for about two years and a half; the body of the *Mansoul the* town was the seat of war; the people of the town *seat of war.* were driven into holes, and the glory of Mansoul was laid in the dust; what rest then could be to the inhabitants, what peace could Mansoul have, and what sun could shine upon it? Had the enemy lain so long without in the plain against the town, it had been enough to famish them; but now when they shall be within, when the town shall be their tent, their trench, and fort against the castle that was in the town, when the town shall be against the town, and shall serve to be a defence to the enemies of her strength and life; I say, when they

* This is an awful representation of the state of a soul overwhelmed with distressing doubts of God's love, and fears of eternal destruction; "torment," and "loss of ease," take possession. The understanding is darkened, and the

The heart. shall make use of the forts and town-holds to secure themselves in, even till they shall take, spoil, and demolish the castle; this was terrible, and yet this was now the state of the town of Mansoul.*

After the town of Mansoul had been in this sad and lamentable condition for so long a time as I have told you, and no petitions that they had presented their prince with (all this while) could prevail, the inhabitants of the town, to wit, the elders, and chief of Mansoul, gather together, and after some time spent in condoling their miserable state, and this miserable judgment coming upon them, they agreed together to draw up yet another petition, and to send it away to Immanuel for relief. But Mr Godly-fear stood up, and answered, "That he knew his lord the prince never did, nor never would receive a petition for these matters from the hand of any whoever, unless the lord secretary's hand was to it (and this, quoth he, is the reason you prevailed not all this while)." Then they said they would draw up one, and get the lord secretary's hand to it. But Mr Godly-fear answered again, "That he knew also that the lord secretary would not set his hand to any petition that himself had not a hand in composing and drawing up; and besides, said he, the prince doth know my lord secretary's hand from all the hands in the world; wherefore he cannot be deceived by any pretence whatever; wherefore my advice is, that you go to my lord and implore him to lend you his aid." (Now he abode in the castle, where all the captains and men at arms were.) So they heartily thanked Mr Godly-fear, took his counsel, and did as he had bidden them; so they departed and came to my lord, and made known the cause of their coming to him; to wit, that since Mansoul was in so deplorable a condition, his highness would be pleased to undertake to draw up a petition for them to Immanuel, the son of the mighty Shaddai, and to their king and his father by him.

Mr Godly-fear's advice about drawing up a petition to the prince.

Then said the secretary to them, "What petition is it that you would have me draw up for you?" But they said, Our lord knows best the state and condition of the town of Mansoul, and how we are backslidden and degenerated from the prince; thou also knowest who is come up to war against us, and how Mansoul is now the seat of war. My lord knows, moreover,

conscience wounded; while a crowd of idle thoughts, vanities, and blasphemies increase the confusion and dismay.

* In the midst of all this misery, the castle is safe, or in other words, the heart remains right with God, Godly-fear being the keeper of it. In many a soul where distressing doubts prevail, perhaps for years, yet the fear of God is in the heart so that it still cleaves to him, and opposes sin.

what barbarous usage our men, women, and children have suffered at their hands, and how our home-bred Diabolonians walk now with more boldness than dare the townsmen in the streets of Mansoul. Let our lord therefore, according to the wisdom of God that is in him, draw up a petition for his poor servants to our prince Immanuel. "Well (said the lord secretary) I will draw up a petition for you, and will also set my hand thereto." Then said they, "But when shall we call for it at the hand of our lord?" He answered, "Yourselves must be present at the doing of it. Yea, you must put your desires to it. True, the hand and pen shall be mine, but the ink and paper must be yours, else how can you say it is your petition! Nor have I need to petition for myself, because I have not offended.

The secretary requested to draw up a petition for Mansoul.

He also added as followeth: "No petition goes from me in my name to the prince, and so to his father by him, but when the people, that are chiefly concerned therein, join in heart and soul in the matter, for that must be inserted therein."*

So they heartily agreed with the sentence of the lord, and a petition was forthwith drawn up for them. But now who shall carry it, that was the next. But the secretary advised that Captain Credence should carry it, for he was a well-spoken man. They therefore called for him, and propounded to him the business. Well, said the captain, I gladly accept of the motion; and though I am lame, I will do this business for you, with as much speed, and as well as I can.† The contents of the petition were to this purpose:

The petition of Mansoul to the prince Immanuel.

"O our lord and sovereign prince Immanuel, the potent, the long-suffering prince! Grace is poured into thy lips, and to thee belong mercy and forgiveness, though we have rebelled against thee. We who are no more worthy to be called thy Mansoul, nor yet fit to partake of common benefits, do beseech thee, and thy father by thee, to do away our transgressions. We confess that thou mightest cast us away for them, but do it not for thy name's sake; let the lord rather take an opportunity, at our miserable condition, to let out his bowels of compassion to us;

---

* This is an illustration of that text, Rom. viii. 26. "The spirit *helpeth* our infirmities, for we know not what we should pray for as we ought," &c. The original word *helpeth* signifies *helping together*, like two persons uniting to lift up a weight. Thus should we ever implore the assistance of the good spirit to indite our petitions; and (blessed be God) it is said, "He will give his holy spirit to them that ask him."

† Credence is a very proper person to carry the petition, for we are to *pray in faith*.

we are compassed on every side, lord; our own backslidings reprove us, our Diabolonians within our town fright us, and the army of the angel of the bottomless pit distress us. Thy grace can be our salvation, and whither to go but to thee we know not.

"Furthermore, O gracious prince, we have weakened our captains, and they are discouraged, sick, and of late some of them grievously worsted, and beaten out of the field by the power and force of the tyrant. Yea, even those of our captains, in whose valour we formerly used to put most of our confidence, they are as wounded men. Besides, lord, our enemies are lively, and they are strong, they vaunt and boast themselves, and threaten to part us among themselves for a booty. They are fallen also upon us, lord, with many thousand Doubters, such as with whom we cannot tell what to do; they are all grim-looked and unmerciful ones, and they bid defiance to us and thee.

"Our wisdom is gone, our power is gone, because thou art departed from us, nor have we what we may call ours, but sin, shame, and confusion of face for sin. Take pity upon us, O lord, take pity upon us, thy miserable town of Mansoul, and save us out of the hands of our enemies. Amen."*

This petition, as was touched afore, was handed by the lord secretary, and carried to the court by the brave and most stout Captain Credence. Now he carried it out at Mouth-gate, for that, as I said, was the sally-port of the town; and he went, and came to Immanuel with it. Now how it came out I do not know, but for certain it did, and that so far as to reach the ears of Diabolus. Thus I conclude, because that the tyrant had it presently by the end, and charged the town of Mansoul with it; saying, "Thou rebellious and stubborn-hearted Mansoul, I will make thee to leave off petitioning: art thou yet for petitioning? I will make thee to leave off." Yea, he also knew who the messenger was that carried the petition to the prince, and it made him both fear and rage. Wherefore he commanded that his drum should be beat again, a thing that Mansoul could not abide to hear: but when Diabolus would have his drum beat, Mansoul must abide the noise. Well, the drum was beat, and the Diabolonians were gathered together.†

Satan cannot abide prayer.

Then said Diabolus, "O ye stout Diabolonians, be it known unto you, that there is treachery hatched against us in the rebellious town of Mansoul; for albeit the town is in our possession, as you see, yet these miserable Mansoulians have attempted to dare, and have been so hardy as yet to send to the court of

---

* An excellent prayer! full of humility and faith.

† When Christians pray Satan rages; for he hates the prayer of faith, and dreads its effect.

Immanuel for help. This I give you to understand, that ye may yet know how to carry it to the wretched town of Mansoul. Wherefore, O my trusty Diabolonians, I command, that yet more and more ye distress this town of Mansoul, and vex it with your wiles, ravish their women, deflower their virgins, slay their children, brain their ancients, fire their town, and do what other mischief you can; and let this be the reward of the Mansoulians from me, for their desperate rebellion against me."

Diabolus is enraged against the town of Mansoul

This you see was the charge, but something stepped in betwixt that and execution, for as yet there was but little more done than to rage.

Moreover, when Diabolus had done thus, he went the next day up to the castle gates, and demanded that, upon pain of death, the gates should be opened to him, and that entrance should be given him, and his men that followed after. To whom Mr Godly-fear replied (for he it was that had the charge of the gate) "That the gate should not be opened unto him, nor to the men that followed after him." He said, moreover, "That Mansoul, when she had suffered awhile, should be made perfect, strengthened and settled."

Then said Diabolus, "Deliver me then the men that petitioned against me, especially Captain Credence that carried it to your prince; deliver that varlet into my hands, and I will depart from the town."*

Satan cannot abide faith.

Then up starts a Diabolonian, whose name was Mr Fooling, and said, "My lord offereth you fair, it is better for you that one man perish, than that your whole Mansoul should be undone."

But Mr Godly-fear made him this replication: "How long will Mansoul be kept out of the dungeon, when she hath given up her faith to Diabolus? As good lose the town as lose Captain Credence, for if one be gone, the other must follow." But to that Mr Fooling said nothing.

Then did my lord-mayor reply, and said, "O thou devouring tyrant, be it known unto thee, we shall hearken to none of thy words; we are resolved to resist thee as long as a captain, a man, a sling, and a stone to throw at thee, shall be found in the town of Mansoul.

But Diabolus answered, "Do you hope, do you wait, do you look for help and deliverance! You have sent to Immanuel, but your wickedness sticks too close in your skirts to let innocent prayer come out of your lips. Think you, that you shall be prevailers, and prosper

Diabolus rages.

---

* Could faith be given up, Satan would obtain all his desire.

in this design? you will fail in your wish, you will fail in your attempts; for it is not only I, but your Immanuel is against you. Yea it is he that hath sent me against you to subdue you; for what then do you hope, or by what means will you escape?"

Then said my lord mayor, "We have sinned indeed, but that shall be no help to thee, for our Immanuel hath said it, and that in great faithfulness, 'And him that cometh to me I will in no wise cast out.' He hath also told us (O our enemy) that 'all manner of sin and blasphemy shall be forgiven to the sons of men.' Therefore we dare not despair, but will look for, and wait for mercy."*

The lord-mayor's speech just at the time of the return of Captain Credence.

And now by this time Captain Credence was come from the court from Immanuel to the castle of Mansoul, and he returned to them with a packet. So my lord-mayor, hearing that Captain Credence was come, withdrew himself from the noise of the roaring of the tyrant, and left him to yell at the wall of the town, or against the gates of the castle. He then came up to the captain's lodgings, and, saluting him, asked him of his welfare, and what was the best news at court? but when he asked Captain Credence that, the water stood in his eyes. Then said the captain, Cheer up, my lord, for all will be well in time. And with that he first produced his packet, and laid it by, but that the lord-mayor and the rest of the captains took for a sign of good tidings. (Now a season of grace being come, he sent for all the captains and elders of the town that were here and there in their lodgings, in the castle, and upon their guard, to let them know that Captain Credence was returned from the court, and that he had something in general, and something in special to communicate to them.) So they all came up to him, and saluted him, and asked him concerning his journey, and what was the best news at court! And he answered them, as he had done the lord-mayor before, that all would be well at last.†

Now when the captain had thus saluted them, he opened his packet, and thence drew out of it several notes for those that he had sent for. And the first note was for my lord-mayor, wherein was signified: "The prince Immanuel had taken it well that my lord-mayor had been so true and trusty in his office, and the great concerns that lay upon him for the town and people of Mansoul. Also he bid him to know that he took it well that he had been so bold for his prince Im-

The packet opened.

A note for my lord-mayor.

---

* Nothing like the precious promises as an answer to Satan. With the word of God our Lord himself silenced the devil in the wilderness.
† This is the proper language of faith, "All shall be well at the last."

manuel, and had engaged so faithfully in his cause against Diabolus. He also signified at the close of his letter, than he should shortly receive his reward."

The second note that came out, was for the noble Lord Will-be-will, wherein there was signified, "That his prince Immanuel did well understand how valiant and courageous he had been for the honour of his lord, now in his absence, and when his name was under contempt by Diabolus. There was signified also, that his prince had taken it well that he had been so faithful to the town of Mansoul, in his keeping of so strict a hand and eye over, and so strict a rein upon the necks of the Diabolonians that still were lurking in their several holes in the famous town of Mansoul.

A note for my Lord Will-be-will.

He signified moreover, that he understood that my lord had with his own hand done great execution upon some of the chiefs of the rebels there, to the great discouragement of the adverse party, and to the good example of the whole town of Mansoul, and that shortly his lordship should have his reward."

The third note came out for the subordinate preacher, wherein was signified, "That his prince took it well from him, that he had so honestly and so faithfully performed his office, and executed the trust committed to him by his lord, while he exhorted, rebuked, and forewarned Mansoul according to the laws of the town." He signified moreover, "that he took it well at his hand, that he called to fasting, to sack-cloth, and ashes, when Mansoul was under her revolt. Also, that he called for the aid of the Captain Boanerges to help in so mighty a work, and that shortly he also should receive his reward."

A note for the subordinate preacher.

The fourth note came out for Mr Godly-fear, wherein his lord thus signified: "That his lordship observed, that he was the first of all the men in Mansoul that detected Mr Carnal-security, as the only one that, through his subtlety and cunning, had obtained for Diabolus a defection and decay of goodness in the blessed town of Mansoul. Moreover, his lord gave him to understand, that he still remembered his tears and mourning for the state of Mansoul." It was also observed by the same note, "that his lord took notice of his detecting this Mr Carnal-security at his table among his guests, in his own house, and that in the midst of his jolliness, even while he was seeking to perfect his villanies against the town of Mansoul. Immanuel also took notice, that this reverend person, Mr Godly-fear, stood stoutly to it at the gates of the castle against all the threats and attempts of the tyrant, and that he had put the towns-

A note for Mr Godly-fear.

men in a way to make their petition to their prince, so as that he might accept thereof, and as that they might obtain an answer of peace; and that therefore shortly he should receive his reward."

A note for the town of Mansoul. After all this, there was yet produced a note which was written to the whole town of Mansoul, whereby they perceived, "That their lord took notice of their so often repeated petitions to him, and that they should see more of the fruits of such their doings in time to come." Their prince also therein told them, "that he took it well, that their heart and mind now at last abode fixed upon him and his ways, though Diabolus had made such inroads upon them, and that, neither flatteries on the one hand, nor hardships on the other, could make them yield to serve his cruel designs. There was also inserted at the bottom of this note, "that his lordship had left the town of Mansoul in the hands of the lord secretary, and under the conduct of Captain Credence; saying, Beware that you yet yield yourselves unto their governance, and in due time you shall receive your reward."*

After the brave Captain Credence had delivered his notes to those to whom they belonged, he retired himself to my lord secretary's lodgings, and there spends his time in conversing with him; for they two were very great one with another, and indeed knew more how things would go with Mansoul than all the townsmen besides. The lord secretary also loved Captain Credence dearly, yea, many a good bit was sent him from my lord's table; also he might have a show of countenance when the rest of Mansoul lay under the clouds; so after some time for converse was spent, the captain betook himself to his chamber to rest. But not long after my lord sent for the captain again; so the captain came to him, and they greeted one another with usual salutations. Then said the captain to the lord secretary, "What hath my lord to say to his servant?" So the lord secretary took him and had him aside, and, after a sign or two of more favour, he said, "I have made thee the lord-lieutenant over all the forces in Mansoul; so that from this day forward all men in Mansoul shall be at thy word, and thou shalt be he that shall lead in, and that shall lead out Mansoul. Thou shalt therefore manage, according to thy place, the war for thy prince, and for the town of Mansoul, against the force and power of Diabolus, and at thy command shall the rest of the captains be."

Captain Credence made lord-lieutenant over all the forces in Mansoul.

---

* In due time believers "shall reap, if they faint not." The Lord observes and approves the works of faith and the labours of love here mentioned, and none of them shall lose its reward. The honest efforts of the understanding, the will, the conscience, and the fear of God, shall, at length, be crowned with success.

Now the townsmen began to perceive what interest the captain had, both with the court and also with the lord secretary in Mansoul; for no man before could speed when sent, nor bring such good news from Immanuel as he. Wherefore what do they (after some lamentation that they made no more use of him in their distress) but send by their subordinate preacher to the lord secretary, to desire him that all that ever they were and had might be put under the government, care, custody, and conduct of Captain Credence."*

The townsmen desire to be put under the government of Captain Credence.

So their preacher went and did his errand, and received this answer from the mouth of his lord, That Captain Credence should be the great doer in all the king's army against the king's enemies, and also for the welfare of Mansoul. So he bowed to the ground, and thanked his lordship, and returned and told his news to the townsfolk. But all this was done with all imaginable secrecy, because the foes had yet great strength in the town. But to return to our story again.

CHAPTER XVI.

A new plot is laid to ruin the town by Riches and Prosperity. Immanuel appears in the Field to assist the Forces of Mansoul, whereby the whole army of Doubters is completely routed. Immanuel enters the town amidst the most joyful acclamations of the inhabitants.

WHEN Diabolus saw himself thus boldly confronted by the lord-mayor, and perceived the stoutness of Mr Godly-fear, he fell into a rage, and forthwith called a council of war, that he might be revenged on Mansoul. So all the princes of the pit came together, and old Incredulity at the head of them, with all the captains of his army. So they consulted what to do. Now the effect and conclusion of the council that day was, how they might take the castle, because they could not conclude themselves masters of the town so long as that was in the possession of their enemies. So one advised this way, and another advised that; but when they could not agree in their verdict, Apollyon, the president of the council, stood up, and thus he began: My brotherhood (quoth he) I have some things to propound unto you; and my first is this: Let us withdraw ourselves from

Different judgments in Diabolus's council of war.

---

* The design of this is, to show that the soul is to live by faith, and not by sense. The spirit of God puts honour upon faith, and makes him chief captain in the town. This is a token for good, now the Doubters prevail in the town This is a prelude of victory over them. The inhabitants are, at length, aware of his abili s, and wish to be under his control. Thus Christians learn, but seldom w   ut painful experience, that they are not to live by their feelings, but by   ir faith.

the town into the plain again, for our presence here will do us no good, because the castle is yet in our enemies' hands; nor is it possible that we should take that, so long as so many brave captains are in it, and this bold fellow **Godly-fear** is made the keeper of the gates of it.

"Now when we have withdrawn ourselves into the plain, they of their own accord will be glad of some little ease, and it may be of their own accord they again may begin to be remiss, and even their so being will give them a bigger blow than we can possibly give them ourselves. But if that should fail, our going forth out of the town may draw the captains out after us, and you know what it cost them when we fought them in the field before. Besides, can we but draw them out into the fields, we may lay an ambush behind the town, which shall, when they are come forth abroad, rush in, and take possession of the castle." But Beelzebub stood up and replied; saying, it is impossible to draw them all off from the castle; some, you may be sure, will lie there to keep that; wherefore it will be but in vain thus to attempt, unless we were sure that they will all come out. He therefore concluded, that what was done must be done by some other means. And the most likely means that the greatest of their heads could invent, was that which Apollyon had advised to before; to wit, to get the townsmen again to sin. For, said he, it is not our being in the town, nor in the field, nor our fighting, nor our killing of their men, that can make us the masters of Mansoul; for so long as one in the town is able to lift up his finger against us, Immanuel will take their parts, and if he shall take their parts, we know what a time a day it will be with us. Wherefore, for my part, quoth he, there is, in my judgment, no way to bring them into bondage to us like inventing a way to make them sin, 2 Pet. ii. 18, 19, 20, 21. Had we, said he, left all our **Doubters** at home, we had done as well as we have done now, unless we could have made them the masters and governors of the castle; for **Doubters** at a distance are but like objections repelled with arguments. Indeed, can we but get them into the hold, and make them possessors of that, the day will be our own. Let us therefore withdraw ourselves into the plain (not expecting that the captains in Mansoul should follow us,) but yet, I say, let us do this; and before we do so, let us advise again with our trusty Diabolonians that are yet in the holds of Mansoul, and set them to work to betray the town to us; for they indeed must do it, or it will be left undone forever. By these sayings of Beelzebub (for I think it was he that gave this counsel,) the whole conclave was

Beelzebub harangues.

Mansoul cannot be taken while the inhabitants do not consent to sin.

forced to be of his opinion; to wit, that the way to get the castle was to get the town to sin. Then they fell to inventing by what means they might do this thing.*

Then Lucifer stood up and said, "The counsel of Beelzebub is pertinent; now the way to bring this to pass, in my opinion, is this: Let us withdraw our force from the town of Mansoul: let us do this: and let us terrify them no more, either with summonses or threats, or with the noise of our drum, or any other awakening means. Only let us lie in the field at a distance, and be as if we regarded them not (for frights I see do but awaken them, and make them stand more to their arms.) I have also another stratagem in my head: you know Mansoul is a market town, a town that delights in commerce; what therefore if some of our Diabolonians shall feign themselves far countrymen, and shall go out and bring to the market of Mansoul some of our wares to sell; and what matter at what rates they sell their wares, though it be but for half the worth? Now let those that thus trade in their market be those that are witty and true to us, and I will lay my crown to pawn, it will do. There are two that are come to my thoughts already, that I think will be arch at this work, and they are, Mr Penny-wise-pound-foolish, and Mr Get-i'th-hundred-and-lose-i'th-shire; nor is this man with the long name at all inferior to the other. What also if you join with them Mr Sweet-world and Mr Present-good, they are men that are civil and cunning, and our true friends and helpers, Rev. iii. 17. Let these, with as many more engage in this business for us, and let Mansoul be taken up in much business, and let them grow full and rich, and this is the way to get ground of them; remember ye not, that thus we prevailed upon Laodicea, and how many at present do we hold in this snare! Now when they begin to grow full they will forget their misery, and, if we shall not afright them, may happen to fall asleep and so be got to neglect their town-watch, their castle-watch as well as their watch at the gates.†

"Yea, may we not by this means so cumber Mansoul with abundance, that they shall be forced to make of their castle a warehouse, instead of a garrison fortified against us, and a receptacle of men of war? Thus if we get our goods and commodities thither, I reckon that

Lucifer proposes another stratagem for the taking of Mansoul.

The deceitfulness of riches.

---

* The great object of temptation is to allure us to sin. Satan cannot hope to possess the heart until it be first brought over to the side of iniquity.

† "Penny-wise and pound-foolish," &c. are proverbial expressions, denoting the folly of those who are anxious to obtain small gains, while they neglect large profits. Satan having found that his doubts and fears did not succeed, but had rather kept men alert, now proposes to try the effect of worldly prosperity, as likely to produce carelessness. And indeed great is the danger, when the castle, (the heart) which should be the temple of the Lord, is turned into a warehouse.

the castle is more than half ours. Besides, could we so order it, that they should be filled with such kind of wares, then, if we made a sudden assault upon them, it would be hard for the captain to take a shelter there. Do you know that of the parable, Luke viii. 14. "The deceitfulness of riches chokes the work." And again, "When the heart is overcharged with surfeiting and drunkenness, and the cares of this life, all mischief comes upon them unawares." Chap. xxi. 84, 35, 36.

"Furthermore, my lords,(quoth he) you very well know that it is not easy for a people to be filled with our things, and not to have some of our Diabolonians as retainers to their houses and services. Where is a Mansoulian that is full of this world, that has not for his servants and waiting-men, Mr Profuse, or Mr Prodigality, or some other of our Diabolonian gang; as Mr Voluptuousness, Mr Pragmatical, Mr Ostentation, or the like? Now these can take the castle of Mansoul, or blow it up, or make it unfit for a garrison for Immanuel, and any of these will do. Yea these, for aught I know, may do it for us sooner than an army of twenty thousand men. Wherefore, to end as I began, my advice is, that we quietly withdraw ourselves, not offering any further force or forcible attempt upon the castle, at least at this time, and let us set on foot our new project, and let us see if that will not make them destroy themselves.*

Lucifer's advice is applauded by all. This advice was highly applauded by them all, and was accounted the very master-piece of hell, to wit, to choke Mansoul with a fulness of this world, and to surfeit her heart with the good things thereof. But see how things meet together. Just as this Diabolonian council was broken up Captain Credence received a letter from Immanuel, the contents of which were these: "That upon the third day he would meet him in the field, in the plains about Mansoul." Meet me in the field! quoth the Captain. What meaneth my lord by this? I know not what he meaneth by meeting me in the field. So he took the note in his hand, and carried it to my Lord Secretary, to ask his thoughts thereupon (for my lord was a seer in all matters concerning the king, and also for the good and comfort of the town of Mansoul. So, he showed my lord the note, and desired his opinion thereon: for my part, quoth Captain Credence, I know not the meaning thereof. So my lord read it, and after a little pause he said, "The Diabolonians have had against Mansoul a great consultation to-day; they have, I say, this day been contriving the utter ruin

A note from Immanuel.

---

* How rarely do men grow rich and prosperous without entertaining those Diabolonians, profusion, prodigality, pride, &c.! These are Satan's best supporters, and more destructive to the soul than an army of external foes.

of the town; and the result of their counsel is, to set Mansoul into such a way, which, if taken, will surely make her destroy herself. And to this end they are making ready for their own departure out of the town, intending to betake themselves to field again, and there to lie till they shall see whether this their project will take or no. But be thou ready with the men of thy Lord (for on the third day they will be in the plain) there to fall upon the Diabolonians; for the prince will by that time be in the field; yea, by that it is break of day, sun rising or before, and that with a mighty force against them. So he shall be before them, and thou shalt be behind them, and betwixt you both their army shall be destroyed."

When Captain Credence heard this, away goes he to the rest of the captains, and tells them what a note he had a while since received from the hand of Immanuel. And, said he, that which was dark therein has my Lord Secretary expounded unto me. He told them moreover, what by himself and by them must be done to answer the mind of their Lord. Then were the captains glad, and Captain Credence commanded, that all the king's trumpeters should ascend on the battlements of the castle, and there in the audience of Diabolus, and of the whole town of Mansoul, make the best music that heart could invent. The trumpeters then did as they were commanded: they got themselves up to the top of the castle, and thus they began to sound. Then did Diabolus start, and said, What can be the meaning of this? they neither sound Boot-and-saddle, nor Horse-and-away, nor a Charge. What do these madmen mean, that yet they should be so merry and glad? Then answered him one of themselves, and said, This is for joy that their prince Immanuel is coming to relieve the town of Mansoul; that to this end he is at the head of an army, and that this relief is near.*

The king's trumpeters commanded to sound from the castle.

The men of Mansoul also were greatly concerned at this melodious charm of the trumpets; they said, yea, they answered one another, saying, This can be no harm to us; surely this can be no harm to us. Then said the Diabolonians, What had we best to do? And it was answered, It was best to quit the town; and that, said one, ye may do in pursuance of your last counsel, and by so doing also be better able to give the enemy battle, should an army from without come upon us. So on the second day they withdrew themselves from Mansoul, and abode in the plains without; but they encamped themselves before Eye-gate, in what terrene and terri-

Diabolus withdraws from the town, and why.

---

* The saints are kept by the power of God. How seasonably is this relief promised! "In the mount it shall be seen." And nothing can so encourage us in our spiritual warfare as the expectation of the Lord's power and presence.

ble manner they could. The reason why they could not abide in the town (besides the reasons that were debated in their late conclave,) was, for that they were not possessed of the strong-hold, and because, said they, we shall have more convenience to fight, and also to fly, if need be, when we are encamped in the open plain. Besides the town would have been a pit for them, rather than a place of defence, had the prince come up and inclosed them fast therein. Therefore they betook themselves to the field, that they might also be out of the reach of the slings by which they were much annoyed all the while they were in the town.

The time come for the captains to fight them. Well, the time that the captains were to fall upon the Diabolonians being come, they eagerly prepared themselves for action; for Captain Credence having told the captains over night, that they should meet their prince in the field to-morrow, was like oil to a flaming fire: for of a long time they had been at a distance; they therefore were for this the more earnest and desirous of the work. So, as I said, the hour being come, Captain Credence, with the rest of the *They draw out into the field.* men of war, drew out their forces before it was day by the sally-port of the town. And being all ready, Captain Credence went up to the head of the army, and gave to the rest of the captains the word, and they to the under officers and soldiers, which was, "The sword of the Prince Immanuel, and the shield of Captain Credence!" which is in the Mansoulian tongue, "The word of God and Faith." Then the captains fell on, and began roundly to front and flank and rear Diabolus's camp.*

Now they left Captain Experience in the town, because he was ill of his wounds which the Diabolonians had given him in the last fight. But when he perceived that the captains were at it, what does he but, calling for his crutches in haste, gets up and away he goes to the battle, saying, Shall I lay here when my brethren are in the fight, and when Immanuel the prince will show himself in the field to his servants? But when the enemy saw the man come with his crutches, they were daunted yet the more, for, thought they, what spirit has possessed these Mansoulians, that they fight us upon their crutches! Well, the captains, as I said, fell on, and bravely handled their weapons, still crying out, and shouting as they laid on blows, "The sword of the Prince Immanuel, and the shield of Captain Credence!"

Now when Diabolus saw that the captains were come out, and that so valiantly they surrounded his men, he concluded, that for the present nothing from them was to be looked for but blows, with the dints of their two-edged swords. Wherefore he also falls

* "The word of God, and Faith." These are invincible weapons.

upon the prince's army with all his deadly force. So the battle was joined. Now who was it that at first Diabolus met with in the fight, but Captain Credence on the one hand, and the Lord Will-be-will on the other; now Will-be-will's blows were like the blows of a giant, for that man had a strong arm, and he fell in upon the Election-doubters, for they were th life-guard of Diabolus, and he kept them in play a good while, cutting and battering shrewdly. Now when Captain Credence saw my lord engaged, he stoutly on the other hand fell upon the same company also, so they put them to great disorder. Now Captain Good-hope had engaged the Vocation-doubters, and they were sturdy men; but the captain was a valiant man: Captain Experience also sent him some aid; for he made the Vocation-doubters retreat.* The rest of the armies were hotly engaged, and that on every side, and the Diabolonians fought stoutly. Then my Lord Secretary commanded that the slings from the castle should be played, and his men could throw stones at a hair's breadth. But after a while those that fled before the captains of the prince began to rally again, and they came up stoutly upon the rear of the prince's army, wherefore the prince's army began to faint; but remembering they should see the face of their prince by and by, they took courage, and a very fierce battle was fought. Then shouted the captains, saying, "The sword of the Prince Immanuel, and the shield of Captain Credence!" and with that Diabolus gave back, thinking that more aid had been come. But no Immanuel as yet appeared. Moreover the battle hung in doubt; and they made a little retreat on both sides. Now in the time of respite, Captain Credence bravely encouraged his men to stand to it, and Diabolus did the like, as well as he could. But Captain Credence made a brave speech to his soldiers, the contents whereof here follow:

"Gentlemen soldiers, and my brethren in his design, it rejoiceth me much to see in the field, for our prince his day so stout and so valiant an army, and faithful lovers of Mansoul. You have hitherto, as hath become you, shown yourselves men of truth and courage against the Diabolonian forces, so that for all their boast, they have not yet cause much to boast of their gettings. Now take to yourselves your wonted courage, and show yourselves men, even this once only; for in a few minutes after the next engagement, this time, you shall see your prince

---

* There may be long and violent conflicts in the soul between doubts and faith; doubt whether or not we are chosen, called, &c. but faith shall at length revive, and Satan with his doubters, retreat.

show himself in the field, for we must make this second assault upon this tyrant Diabolus, and then Immanuel comes."

No sooner had the captain made this speech to the soldiers, but one Mr Speedy came post to the captain from the prince, to tell him that Immanuel was at hand. This news when the captain had received, he communicated to the other field officers, and they again to their soldiers and men of war. Wherefore, like men raised from the dead, so the captains and their men arose, made up to the enemy, and cried as before, "The sword of the Prince Immanuel, and the shield of Captain Credence!"

Immanuel's approach announced.

The Diabolonians also bestirred themselves, and made resistance as well as they could, but in this last engagement they lost their courage, and many of the Doubters fell down dead to the ground. Now when they had been in heat of battle about an hour or more, Captain Credence lifted up his eyes, and beheld Immanuel coming, and he came with colours flying, trumpets sounding, and the feet of his men scarce touched the ground, they hasted with that celerity towards the captains that were engaged. Then Captain Credence wheeled his men to the townward, and gave to Diabolus the field. So Immanuel came upon him on the one side, and the enemies' place was betwixt them both; then again they fell to it afresh, and a little while afterwards Immanuel and Captain Credence met, still trampling down the slain as they came.

But when the captains saw that their prince was come, and that he fell upon the Diabolonians on the other side, and that Captain Credence and his Highness had got them up betwixt them, they shouted (they so shouted, that the ground rent again,) saying, "The sword of Immanuel, and the shield of Captain Credence!" Now when Diabolus saw that he and his forces were so hard beset by the prince and his princely army, what does he, and the lords of the pit that were with him, but make their escape, and forsake their army, and leave them to fall by the hand of Immanuel, and of his noble Captain Credence;* so they fell all down slain before them, before the prince, and before his royal army; there was not left so much as one Doubter alive; they lay spread upon the ground like dead men, as one would spread dung upon the land.

Diabolus and his lords make their escape.

When the battle was over, all things came in order in the camp; then the captains and elders of Mansoul came together to salute

---

* The presence of the Lord decides the contest. Doubts and fears cannot stand before the gracious manifestation of himself to the soul.

"But if Immanuel's face appear,
My hope my joy begins;
His name forbids my slavish fear,
His grace removes my sins."

; without the corporation; so they saluted him,
m, and that with a thousand welcomes, for that he
borders of Mansoul again. So he smiled upon
peace be unto you." Then they addressed them-
e town; they went then to go up to Mansoul, they,
all the new forces that now he had brought with

Also all the gates of the town were set open for
glad were they of his blessed return. And this
and order of his going into Mansoul.

l, all the gates of the town were set open, yea, the
e; the elders too of the town of Mansoul placed
e gates of the town, to salute him at his entrance
hey did, for as he drew near and approached towards the gate, they said, "Lift up your heads,
O ye gates, and be lift up ye everlasting doors,
and the King of glory shall come in." And they
answered again, "Who is the King of glory?"
And they made return to themselves, "The Lord
ty, the Lord! is mighty in battle. Lift up your
s, even lift them up ye everlasting doors," &c.

as ordered also by those of Mansoul, that all the
town-gates to those of the castle, his blessed
be entertained with the song, by them that had
c in all the town of Mansoul; then the elders, and
en of Mansoul answered one another as Immanuel
l, till he came to the castle-gates, with songs and
s, saying, "They have seen thy goings, O God,
of my God, my King, in the sanctuary. So the
re, the players on instruments followed after, and
e the damsels playing on timbrels."

the captains (for I would speak a word for them)
ited on the prince as he entered into the gates of
n Credence went before, and Captain Good-hope
n Charity came behind, with other of his com-
tain Patience followed after all, and the rest of
e on the right hand, and some on the left, ac-
nuel into Mansoul. And all the while the colours
the trumpets sounded, and continual shoutings
soldiers. The prince himself rode into the town
hich was all of beaten gold; and his chariot, the
of silver, the bottom thereof of gold, the covering
e, the midst thereof being paved with love for the
town of Mansoul.

en the prince was come to the entrance of Mansoul, he found all the streets strewed with lilies and flowers, curiously decked with boughs and branches from the green trees, that stood round about the town. Every door also was filled with persons who had adorned every one their fore-part against their house with something of variety and singular excellency to entertain him withal as he passed in the streets; they also themselves, as Immanuel passed by, welcomed him with shouts and acclamations of joy, saying, "Blessed be the prince that cometh in the name of his father Shaddai."*

Fifthly. At the castle-gates the elders of Mansoul, to wit, my Lord-mayor, Lord Will-be-will, the subordinate preachers, Mr Knowledge, and Mr Mind, with other of the gentry of the place, saluted Immanuel again; they bowed before him, they kissed the dust of his feet, they thanked, they blessed and praised his highness for not taking advantage against them for their sins, but rather had pity upon them in their misery, and returned to them with mercies, and to build up their Mansoul for ever. Thus was he had up straightway to the castle; for that was the royal palace, and the place where his honour was to dwell; which was ready prepared for his highness by the presence of the Lord Secretary, and the work of Captain Credence. So he entered in.

Sixthly, Then the people and commonalty of the town of Mansoul came to him into the castle to mourn, weep, and lament for their wickedness, by which they had forced him out of the town. So they, when they were come, bowed themselves to the ground seven times, they also wept, they wept aloud, and asked forgiveness of the prince, and prayed that he would again, as of old, confirm his love to Mansoul.

Immanuel comforts the inhabitants of Mansoul.

To which the great prince replied, "Weep not, but go your way, eat the fat and drink the sweet, and send portions to them for whom nought is prepared, for "the joy of your Lord is your strength." I am returned to Mansoul with mercies, and my name shall be set up, exalted, and magnified by it." He also took these inhabitants, and kissed them, and laid them in his bosom.†

Moreover, he gave to the elders of Mansoul, and to each town-officer, a chain of gold and a signet. He also sent to their wives ear

---

* How gladly is Jesus received! how delightful and welcome is his presence to the soul that has long been vexed with an army of doubts. O let christians beware of sin and unbelief, which caused him to withdraw, and the doubts to enter. Well may the soul be humbled to the dust, in the recollection of its backsliding.

† "The joy of the Lord is our strength;" when this is possessed there will be double diligence in searching out and destroying our sins.

rings and jewels, and bracelets, and other things. He also bestowed upon the true-born children of Mansoul many precious things.

When Immanuel the prince had done all these things for the famous town of Mansoul, than he said unto them, "First, wash your garments, then put on your ornaments, and then come to me into the castle of Mansoul," Eccles. ix. 8. So they went to the fountain that was set open for Judah and Jerusalem to wash in and there they washed, and there they made their garments white, and came again to the prince into the castle, and thus they stood before him, Zech. xiii. 1. Rev. vii. 14, 15.

And now there was music and dancing throughout the whole town of Mansoul: and that because their prince had again granted to them his presence, and light of his countenance; the bells also rung, and the sun shone comfortably upon them for a great while together.

The town of Mansoul also now more thoroughly sought the destruction and ruin of all remaining Diabolonians, that abode in the walls, and the dens (that they had in the town of Mansoul), for there was of them that had to this day escaped with life and limb from the hand of their suppressors in the famous town of Mansoul.

But my Lord Will-be-will was a greater terror to them now than ever he had been before, forasmuch as his heart was yet more fully bent to seek, contrive, and pursue them to the death, he pursued them night and day, and put them now to sore distress, as will afterwards appear.

After things were thus far put into order in the famous town of *Orders given out to bury the dead.* Mansoul, care was taken, and order given by the blessed prince Immanuel, that the townsmen should, without further delay, appoint some to go forth into the plain to bury the dead that were there; the dead that fell by the sword of Immanuel, and by the shield of Captain Credence, lest the fumes and ill savours that would arise from them, might infect the air, and so annoy the famous town of Mansoul. This also was a reason of this order, to wit, that as much as in Mansoul lay, they might cut off the name and being and remembrance of those enemies from the thought of the famous town of Mansoul and its inhabitants.

So order was given out by the lord-mayor, that wise and trusty friend of the town of Mansoul, that persons should be employed about this necessary business; and Mr Godly-fear, and one Mr Upright were to be overseers about this matter; so persons were put under them to work in the fields, and to bury the slain that

The burial of the Diabolonian Doubters that had been slain.

lay dead in the plains. And these were their places of employment; some were to make the graves, some were to bury the dead, and some were to go to and fro in the plains, and also round about the borders of Mansoul, to see if a skull or a bone, or a piece of a bone of a Doubter, was yet to be found above-ground any where near the corporation; and if any were found, it was ordered that the searchers that searched should set up a mark thereby and a sign, that those that were appointed to bury them might find it, and bury it out of sight, that the name and remembrance of a Diabolonian Doubter might be blotted out from under heaven. And that the children and they that were to be born in Mansoul might not know (if possible) what a skull, what a bone, or a piece of a bone of a Doubter was. So the buriers, and those that were appointed for that purpose, did as they were commanded; they buried the Doubters, and all skulls and bones, and pieces of bones of Doubters, wherever they found them, and so they cleansed the plains. Now also Mr God's-peace took up his commission, and acted again as in former days.

Thus they buried in the plains about Mansoul, the Election-Doubters, the Vocation-Doubters, the Grace-Doubters, the Perseverance-Doubters, the Resurrection-Doubters, the Salvation-Doubters, and the Glory-Doubters, whose captains were, Captain Rage, Captain Cruel, Captain Damnation, Captain Insatiable, Captain Brimstone, Captain Torment, Captain No-Ease, Captain Sepulchre, and Captain Past-hope: and old Incredulity was under Diabolus their general; there were also the seven heads of their army, and they were the Lord Beelzebub, the Lord Lucifer, the Lord Legion, the **Lord Apollyon**, the Lord Python, the Lord Cerberus, and the **Lord Belial**. But the princes and the captains, with old Incredulity their general, all made their escape; so their men fell down upon the slain by the power of the prince's forces, and by the hands of the men of the town of Mansoul. They also were buried, as is before related, to the exceeding great joy of the town of Mansoul: they that buried them, buried also with them their arms, which were cruel instruments of death (their weapons were arrows, darts, mauls, firebrands, and the like;) they buried also their armour, colours, and banners, with the standard of Diabolus, and what else soever they could find that did but smell of a Diabolonian Doubter.*

---

* Thus was the victory completed. All doubts of God's grace and love were utterly destroyed; and pains were taken that, if possible, the succeeding generation might never be plagued with the name of a Doubter. The design of all this is to show that doubt and distress of the love of Christ, contrary to the declarations of his word, should be utterly suppressed, as being infinitely dishonourable to our faithful covenant with God, and unspeakably pernicious to our own souls.

CHAPTER XVII.

A new army of Bloodmen, or Persecutors, attack the town, but are surrounded by the Mansoulians, headed by Faith and Patience. The examination of some of the leaders. Evil-questioning entertains some of the Doubters, but is discovered by Diligence. The principal Doubters tried, convicted and executed.

NOW when the tyrant was arrived at Hellgate-hill, with his old friend Incredulity, they immediately descended the den, and having there with their followers for a while condoled their misfortune, and the great loss they sustained before the town of Mansoul, they fell at length into a passion, and revenged they would be for the loss that they sustained before the town of Mansoul;

The tyrant resolves to have yet a bout with Mansoul. wherefore they presently call a council to contrive yet further what was to be done against the famous town of Mansoul; for their yawning paunches could not wait to see the result of their Lord Lucifer's and their Lord Apollyon's counsel that they had given before, their raging gorge thought every day even as long as a short for-ever, until they were filled with the body and soul, with the flesh and bones, and with all the delicacies of Mansoul. They therefore resolved to make another attempt upon the town of Mansoul, and that by an army mixed, and made up partly of Doubters and partly of Blood-men. A more particular account now take of both.*

The Doubters are such as have their name from their nature, as well as from the lord and kingdom where they were born; their nature is to put a question upon every one of the truths of Immanuel, and their country is the Land of Doubting, and that

Description of the Land of Doubting. land lieth off, and furthest remote to the north, between the Land of Darkness, and that called the Valley of the Shadow of Death.

For though the Land of Darkness, and that called the Land of the Shadow of Death, be sometimes called as if they were one and the self-same place; yet indeed they are two, lying but a little way asunder, and the Land of Doubting points in, and lieth between them. This is the Land of Doubting, and those that came with Diabolus to ruin the town of Mansoul, are the natives of that country.

The character of the blood-men. The Blood-men are a people that have their name derived from the malignity of their nature, and from the fury that is in them to execute it

---

* By Blood-men (or bloody-men, so called Psalm cxxxix. 19.) the author seems to intend *Persecutors;* men under the power of that carnal mind which is enmity against God, and against his image in the soul of man. Here a new set of enemies arise, and may signify that opposition to religion which, more or less every christian must expect, for " they who live godly, in Christ Jesus, shall suffer persecution."

upon the town of Mansoul; their land lieth under the Dog-star, and by that they are governed as to their intellectuals. The name of their country is the province of Loath-good, the remote parts of it are far distant from the Land of Doubting, yet they do both butt and bound upon the hill called Hellgate-hill. These people are always in league with the Doubters, for they jointly make question of the faith and fidelity of the men of the town of Mansoul, and so are both alike qualified for the service of their prince.

Now of these two countries did Diabolus by the beating of his drum raise another army against the town of Mansoul, of five-and-twenty thousand strong. There were ten thousand Doubters, and fifteen thousand Blood-men, and they were put under several captains for the war, and old Incredulity was again made general of the army.

As for the Doubters, their captains were five of the seven that were heads of the last Diabolonian army, and these are their names: Captain Beelzebub, Captain Lucifer, Captain Apollyon, Captain Legion, and Captain Cerberus, and the captains that they had before were some of them made lieutenants and some ensigns of the army.

But Diabolus did not count that in this expedition of his, these Doubters would prove his principal men, for their manhood had been tried before; also the Mansoulians had put them to the worst, only he brought them to multiply a number, and to help, if need was, at a pinch; but his trust he put in his Blood-men, for they were all rugged villains, and he knew that they had done feats heretofore.

The captains of the Blood-men. As for the Blood-men, they also were under command, and the names of their captains were, Captain Cain, Captain Nimrod, Captain Ishmael, Captain Esau, Captain Saul, Captain Absalom, Captain Judas and Captain Pope.

1. Captain Cain was over two bands, to wit, the Zealous and the Angry Blood-men; his standard-bearer bore the red colours, and his scutcheon was the murdering club, Gen. iv. 8.

Their bands, standard-bearers, and colours. 2. Captain Nimrod was captain over two bands, to wit, the Tyrannical and Incroaching Blood-men; his standard-bearer bore the red colours, and his scutcheon was the great blood-hound, Gen. x, 8, 9.

3. Captain Ishmael was captain over two bands, to wit, over the Mocking and Scorning Blood-men; his standard bearer bore the red colours, and his scutcheon was one mocking at Abraham's Isaac, Gen. xxi. 9. 10.

4. Captain Esau was captain over two bands, to wit, the Blood-men that grudged that another should have the blessing; also over the

Blood-men that are for executing their private revenge upon others, his standard-bearer bore the red colours, and his scutcheon was one privately lurking to murder Jacob, xxvii. 42, 43, 44, 45.

5. Captain Saul was captain over two bands, to wit, the Groundlessly Jealous and the Devilishly Furious Blood-men; his standard-bearer bore the red colours, and his scutcheon was three bloody darts cast at harmless David, 1 Sam. xviii. 11.

6. Captain Absalom was captain over two bands, to wit, over the Blood-men that will kill a father or a friend, for the glory of this world: also over those Blood-men that hold one fair in hand with words, till they shall have pierced him with their swords; his standard-bearer bore the red colours, and his scutcheon was the son pursuing the father's blood, 2 Sam. xv. 13, 14. xvii. 16.

7. Captain Judas was over two bands, to wit, the blood-men that will sell a man's life for money, and those also that will betray their friend with a kiss; his standard-bearer bore the red colours, and his scutcheon was thirty pieces of silver, and the halter, Matt. xxvi. 14, 15, 16.

8. Captain Pope was captain over one band, for all these spirits are joined in one under him; his standard-bearer bore the red colours, and his scutcheon was the stake, the flame, and the good man in it, Rev. xiii. 7, 8. Dan. xi. 33.*

Now the reason why Diabolus so soon rallied another force after he had been beaten out of the field, was, for that he put mighty confidence in this army of Blood-men, for he put a great deal of more trust in them than he did before in his army of Doubters, though they had also often done great service for him in the strengthening of him in his kingdom. But those Blood-men he had often proved, and their swords seldom returned empty. Besides, he knew that these, like mastiffs, would fasten upon any; upon father, mother, brother, sister, prince, or governor, yea, upon the prince of princes. And that which encouraged him the more was, for that they once forced Immanuel out of the kingdom of Universe; and why, thought he, may they not drive him from the town of Mansoul?†

So this army of five-and-twenty thousand strong, was by their gene-

---

* The names of some ancient persecutors and oppressors are here mentioned, beginning with Cain, the first blood-man, and ending with his Holiness of Rome, who has been, in these later ages, the most bloody scourge of the true church of God.

† Diabolus, with no small cause, puts much confidence in bloody persecutors, for their rage has seldom been in vain. Though the true disciples of Christ have been enabled to stand their ground; a great multitude of professors become apostates through fear of death. Satan also well remembers that his Jewish blood-men prevailed by divine permission) to force Immanuel himself out of the world. Incredulity is deservedly put at the head of this army.

Lord Incredulity leads the army of Blood-men. ral, the great Lord Incredulity, led up again the town of Mansoul. Now Mr Prywell, the scout-master-general, went out to spy, and he brought Mansoul tidings of their coming. Wherefore they shut up their gates, and put themselves in a posture of defence against these new Diabolonians that came up against the town.

So Diabolus brought up his army, and beleaguered the town of Mansoul; the Doubters were placed about Feel-gate, and the Blood-men set down before Eye-gate and Ear-gate.

Now when this army had thus encamped themselves, Incredulity, in the name of Diabolus, in his own name, and in the name of the Blood-men and the rest that were with him, sent a summons as hot as a red-hot iron to Mansoul, to yield to their demands, threatening, that if they still stood it out against them, they would presently burn down Mansoul with fire. *The town summoned by Incredulity to surrender to Diabolus.* For you must know, that as for the Blood-men, they were not so much that Mansoul should be surrendered, as that Mansoul should be destroyed, and cut off out of the land of the living. True, they sent to them to surrender; but should they so do, that would not quench the thirsts of these men: they must have blood, the blood of Mansoul, else they die; and it is from hence that they have their name. Wherefore these Blood-men he reserved while now, that they might, when all his engines proved ineffectual, as his last and sure card, be played against the town of Mansoul, Psalm xxix. 10. Isa. lix. 7. Isa. xxii. 17.*

Now when the townsmen had received this red-hot summons, it begat in them at present some changing and interchanging thoughts; but they jointly agreed, in less than half an hour, to carry the summons to the prince, which they did when they had writ at the bottom of it, Lord, save Mansoul from bloody men, Psalm lix. 2.

So he took it, and looked upon it, and considered it, and took notice also of that short petition that the men of Mansoul had written at the bottom of it, and called to him the noble Captain Credence, and bid him go and take Captain Patience with him, and go and take care of that side of Mansoul that was beleaguered by the Blood-men, Heb. vi. 12. ver. 15. So they went and did as they were commanded! then Captain Credence went and took Cap-

---

* Persecution will be satisfied with nothing less than the utter destruction of the christian. Even a surrender will not suffice, as some too yielding professors have found to their cost; witness good Archbishop Cranmer, who recanted through fear, and yet was put to death by the bloody papists.

tain Patience, and they both secured that side of Mansoul that was besieged by the Blood-men.*

Immanuel gives directions for the security of the town.

Then he commanded that Captain Good-hope and Captain Charity, and my Lord Will-be-will should take charge of the other side of the town; and I, said the prince, will set my standard upon the battlements of your castle, and do you three watch against the Doubters. This done, he again commanded that the brave Captain Experience should draw up his men in the market-place, and that there also he should exercise them day by day before the people of the town of Mansoul. Now the siege was long, and many a fierce attempt did the enemy, especially those called Blood-men, make upon the town of Mansoul, and many a shrewd brush did some of the townsmen meet with from them; especially Captain Self-denial; who, I should have told you before, was commanded to take the care of Ear-gate and Eye-gate now against the Blood-men. This Captain Self-denial was a young man, but stout, and a townsman in Mansoul, as Captain Experience also was; and Immanuel, at his second return to Mansoul, made him a captain over a thousand of the Mansoulians, for the good of the corporation. This captain, therefore, being a hardy man, a man of great courage, and willing to venture himself for the good of the town of Mansoul, would now and then sally out upon the Blood-men, and give them many notable alarms, and had several skirmishes with them, and also did some execution upon them; yet you must think that this could not easily be done, but he must meet with brushes himself, for he carried several of their marks in his face; yea, and some in other parts of his body.†

Immanuel prepares to give the enemy battle.
How he ordereth his men.

So after some time spent for the trial of the faith, hope, and love of the town of Mansoul, the Prince Immanuel upon a day calls his captains and men of war together, and divides them into two companies; this done, he commands them at a time appointed, and that in the morning very early, to sally out upon the enemy; saying, "Let half of you fall upon the Doubters, and half of you fall upon the Blood-men. Those of you that go out against the Doubters, kill and slay, and cause to perish so many of them as by any means you can lay hands on; but for you that go out against the Blood-men, slay them not, but take them alive."‡

* It was through faith and patience that the ancient believers inherited the promises. These graces therefore are judiciously opposed to the persecutors, and nothing less will sustain the soul in the time of trial.

† A time of persecution loudly calls for the exercise of self-denial. When this prevails the terrors of persecution are diminished.

‡ Christianity forbids us to kill our persecutors; on the contrary we are to return good for evil.

Accordingly at the time appointed, betimes in the morning, the captains went out as they were commanded against the enemies: Captain Good-hope, Captain Charity, and those that were joined with them, as Captain Innocent, and Captain Experience, went out against the Doubters; and Captain Credence, and Captain Patience with Captain Self-denial, and the rest that were to join with them, went out against the Blood-men.

Now those that went out against the Doubters, drew up in a body before the plain, and marched on to bid them battle: but the Doubters, remembering their last success, made a retreat, not daring to stand the shock, but fled from the prince's men; wherefore they pursued them, and in their pursuit slew many, but they could not catch them all. Now those that escaped went some of them home; and the rest, by fives, nines, and seventeens, like wanderers, went straggling up and down the country, where they showed and exercised many of their Diabolonian actions upon the barbarous people; nor did these people rise up in arms against them, but suffered themselves to be enslaved by them. They would also after this show themselves in companies before the town of Mansoul, but never to abide it; for if Captain Credence, Captain Good-hope, or Captain Experience did but show themselves, they fled.

Those that were against the Blood-men, did as they were commanded, they forbore to slay any, but sought to compass them about. But the Blood-men, when they saw that no Immanuel was in the field, concluded also that no Immanuel was in Mansoul, wherefore they looking upon what the captains did, to be, as they called it, a fruit of the extravagancy of their wild and foolish fancies, *Immanuel's captains surround the Blood-men, and take them prisoners.* rather despised than feared them; but the captains minding their business, at last compassed them round; they also that had routed the Doubters, came in amain to their aid; so in fine, after some little struggling (for the Blood-men also would have run for it, only now it was too late; for though they are mischievous and cruel where they can overcome, yet all Blood-men are chicken-hearted men, when they once come to see themselves matched and equalled,) so, I say, the captains took them, and brought them to the prince.

Now when they were taken, had before the prince, and examined, he found them to be of three several counties, though they all came out of one land.

1. One sort of them came out of Blindmanshire, and they were such as did ignorantly what they did.

The prisoners examined and described. 2. Another sort of them came out of Blindzealshire and they did superstitiously what they did

3. The third sort of them came out of the town of

CAPTAIN EXPERIENCE. P. 216.

Malice, in the county of Envy, and they did what they did out of spite and implacableness.*

For the first of these, to wit, they that came out of Blindmanshire, when they saw where they were, and against whom they had fought, trembled, and cried as they stood before him; and as many of those as asked him mercy, he touched their lips with his golden sceptre. They that came out of Blindzealshire did not as their fellows, for they pleaded that they had a right to do what they did, because Mansoul was a town whose laws and customs were diverse from all that dwelt thereabouts; very few of these could be brought to see their evil, but those that did, and asked mercy, they also obtained favour.

Now they that came out of the town of Malice, that is in the county of Envy, they neither wept nor disputed, but stood gnawing of their tongues before him for anguish and madness, because they could not have their will upon Mansoul. Now those last, with all those of the other two sorts that unfeignedly asked pardon for their faults; those he made to enter into sufficient bond to answer for what they had done against Mansoul, and against her king, at the great and general assizes to be holden for our lord the king, where he himself should appoint for the country and kingdom of Universe. So they came bound, each man for himself, to come in when called upon, to answer before our lord the king for what they had done before.†

And thus much concerning this second army that was sent by Diabolus to overthrow Mansoul.

But there were three of those that came from the land of Doubting, *Three or four of the Doubters go into Mansoul, are entertained, and by whom.* who, after they had wandered and ranged the country awhile, and perceived that they had escaped, were so hardy as to thrust themselves, knowing that yet there were in the town some who took part with Diabolus; I say, they were so hardy as to thrust themselves into Mansoul among them. (Three did I say? I believe there were four.) Now to whose house should these Doubters go, but to the house of an old Diabolonian in Mansoul, whose name was Evil-questioning: a very great enemy he was to Mansoul, and a very great doer among the Diabolonians there. Well, to this Evil-questioning's house, as was said, did these Diabolonians come (you may be sure that they had their directions how to find their way thither) so he made them welcome,

---

* The spirit of persecution will be found to originate, either in a blind understanding or superstitious zeal, or cruel malice and envy. To the two former, Immanuel showed mercy to Saul, who was once a bloody man; but he obtained mercy because he did it ignorantly.

† Malicious persecutors are bound over to appear at the great assize, when these ungodly men shall be judged for all their ungodly deeds, and all their hard speeches against Christ in his members. Jude, 15.

pitied their misfortune, and succoured them with the best he had in his house. Now after a little acquaintance, and it was not long before they had that, this Evil-questioning asked the Doubters if they were all of a town (he knew that they were all of one kingdom,) and they answered, No, nor of one shire neither; for I, said one, am an election-doubter; and I, said another, am a vocation-doubter; then said the third, I am a salvation-doubter; and the fourth said, he was a grace-doubter. Well, quoth the old gentlemen, be of what shire you will, I am persuaded that you are town-boys, you have the very length of my foot, are one with my heart, and shall be welcome to me. So they thanked him, and were glad that they had found themselves a harbour in Mansoul. Then said Evil-questioning

Talk betwixt the Doubters and old Evil-questioning.

to them, How many of your company might there be that came with you to the siege of Mansoul? And they answered, There were but ten thousand Doubters in all, for the rest of the army consisted of fifteen thousand Blood-men: these blood-men, quoth they, border upon our country; but, poor men, we hear, they were every one taken by Immanuel's forces. Ten thousand! quoth the old gentleman, I'll promise you, that's a round company. But how came it to pass, since you were so mighty a number, that you fainted, and durst not fight your foes? Our general, said they, was the first man that ran for it. Pray, quoth their landlord, who was that your cowardly general? He was once the lord-mayor of Mansoul said they. But pray call him not a cowardly general, for whether any from the east to the west has done more service for our prince Diabolus than has my Lord Incredulity, will be a hard question for you to answer. But had they catched him, they would for certain have hanged him, and we promise you hanging is but a bad business.*

Then said the old gentleman, I would that all the ten thousand Doubters were now well armed in Mansoul, and myself at the head of them, I would see what I could do. Ah, sa'd they, that would be well, if we could see that: but wishes, alas! what are they? And these words were spoken aloud. Well, said old Evil-questioning, take heed that ye talk not too loud, you must be quiet and close, and must take care of yourselves while you are here, or I will assure you, you will be snapped.

Why? quoth the Doubters.

Why? quoth the old gentleman: why, because both the prince and lord secretary, and their captains and soldiers, are all at present in town; yea, the town is as full of them as it can hold. And

---

* Doubts will return again and again, and while there is such a thing as *evil-questioning* in the heart, they will find a harbour there. Unbelief, however, was obliged to fly.

one whose name is Will-be-will, a most cruel
and him the prince hath made keeper of the gates,
nded him, that with all the diligence he can, he
search out, and destroy all manner of Diabolonians.
h upon you, down you go, though your heads be

see how it happened, one of the Lord Will-be-
's faithful soldiers, whose name was Mr Diligence,
d all the while listening under old Evil-question
; eaves, and heard all the talk that had been be-
he Doubters that he entertained under his roof.
is a man that my lord had much confidence in,
d dearly, and that both because he was a man of
o a man that was unwearied in seeking after Dia-
rehend them.
a, as I told you, heard all the talk that was be-
-questioning and these Diabolonians; wherefore
ut goes to his Lord, and tells him what he had
rest thou so, my trusty? quoth my lord. Ay,
that I do, and if your lordship will be pleased to
shall find it as I have said. And are they there?
I know Evil-questioning well, for he and I were
e of our apostacy; I know not where he dwells.
is man, and if your lordship will go, I will lead
is den. Go! quoth my lord, that I will. Come,
t us go find them out. So my lord and his man
e direct way to his house. Now his man went
him the way, and they went till they came even
Evil-questioning's wall. Then said Diligence,
do you know the old gentleman's tongue when you
id my lord, I know it well, but I have not seen him
is I know; he is cunning. I wish he may not give
t me alone for that, said his servant Diligence.
e find the door? quoth my lord. Let me alone
d his man. So he had my Lord Will-be-will
ed him the way to the door. Then my lord, with-
roke open the door, rushed into the house, and
ive together, even as Diligence his man had told
  him. So my lord apprehended them, and led
  them away, and committed them to the hand of
  Mr Trueman the gaoler, and he commanded, and
  put them in ward. This done, my lord-mayor
  a the morning with what my Lord Will-be-will

ice is of special use in detecting sin. 2 Pet. i. 10.

had done over night, and his lordship rejoiced much at the news, not only because there were Doubters apprehended, but because that old Evil-questioning was taken; for he had been a very great trouble to Mansoul, and much affliction to my lord-mayor himself. He had also been sought for often, but no hand could ever be laid upon him till now.

Well, the next thing was, to make preparations to try these five that by my lord had been apprehended, and that were in the hands of Mr Trueman, the gaoler. So the day was set, and the court called and came together, and the prisoners brought to the bar. My lord Will-be-will had power to have slain them when at first he took them, and that without any more ado, but he thought it at this time more for the honour of the prince, the comfort of Mansoul, and the discouragement of the enemy, to bring them forth to public judgment. But I say, Mr Trueman brought them in chains to the bar, to the town-hall, for that was the place of judgment. So, to be short, the jury was pannelled, the witnesses sworn, and the prisoners tried for their lives; the jury was the same that tried Mr No-truth, Pitiless, Haughty, and the rest of their companions.

They are brought to trial.

And first, old Evil-questioning himself was set to the bar; for he was the receiver, the entertainer, and comforter of these Doubters, that by nation were outlandish men; then he was bid to hearken to his charge, and was told that he had liberty to object, if he had aught to say for himself. So his indictment was read, the manner and form here follows: "Mr Questioning, Thou art here indicted by the name of Evil-questioning, an intruder upon the town of Mansoul, for that thou art a Diabolonian by nature, and also a hater of the prince Immanuel, and one that has studied the ruin of Mansoul. Thou art also here indicted, for entertaining the king's enemies, after wholesome laws made to the contrary: For, 1. Thou hast questioned the truth of her doctrine and state. 2. In wishing that ten thousand Doubters were in her. In receiving, entertaining, and encouraging of her enemies, that came from their army unto thee. What sayest thou to this indictment? art thou guilty, or not guilty?"

My lord, quoth he, I know not the meaning of this indictment, forasmuch as I am not the man concerned in it; the man that standeth by this charge accused before this bench, is called by the name of Evil-questioning, which name I deny to be mine, mine being Honest-inquiring.* The one indeed sounds like the other, but I trow, your lordships know that between these two there is a wide differ-

Evil-questioning denies his name.

---

* Evil-questioning denies his name, and would fain pass for *Honest-inquiry*. So all the enemies of truth shelter themselves under the pretence of free-inquiry and free-thinking.

DILIGENCE ON THE WATCH.   P. 241.

ence; for I hope, that a man, even in the worst of times, and that too amongst the worst of men, may make an honest inquiry after things, without running the danger of death.

Then spake my Lord Will-be-will, for he was one of the witnesses: "My Lord, and you the honourable bench and magistrates of the town of Mansoul, you all have heard with your ears, that the prisoner at the bar has denied his name, and so thinks to shift from the charge of the indictment. But I know him to be the man concerned; and that his proper name is Evil-questioning. I have known him, my Lord, above these thirty years, for he and I (a shame it is for me to speak it) were great acquaintance, when Diabolus, that tyrant, had the government of Mansoul; and I testify, that he is a Diabolonian by nature, an enemy to our prince, and an hater of the blessed town of Mansoul. He has, in times of rebellion, been at, and lain in my house, my lord, not so little as twenty nights together, and we used to talk then (for the substance of talk) as he and his Doubters have talked of late. True, I have not seen him many a-day; I suppose that the coming of Immanuel to Mansoul has made him change his lodgings, as this indictment has driven him to change his name; but this is the man, my lord."

Lord Will-be-will a witness against them.

Then said the court unto him, Hast thou any more to say?

Yes, quoth the old gentlemen, that I have; for all that has yet been said against me is but by the mouth of one witness; and it is not lawful for the famous town of Mansoul, at the mouth of one witness, to put any man to death.

Then stood forth Mr Diligence, and said, "My lord, as I was upon my watch such a night, at the head of Bad-street, in this town, I chanced to hear a muttering within the gentleman's house; then thought I, What's to do here? So I went up close, but very softly, to the side of the house to listen, thinking, as indeed it fell out, that there I might light of some Diabolonian conventicle. So, as I said, I drew nearer and nearer, and when I was got up close to the wall, it was but a while before I perceived that there were outlandish men in the house (but I understood their speech, for I have been a traveller myself;) now, hearing such language in such a tottering cottage this old gentleman dwelt in, I clapped mine ear to a hole in the window, and there heard them talk as followeth. This old Mr Questioning asked these Doubters what they were, whence they came, and what was their business in these parts? And they answered him to all these questions, yet he entertained them. He also asked what numbers there were of them; and they told him, ten thousand men. He then asked them why they made no more manly assault upon Mansoul, and they told him; so he

The evidence of Mr Diligence, another witness.

called their general coward, for marching off when he should have fought for his prince. Further, this old Evil-questioning wished, and I heard him wish, Would all the ten thousand Doubters were now in Mansoul, and himself at the head of them! He bid them also take heed and lie quiet; for if they were taken they must die, although they had heads of gold."

Then said the court, Mr Evil-questioning, here is now another witness against you, and his testimony is full: 1. He swears that you received these men into your house, and that you nourished them there, though you knew that they were Diabolonians, and the king's enemies. 2. He swears that you wished ten thousand of them in Mansoul. 3. He swears that you gave them advice to be quiet and close, lest they were taken by the king's servants. All which manifesteth that thou art a Diabolonian; but hadst thou been a friend to the king, thou wouldst have apprehended them.

Then said Evil-questioning, to the first of these I answer, The men that came into mine house were strangers, and I took them in; and is it now become a crime in Mansoul for a man to entertain strangers? That I also nourished them is true; and why should my charity be blamed? As for the reason why I wished ten thousand of them in Mansoul, I never told it to the witnesses, nor to themselves. I might wish them to be taken, and so my wish might mean well to Mansoul, for aught that any yet knows. I also bid them take heed that they fell not into the captain's hands, but that might be because I am unwilling that any man should be slain, and not because I would have the king's enemies, as such, escape.*

Evil-questioning sets up a defence.

My lord-mayor then replied, that though it was a virtue to entertain strangers, yet it was treason to entertain the king's enemies. And for what else thou hast said, thou dost by words but labour to evade, and defer the execution of judgment. But could there be no more proved against thee but that thou art a Diabolonian, thou must for that die the death of the law; but to be a receiver, a nourisher, a countenancer, and a harbourer of others of them, yea of outlandish Diabolonians; yea, of them that come from far, on purpose to cut off and destroy our Mansoul; this must not be borne.

Then said Evil-questioning, I see how the game will go. I must die for my name, and for my charity. And so held his peace.

Then they called the outlandish Doubters to the bar, and the first of them that was arraigned was the Election-Doubter; so his indictment was read, and because he was an outlandishman, the substance of it was told to him by an interpreter; to wit, "that he was there charged

The trial of Mr Election-Doubter.

---

* He answers with much subtlety, and pretends to great charity, but he is a true Diabolonian, and ought to die.

with being an enemy to Immanuel the prince, a hater of the town of Mansoul, and an opposer of her most wholesome doctrine.

Then the judge asked him if he would plead; but he said only this, "That he confessed that he was an Election-Doubter, and that was the religion that he had ever been brought up in. And said moreover, If I must die for my religion, I trow I shall die a martyr, and so I care the less."

Then the judge replied, To question election is to overthrow a great doctrine of the gospel; to wit, the omniscience, and power, and will of God, to take away the liberty of God with his creature, to stumble the faith of the town of Mansoul, and to make salvation to depend upon works, and not upon grace. It also belied the word, and disquieted the minds of the men of Mansoul, therefore by the best of laws he must die.*

Vocation-doubter set to the bar. Then was the Vocation-doubter called, and set to the bar; and his indictment for substance was the same with the other, only he was particularly charged with denying the calling of Mansoul.

The judge asked him also what he had to say for himself?

So he replied, "That he never believed that there was any such thing as a distinct and powerful call of God to Mansoul, otherwise than by the general voice of the word, nor by that neither, otherwise than as it exhorted them to forbear evil, and to do that which is good, and in so doing a promise of happiness is annexed."

Then said the judge, Thou art a Diabolonian, and hast denied a great part of one of the most experimental truths of the prince of the town of Mansoul; for he has called, and she has heard a most distinct and powerful call of her Immanuel, by which she has been quickened, awakened, and possessed with heavenly grace to desire to have communion with her prince, to serve him, and to do his will, and to look for her happiness merely of his good pleasure. And for thine abhorrence of this good doctrine thou must die the death.†

Grace-Doubter. Then the Grace-Doubter was called, and his indictment was read, and he replied thereto, That though he was of the land of Doubting, his father was the offspring of a Pharisee, and lived in good fashion among his neighbours, and that he taught them to believe (and I believe I do and will) that Mansoul shall never be saved freely by grace.

Then said the judge, Why, the law of the prince is plain; negatively, "not of works:" 2. Positively, "By grace you are saved," Rom. iii. Eph. ii. And thy religion settleth in and upon the works

* Those who deny election deny (though perhaps unwittingly) the omniscience and sovereignty of God, and unavoidably assert, (sometimes without perceiving it) that salvation is not of grace, but of works.

† The enemies of effectual calling by the influence of the Holy Spirit are advocates for salvation by works; that dangerous leaven of the Pharisees.

of the flesh; for the works of the law are the works of the flesh. Besides, in saying, "Thou hast done," thou hast robbed God of his glory, and given it to a sinful man; thou hast robbed Christ of the necessity of his undertaking, and the sufficiency thereof, and hast given both these to the work of the flesh. Thou hast despised the work of the Holy Ghost, and hast magnified the will of the flesh, and of the legal mind. Thou art a Diabolonian, the son of a Diabolonian; and for thy Diabolonian principles thou must die.*

The prisoners are found guilty, and sentenced to death.

The court then having proceeded thus far with them, sent out the jury, who forthwith brought them in guilty of death. Then stood up the recorder, and addressed himself to the prisoners: You, the prisoners at the bar, you have been here indicted, and proved guilty of high crimes against Immanuel our prince, and against the welfare of the famous town of Mansoul: crimes for which you must be put to death; and die ye accordingly.

So they were sentenced to the death of the cross: the place assigned them for execution was that where Diabolus drew up his last army against Mansoul; save only that old Evil-questioning was hanged at the top of Bad-street, over against his own door.†

CHAPTER XVIII.

More Diabolonians tried and condemned. The work concludes with an admirable speech of Immanuel to the inhabitants, in which he recites his gracious acts, and informs them that he intends to rebuild the town in a more glorious manner, recommending, in the mean time, a suitable conduct.

WHEN the town of Mansoul had thus far rid themselves of their enemies, and of the troublers of their peace, in the next place a strict commandment was given out, that yet my Lord Willbe-will should, with Diligence his man, search for, and do his best to apprehend what town Diabolonians were yet left alive in Mansoul. The names of several of them were,

A commission granted to apprehend the rest of the Diabolonians.

Mr Fooling, Mr Let-good-slip, Mr Slavish-fear, Mr No-love, Mr Mistrust, Mr Flesh, and Mr Sloth. It was also commanded that he should apprehend Mr Evil-questioning's children that he left behind him, that they should demolish his house there; Mr Doubt was his eldest son; the next to him was Legal-life, Unbelief, Wrong-thoughts-of-Christ, Clip-promise,

---

* To insist upon salvation by works is utterly to deny grace: for, as the apostle argues, Gall. ii. 21. "If righteousness come by the law, then Christ is dead in vain," and thus the grace of God is entirely frustrated.

† The author does not mean that persons maintaining these opinions ought to be put to death; he designs only the death or destruction of those pernicious errors, which, even as the lusts of the flesh, must be mortified.

Carnal-sense, Live-by-feel, Self-love. All these he had by one wife, and her name was No-hope, she was the kinswoman of old Incredulity, for he was her uncle, and when her father, old Dark was dead, he took her and brought her up, and when she was marriageable, he gave her to this old Evil-questioning to wife.*

Now the Lord Will-be-will put into execution his commission, with Great Diligence his man. He took Fooling in the streets, and hanged him up in Want-wit-alley, over against his own house. This Fooling was he that would have had the town of Mansoul deliver up Captain Credence into the hands of Diabolus, provided that then he would have withdrawn his force out of the town: he also took Mr Let-good-slip one day as he was busy in the market, and executed him according to law. Now there was an honest poor man in Mansoul, and his name was Mr Meditation, one of no great account in the days of apostacy; but now of repute with the best of the town. This man therefore we were willing to prefer. Now Mr Let-good-slip had a great deal of wealth heretofore in Mansoul, and at Immanuel's coming it was sequestered to the use of the prince; this therefore was now given to Mr Meditation to improve for the common good, and after him to his son Mr Think-well; this Think-well he had by Mrs Piety his wife, and she was the daughter of Mr Recorder.†

Clip-promise apprehended, tried, and convicted.

After this my lord apprehended Clip-promise; now because he was a notorious villain (for by his doings much of the king's coin was abused,) therefore he was made a public example. He was arraigned, and adjudged to be first set in the pillory, and then to be whipped by all the children and servants in Mansoul, then to be hanged till he was dead. Some may wonder at the severity of this man's punishments, but they that are honest traders in Mansoul, are sensible of the great abuse that one clipper of promises in little time may do to the town of Mansoul. And truly my judgment is, that all those of his name and life should be served even as he.‡

Carnal-sense.

He also apprehended Carnal-sense, and put him in hold; but how it came about I cannot tell, but he broke prison, and made his escape. Yea, and the bold villain will not yet quit the town, but lurks in the Diabolonian dens a-days,

* The names of these gentry will sufficiently show the necessity of destroying them; they are all enemies to soul-prosperity.
† Great is the advantage of meditation; a practice, alas! in which Christians in general are too backward. And O how much is lost by letting the word slip, which ought to be laid up, and pondered in the heart. This is the way to become spiritually rich.
‡ To curtail or diminish the precious promises, which are as valuable to a spiritual life as the sterling coin of the kingdom to commerce, is highly criminal.

and haunts like a ghost honest men's houses a-nights. Wherefore there was a proclamation set up in the market-place in Mansoul, signifying, that whosoever could discover Carnal-sense, and apprehend him and slay him, should be admitted daily to the prince's table, and should be made keeper of the treasure of Mansoul. Many therefore bent themselves to do this thing: but take him and slay him they could not, though he was often discovered. But my Lord took Mr Wrong-thoughts-of-Christ, and put him in prison, and he died of a lingering consumption.*

Self-love taken into custody and executed by Mr Self-denial.

Self-love was also taken and committed to custody, but there were many that were allied to him in Mansoul, so his judgment was deferred; but at last Mr Self-denial stood up and said, If such villains as these may be winked at in Mansoul, I will lay down my commission. He also took him from the crowd, and had him among his soldiers, and there he was brained. But some in Mansoul muttered at it, though none durst speak plainly, because Immanuel was in the town. But this brave act of Captain Self-denial came to the prince's ears, so he sent for him and made him a lord in Mansoul. My Lord Will-be-will also obtained great commendations of Immanuel for what he had done for the town of Mansoul.

Then my Lord Self-denial took courage, and set to the pursuing of the Diabolonians with my Lord Will-be-will; and they took Live-by-feeling, and they took Legal-life, and put them in hold till they died. But Mr Unbelief was a nimble Jack, him they could never lay hold of, though they attempted to do it often. He therefore, and some few more of the subtlest of the Diabolonian tribe, yet remained in Mansoul, to the time that Mansoul left off to dwell any longer in the kingdom of Universe. But they kept them to their dens and holes; if one of them appeared, or happened to be seen in any of the streets of the town of Mansoul, the whole town would be in arms after them, yea, the very children in Mansoul would cry out after them as after a thief, would wish that they might stone them to death with stones. And now Mansoul arrived to some degree of peace and quiet, her prince also abode within her borders, her captains also, and her soldiers did their duties, and Mansoul minded her trade that she had with the country afar off; also she was busy in her manufacture. Isa. xxxiii. 17. Phil. iii. 20. Prov. xxx. 10, &c.†

---

* Carnality, seated in the corporal senses, is a bitter enemy; and very difficult to be detected and destroyed. The holiest believer may say, with St Paul, "I am (comparatively) carnal." But wrong thoughts of Christ, which are also singularly injurious, will gradually decline in the heart of a true believer.

† Self-denial must be opposed to self-love. "If, through the spirit, we mortify the deeds of the body, we shall live," and shall also haply experience, "that to be

When the town of Mansoul had thus far rid themselves of so many of their enemies, and the troublers of their peace, the prince sent to them, and appointed a day wherein he would meet the whole people at the market-place, and there give them in charge concerning the future matters, that, if observed, would tend to their farther safety and comfort, and to the condemnation and destruction of their home-bred Diabolonians. So the day appointed was come, and the townsmen met together; Immanuel also came down in his chariot, and all his captains in their state attending of him on the right hand, and on the left. Then was an O yes made for silence, and, after some mutual carriages of love, the prince began, and thus proceeded:

Immanuel's speech to Mansoul. "You, my Mansoul, and the beloved of mine heart, many and great are the privileges that I have bestowed upon you: I have singled you out from others, and have chosen you to myself, not for your worthiness, but for mine own sake. I have also redeemed you, not only from the dread of my father's law, but from the hand of Diabolus. This I have done, because I loved you, and because I have set my heart upon you to do you good. I have also, that all things that might hinder thy way to the pleasures of paradise might be taken out of the way, laid down for thee, for thy soul, a plenary satisfaction, and bought thee for myself; a price not of corruptible things, as of silver and gold, but a price of blood, mine own blood, which I have freely spilt upon the ground to make thee mine. So I have reconciled thee, O my Mansoul, to my Father, and intrusted thee in the mansion-houses that are with my Father in the royal city, where things are, O my Mansoul, that eye hath not seen, nor hath entered into the heart of man to conceive.

Immanuel's great love to Mansoul. "Besides, O my Mansoul, thou seest what I have done, and how I have taken thee out of the hand of thine enemies; unto whom thou hadst deeply revolted from my Father, and by whom thou wast content to be possessed, and also to be destroyed. I came to thee first by my law, then by my gospel, to awaken thee and show thee my glory. And thou knowest what thou wast, what thou saidst, what thou didst, and how many times thou rebelledst against my father and me; yet I left thee not, as thou seest this day, but came to thee, have bore thy manners, have waited upon thee, and, after all, accepted of thee even of my mere grace and favour; and would not suffer thee to be lost, as thou most willingly wouldst have been. I also compassed thee about, afflicted thee on every side, that I might

---

spiritually minded is life and peace." But after all, that villain Unbelief, the worst of all the gang, still lurks secretly in the soul, yet is uniformly opposed whenever he dares to appear.

make thee weary of thy ways, and bring down thy heart with molestation to a willingness to close with thy good and happiness. And when I had gotten a complete conquest over thee, I turned it to thy advantage.

"Thou seest also what a company of my father's host I have lodged within thy borders, captains, and rulers, soldiers, men of war, engines, and excellent devices, to subdue and bring down thy foes; thou knowest my meaning, O Mansoul. And they are my servants, and thine too, Mansoul. Yea, my design of possessing of thee with them, and the natural tendency of each of them, is to defend, purge, strengthen, sweeten thee for myself, O Mansoul, and to make thee meet for my father's presence, blessing, and glory; for thou, my Mansoul, art created to be prepared unto these.

"Thou seest moreover, my Mansoul, how I have passed by thy backslidings, and have healed thee. Indeed I was angry with thee, but I have turned away my anger, and mine indignation is ceased in the destruction of thine enemies, O Mansoul. Nor did thy goodness fetch me again unto thee, after that I for thy transgressions had hid my face, and withdrawn my presence from thee. The way of backsliding was thine, but the way and means of recovery was mine. I invented the means of thy return; it was I that made a hedge and a wall, when thou wast beginning to turn to things in which I delighted not. It was I that made thy sweet bitter, thy day night, thy smooth way thorny, and that also confounded all that sought thy destruction. It was I that set Mr Godly-fear to work in Mansoul. It was I that stirred up thy conscience and understanding, thy will and thy affections, after thy great and woful decay. It was I that put life into thee, O Mansoul, to seek me, that thou mightest find me, and, in thy finding, find thine own health, happiness, and salvation. It was I that fetched the second time the Diabolonians out of Mansoul; it was I that overcame them, and that destroyed them before thy face.

Mansoul saved from her enemies by Immanuel's power and mercy.

"And now, my Mansoul, I am returned to thee in peace, and thy transgressions against me are as if they had not been. Nor shall it be with thee as in former days, but I will do better for thee than at thy beginning. For yet a little while, O my Mansoul, even after a few more times are gone over thy head, I will (but be not thou troubled at what I say) take down this famous town of Mansoul, stick and stone, to the ground. And I will carry the stones thereof, and the timber thereof, and the walls thereof, and the dust thereof, and inhabitants thereof, into mine own country, even into the kingdom of my father: and will there set it up in such strength

The death of the body.

The resurrec-

tion unto life eternal. and glory as it never did see in the kingdom w ere now it is placed. I will even there set it up for my father's habitation, because for that purpose it was at first erected in the kingdom of Universe; and there will I make it a spectacle of wonder, a monument of mercy. There shall the natives of Mansoul see all that of which they have seen nothing here; there shall they be equal to those unto whom they have been inferior here. And there shalt thou, O my Mansoul, have such communion with me, with my father, and with your lord secretary, as is not possible here to be enjoyed, nor ever could be, shouldst thou live in Universe the space of a thousand years.

"There, O my Mansoul, thou shall be afraid of murderers no more; of Diabolonians no more. There shall be no more plots, nor contrivances, nor designs against thee, O my Mansoul. There thou shalt no more hear of evil tidings, or the noise of the Diabolonian drum. There thou shalt not see the Diabolonian standard-bearers, nor yet behold Diabolus's standard. No Diabolonian mount shall be cast up against thee there, nor shall there the Diabolonian standard be set up to make thee afraid. There thou shalt meet with no sorrow nor grief, nor shall it be possible that any Diabolonian should again (for ever) be able to creep into thy skirts, burrow in thy walls, or be seen within thy borders all the days of eternity. Life shall there last longer than here you are able to desire it should, and yet it shall always be sweet and new, nor shall any impediment attend it for ever.

All shall be peace and happiness in heaven.

"There, O Mansoul, thou shalt meet with many of those that have been like thee, and that have been partakers of thy sorrows; even such as I have chosen and redeemed, and set apart, as thou, for my father's court and city royal. All they will be glad in thee; and thou, when thou seest them, shalt be glad in thine heart.

"There are things, O Mansoul, even things of thy father's providing and mine, that never were seen since the beginning of the world, and they are laid up with my father, and sealed up among his treasures for thee, till thou shalt come thither to them. I told you before that I would remove my Mansoul, and set it up elsewhere; and where I will set it, there are those that love thee, and those that rejoice in thee now, but much more when they see thee exalted to honour. My father will then send them for you to fetch you; and their bosoms are chariots to put you in. And thou, O my Mansoul, shalt ride upon the wings f the wind, Psal. lxviii. 17. They will come to convey, conduct, and bring you to that, when your eyes see more, that will be your desired haven.

" And thus, O my Mansoul, I have showed unto thee what shall be done to thee hereafter, if thou canst understand; and now I will tell thee what at present must be thy duty and practice, until I shall come and fetch thee to myself according as is related in the scriptures of truth.

" First, I charge thee that thou dost hereafter keep more white and clean the liveries which I gave thee before my last withdrawing from thee. Do it, I say, for this will be thy wisdom. They are in themselves fine linen, but thou must keep them white and clean. This will be your wisdom, your honour: and will be greatly for my glory. When your garments are white, the world will count you mine. Also when your garments are white, then I am delighted in your ways; for then your goings to and fro will be like a flash of lightning, that those that are present must take notice of, also their eyes will be made to dazzle thereat. Deck thyself therefore according to my bidding, and make thyself by my law straight steps for thy feet, so shall thy king greatly desire thy beauty, for he is thy Lord, and worship thou him.

Fine linen, the righteousness of the saints.

" Now that thou mayest keep them as I have bid thee, I have, as I before told thee, provided for thee an open fountain to wash thy garments in. Look therefore that thou wash often in my fountain, and go not in defiled garments; for as it is to my dishonour, and my disgrace, so it will be to thy discomfort, when you shall walk in filthy garments, Zech. iii. 3, 4. Let not therefore my garments, your garments, the garments that I gave thee, be defiled or spotted by the flesh, Jude ver. 23. Keep thy garments always white, and let thy head lack no ointment.

Purity of life recommended.

" My Mansoul, I have oft-times delivered thee from the designs, plots, attempts, and conspiracies of Diabolus, and for all this I ask thee nothing, but that thou render not to me evil for good, but that thou bear in mind my love, and the continuation of my kindness to my beloved Mansoul, so as to provoke thee to walk, in thy measure, according to the benefit bestowed on thee. Of old the sacrifices were bound with cords to the horns of the golden altar. Consider what is said to thee, O my blessed Mansoul.

" O my Mansoul, I have lived, I have died; I live, and will die no more for thee, I live, that thou mayest not die. Because I live thou shalt live also. I reconciled thee to my father by the blood of my cross, and being reconciled thou shalt live through me. I will pray for thee, I will fight for thee, I will yet do thee good.

"Nothing can hurt thee but sin, nothing can grieve me but sin:

Sin their great enemy.

nothing can make thee base before thy foes but sin. take heed of sin my Mansoul.

"And dost thou know why I at first, and do still suffer Diabolonians to dwell within thy walls, O Mansoul? It is to keep thee waiting, to try thy love, to make thee watchful, and to cause thee yet to prize my noble captains, their soldiers, and my mercy.

"It is also that yet thou mayest be made to remember what a deplorable condition thou once wast in, I mean when, not some, but all did dwell, not in thy wall, but in thy castle, and in thy strong hold, O Mansoul.

"O my Mansoul, should I slay all them within, many there be *Watchfulness recommended.* without that would bring thee into bondage; for were all these within cut off, those without would find thee sleeping, and then as in a moment they would swallow up my Mansoul. I therefore left them in thee, not to do thee hurt (the which they yet will, if thou hearken to them, and serve them,) but to do thee good, the which they must, if thou watch and fight against them. Know therefore, that whatever they shall tempt thee to, my design is, that they should drive thee, not further off, but nearer to my father, to learn thee war, to make petitioning desirable to thee, and to make thee little in thy own eyes. Hearken diligently to this my Mansoul.

"Show me then thy love, my Mansoul, and let not those that are within thy walls, take thy affection off from him that hath redeemed thy soul. Yea, let the sight of a Diabolonian heighten thy love to me. I came once, and twice, and thrice, to save thee from the poison of those arrows that would have wrought thy death; stand for me, my friend, my Mansoul, against the Diabolonians, and I will stand for thee before my Father, and all his court. Love me against temptation; and I will love thee, notwithstanding thine infirmities.

"O my Mansoul, remember what my captains, my soldiers, and mine engines have done for thee. They have fought for thee, they have borne much at thy hands to do thee good, O Mansoul. Hadst thou not had them to help thee, Diabolus had certainly made a hand of thee. Nourish them therefore, my Mansoul. When thou dost well, they will be well; when thou dost ill, they will be ill, and sick and weak. Make not my captains sick, O Mansoul; for if they be sick, thou canst not be well; if they be weak, thou canst not be strong; if they be faint, thou canst not be stout and valiant for *Mansoul is to live by the word of God.* thy king, O Mansoul. Nor must thou think always to live by sense, thou must live upon my word. Thou must believe, O my Mansoul, when I am for thee, that yet I love and bear thee upon mine heart for ever

"Remember therefore, O my Mansoul, that thou art beloved of me: as I have therefore taught thee to watch, to fight, to pray, and to make war against my foes, so now I command thee to believe that my love is constant to thee. O my Mansoul, now have I set my heart, my love upon thee, watch: "Behold I lay none other burden upon thee, than what thou hast already, hold fast till I come," Rev. ii. 24, 25."*

* In this sweet and truly evangelical speech, the dear Lord Jesus is represented as making a recapitulation of his gracious dealings with the souls of his people. Salvation is uniformly ascribed to the free mercy of the father and the precious blood of the son. Every gracious soul will cordially say, Not unto me, not unto me, O Lord, but to thy name be all the glory.

Immanuel then informs them of his intention to take down the present town of Mansoul, and to rebuild it in a more glorious manner; in other words, to remove the believer to glory, and raise up his mortal body to everlasting honour and happiness, when sin, sorrow and temptation shall never more be known.

Till this event take place, he directs his people to keep their garments white and clean—that is, to be holy in all manner of conversation and godliness; to watch carefully against sin, which is the only thing that can hurt them, and to live every day by faith in the word of God.

Thus have we followed the ingenious and judicious author through this truly excellent work, making use of his own marginal key to unlock the curious cabinet, and expose the valuable contents. May every reader be found among those who are restored by grace to the kingdom of Immanuel, and who, having overcome, shall sit down with him on his throne of glory. To Him, even to the Lamb that was slain, who hath redeemed us to God by his blood; to Him be glory, in all the churches, world without end. Amen.

THE END.

www.ingramcontent.com/pod-product-compliance
Lightning Source LLC
Chambersburg PA
CBHW032205230426
43672CB00011B/2512